A SURVEY OF MUSLIM INSTITUTIONS AND CULTURE

A SURVEY OF MUSLIM INSTITUTIONS AND CULTURE

MANZOOR AHMAD HANIFI
M.A., (Cal.)
Professor of Islamic History and Culture

KITAB BHAVAN
New Delhi-110002

KITAB BHAVAN
Exporters & Importers
1784, Kalan Mahal, Daryaganj
New Delhi-110002 [India]
Phones : 3274686, 3263383
Telex : 31-63106 ALI IN

ISBN 81-7151-144-9

First Edition 1962
2nd Edition 1992

Published by:
Nusrat Ali Nasri for Kitab Bhavan
1784, Kalan Mahal, Daryaganj
New Delhi-110002 [India]

Printed in India at:
Nazia Printers
Rodgran, Lal Kuan
Delhi-110006

To

MY REVERED TEACHER

A. M. A. R. FATMI, M.A.,

PRINCIPAL

QUAID-I-AZAM COLLEGE

DACCA

PREFACE TO THE SECOND EDITION

A thousand copies of the book are now in the hands of its readers, and it is a great encouragement to me that the book has been well received by the students and the general readers.

I have taken great pains in preparing the new edition. The whole of the material has been re-examined and a lot of fresh matter has been added. Besides this, additional chapters on al-Ghazzali, Sufism, Muslim Indebtedness to the Greek and Indian knowledge of Science and Music have been included in the present edition. It is hoped that it will meet with the same warm reception that was accorded to its first edition.

I am greatly indebted to my publisher, Sh. Muhammad Ashraf for rushing through the printing of the book to make it available to students in time. I am also highly indebted to Mr. Muhammad Kamaluddin, B.A., (Hons.), M.A., (Alig.) and my student Mr. Muhammad Aley Nabi, B.A. for other helpful suggestions.

Further suggestions for the improvement of the book will be greatly welcomed.

M. A. Hanifi

PREFACE TO THE FIRST EDITION

In order to restore the ideals of Islam and regulate the life of Muslims on the teachings of the Quran and Traditions of the Prophet of Islam, which were absent during the British regime, the Pakistani Universities included Islamic History and Culture as one of the subjects in the syllabus.

The book, as its name indicates, is meant to be a useful one for Degree students. It is comprehensive enough to cover the entire syllabi of Degree Classes of the Dacca and Rajshahi Universities in Islamic History and Culture Paper II.

As to the subject matter, I have tried to make the exposition clear and concise, without going into unnecessary details. In order to understand the meaning and significance of Islamic History and Culture, I would like to explain each term clearly for the better understanding of the students, who offer this as one of their subjects in B.A. Class.

Islam is derived from the root word 'sl'm' in the paradign of 'Ifa'al', which means a state of health. It may also mean nature. The word Islam from which the adjective Islamic is derived means to submit to the will of Allah. The secondary meaning of the word Islam would indicate the state of being at peace or of entering into a state of peace. This signifies that one can achieve real peace of body and mind only through submission and obedience to Allah. Such a life of obedience brings in peace of mind and establishes real peace in the society at large.

To a layman Islam stands for a religion or a dogma preached by Hazrat Muhammad (صلعم) and practised by a large section of mankind all over the whole world. This system preaches the unity of God (Tauhid) and propounds a code of morals and behaviour as a means of salvation.

To an Historian, the word Islam suggests more than a system of theology. It stands for a distinctive civilization and socio-politico-economic order, based on a form of practical theology. It has been evolving since the days of the Holy Prophet and spreading in all corners of the world.

To an ordinary Muslim, the word Islam is conceived as the name of his religion and as such comprising a system of life, guiding its followers individually and socially, whilst binding its members into a fraternity which transcends the boundaries of state, language, race, colour, and local traditions—an order that regulates the relations between men and women from the point of view of their worldly welfare, besides regulating the relations of the individual to his or her concept of Allah. Thus Islam is the most comprehensive code of life.

In order to get a clear conception of the great contribution of the Muslims to the study and writing of history, a definition of history is needed. There are many definitions but the most general one can be stated as follows :

History is the mirror of the people. It is through this mirror of history that they see themselves and the performances of their predecessors of the past.

Historians define history not as the record of days and kingdoms, but as a science dealing with the causes, results and process of the rise and fall of nations. History in Ibn Khaldun's opinion is not an end but a means to understand society. Cervantes says: "History ought to be precise, faithful and unprejudiced and neither interest nor fear, hatred nor affection, should make a historian swerve from the path of truth."

The Islamic interpretation of history is as scientific as one could imagine. Islam views history as a pageant of countless peoples, flitting across the stage of history and making their mark to the extent to which they mould their lives in conformity with the immutable spiritual and physical laws. Apart from the inexorable logic of those laws, there is no dire necessity or determination in history. There is nothing mystical about these laws. They operate with perfect impartiality and with a grim vengeance, so that every people has to bless or blame itself for the role assigned to it by history.

By the word Culture is generally meant "the training and refinement of mind, tastes and manners or the condition of being thus trained. It is the intellectual side of civilization." (vide "Culture", The Shorter Oxford English Dictionary.)

According to I.M. Baldwin, "Culture refers to the comprehensive changes in individual and social life due to the continued and systematic influences of mental improvement and refinement. Considered from a strictly sociological point of view, it is civilization, but anthropologists make culture the broader term. Whatever affects the intellectual status of man, whether directly or indirectly, may be said to be an element in culture. Arts, science, language and literature, education and Government, social customs, ethics and religion, contribute directly to the culture of a people."

But Islamic culture stands altogether on a different footing. Here religion is not only a single factor out of many but it is the sole basis ; other factors such as literature, education, social customs, ethics, etc., which contribute to the culture of Muslims being included in Islamic religion itself. Those who count religion as one of the many agents of culture mean by the term 'Religion' simply a dogma, which a man must accept if he wants to escape everlasting damnation or at the best, the ways of devotion and means to attain communion with God. Such a misconception of religion has been responsible for much of the antagonistic views held by modern people against religion, who find it useless and even harmful for human society. The application of such a narrow definition will be far from truth.

Religion, according to Islam, is therefore neither a dogma nor a bundle of theoretical beliefs, but it is the real motive force to lead a man to his full development, the fruits of which are enjoyed by the society. It is not one out of many agents which contribute to the culture of a people, but the very basis of culture.

Tauhid or faith in one God and the faith in the Risalat (messengership of the Prophet Muhammad (صلعم) are the chief fundamentals of Islam. Islamic culture is based on this fundamental and on the firm faith in a life-after-death where one shall have to reap the fruits of one's activities in this life.

This book comprises two parts—the first part begins with the history of the Quran and the Hadith, the basis of Islamic code and conduct, surveys the principal institutions of the religion, showing the breaking up of the Muslims into different hostile schools and ends with the idea of future existence; and the second part with the arts, literature, architecture, philosophical speculations, scientific discoveries, women in Islam, Muslim festivals and other cultural achievements.

I am greatly indebted to Moulana Muhammad Ali, Amir Ali, Khuda Bakhsh Khan, Shustery, P. K. Hitti, Joseph Hell and other acknowledged authorities whose works I have freely consulted in writing this book.

My thanks are due to my friend Prof. Azimuddin Ahmed for going through the manuscript before it was sent to the press. I am thankful to my publisher and printer for the interest they have taken in bringing out the book within a very short time.

Any suggestions towards the improvement of the book from the teachers and general readers will be gratefully received.

M. A. Hanifi
February 10, 1962

CONTENTS

PART I

INSTITUTIONS

CHAPTER I

CHAPTER II

CHAPTER III

CHAPTER IV

CHAPTER V

CHAPTER VI

CHAPTER VII

CHAPTER VIII

CHAPTER IX

CHAPTER X

PART II

CULTUTAL HISTORY

CHAPTER XI

CHAPTER XII

CHAPTER XIII

CHAPTER XIV

CHAPTER XV

APPENDIX—A

APPENDIX—B

PART I
INSTITUTIONS

CHAPTER I

HISTORY OF THE HOLY QURAN

Implication of the term Quran

Al-Quran is the sacred book of the Muslims. "Of all the religious scriptures of all ages and all climes which are the fountains of spiritual drink in the world, the Quran alone stands unique and unrivalled, not only for remaining pure and unadulterated from corruptions of ages but for its completeness of teachings, catholicity of views and universality of principles."[1] The original source from which all principles and ordinances of Islam are drawn is the Holy Book called 'Al-Quran.' According to the belief of every Muslim, the Quran is a divinely revealed book and as such, all positive laws given therein have superiority over man-made laws. It is a historical fact that the text of the Quran has not undergone even the slightest change. It is the real foundation on which the whole superstructure of Islam rests, and being the only absolute and final authority in every discussion relating to the principles and laws of Islam, it is to say that the Holy Quran is the sole source from which all the teachings and practices of Islam are drawn.

The Quran is the word of Allah, dictated through the Holy Spirit or Gabriel to Muhammad (صلعم). "Let none touch it but the purified" (56 : 78). It was revealed in the month of Ramazan on a certain night which thenceforward received the name of *Lailat al-Qadr*[2] or

1. F. Karim : *Al-Hadis*, Book I, p. 1.

2. The *Lailat al-Qadr* is one of the three nights in the month of Ramazan, *viz.*, 25th, 27th, or 29th, *i.e.*, the night preceding any of these dates (Bukhari). The Holy Prophet was, at the time when the revelation first came to him, forty years of age.

the Grand Night. It is generally held that on the 27th of Ramazan, the Quran was first revealed. It was revealed in Arabia and in the Arabic language. "So We have made it easy in their tongue that they may be mindful."

The word 'Quran' is derived from the root *qara'a* which signifies primarily 'he collected together.' It also signifies 'he read' or 'recited', because in reading and reciting, letters and words are joined to each other in a certain order. "The Book is so called both, because it is a collection of all best religious teachings and because it is a Book that is or should be read." The Quran speaks of itself under various other names. It is called 'al-Kitab', a writing which is complete in itself; 'al-Furqan' or the Distinguisher between right and wrong, between truth and falsehood; 'al-Zikr' or the Reminder; 'al-Tanzil' or the Revelation from on High; 'al-Hukm' or the Judgment; 'al-Hikmah' or the Wisdom; 'al-Shifa' or the Healing; 'al-Rahmat' or the Mercy; 'al-Khair' or the Goodness; 'al-Ruh' or the Spirit; 'al-Bayan' or the Explanation; 'al-Burhan' or the Argument; 'al-Nur' or the Light; 'al-Haqq' or the Truth; 'Ahsan-al-Hadith' or the Best Saying, etc.

The Book is not only the heart of the religion, or the guide to the kingdom of Heaven, but a compendium of science and a political document, embodying a Code of laws for a kingdom on earth.[1]

The Composition of the Quran

The Holy Quran was revealed in portions, every portion being written and committed to memory as soon as it was revealed. It was spread over 23 years of the Holy Prophet's life. As the Quran was revealed piecemeal, its verses and chapters were preserved on palm leaves, leather, shoulder bones of goats and

1. P. K. Hitti : *The Arabs, A Short History*, p. 33.

on parchments of papers, as they were dictated by the Prophet to his secretaries, especially Zaid bin Thabit. The chapters were arranged under the personal direction of the Holy Prophet who used to ask the scribes present to insert the revealed verses in their specified places. The chapters were not arranged in chronological order, not by oversight, but as commanded by the Prophet. The practice with the Holy Prophet was that, whenever a verse of the Holy Book was revealed, he specified, under Divine guidance, the place of the verse, and thus the arrangement of the verses in each chapter was entirely his work.

The Holy Quran is divided into 114 chapters, each of which is called a Surah, meaning literally eminence or high degree.[1] The Surahs are of varying lengths, the longest comprising one-twelfth of the entire Book. All the Surahs are divided into sections (*Ruku*) each section dealing with one subject. The sections (*Ruku*) are again sub-divided into a number of verses (*Ayats*) meaning originally a sign or a communication from Allah. The highest number of *ayats* in a Surah is 286 and the smallest only three. The total number of *ayats* in the Quran is 6,240, or including the 113 *Bismillah ayats* with which the chapters (Surahs) open, 6,353.[2] The Quran is again divided into thirty equal parts, each of which is called a *Juz* (meaning part).[3] Every *Juz* is again sub-divided into four equal parts. It is also divided into seven *Manzils* or portions. But all these divisions were mainly for facilitating the recitation of the Quran and they have nothing to do with the subject-matter.

1. Imam Abul Qasim al-Hussain ibn Abul Fazl al-Raghib: *Al-Mufradat fi Gharibi'l-Quran.*

2. Every chapter of the Holy Quran begins with *Bismillah* except the ninth.

3. Hughes writes in his *Dictionary of Islam*, p. 489: "The Quran is divided into Haruf (letters), Kalimat (words) Ayah (verse), Surahs (chapters Ruku' (Siparah having ten verses), Rub' (¼ Siparah), Nisf (½ Siparah), Suls (¾ Siparah), Juz (Persian, Siparah) and Manzil (Stages, 7 in number).

The arrangement of the chapters (Surahs) is mechanical in the order of their length. Out of the total of 114 chapters, into which the Quran is divided, 92 were revealed during the Meccan period and 22 during the Medinite period. Generally Medinite Surahs are longer and they comprise one-third of the Quran. The Quran opens with a Meccan Surah, 'The Fateha' or the opening. In arrangement, the Meccan Surahs are intermingled with that of the Medinite.

The Meccan Surahs are mostly short, incisive, fiery, impassioned in style and replete with prophetic feeling. They deal chiefly with faith in Allah and are particularly devoted to grounding the Muslims in that faith. The Medinite Surahs are mostly long, verbose and rich in legislative materials. In them theological dogmas and ceremonial regulations relating to the institutions of prayer, fasting, pilgrimage and the sacred months are laid down. In short, the Medinite Surahs are chiefly intended to translate that faith into action.

Methods of Revelation

According to the need pieces from the Quran were selected by Allah and sent down to the Prophet through an angel, who was called sometimes the Spirit, sometimes Holy Spirit and at a later date Gabriel. The angel recited the revelation to the Prophet, who read it after him and afterwards circulated it among his Ummat.

Sometimes the Prophet, in a wrapped condition, received the Divine Message through Gabriel, who came down to him like a human figu reattired in white dress and interpreted it in purely Arabic language. As to the nature of revelation, there are only four forms in which it came to the Prophet.

Wahy (inspiration) is the indirect way of experiencing symbols of Reality through intuitive faculties. The first method of revelation of the Holy Word was *Wahy* which signifies hasty suggestion thrown into the minds of men or *ilqa fi'l rau.* Infusing an idea into the hearts is a mode of God's speaking to man. In *Wahy* an idea is conveyed to the mind and the subject referred to is illuminated by a flash of lightning. It is not a message in words but simply an idea which clears up a doubt or a difficulty, and it is not the result of meditation.

The second remarkable method of revelation of God to man was from 'behind the veil,' which refers to *Kashf* (visions), *Ru'ya* (dream) and *Ilham* or voice heard or uttered in a state of trance by the inspired neither being asleep nor awake. *Kashf* means uncovering anything covered or manifestation. *Ru'ya* refers to a dream or a vision. This term is used in the Quran for vision of prophets. According to Hazrat Ayesha, in the beginning the revelation was delivered to Hazrat Muhammad (صلعم) in dreams. Inward perception, internal purity, deep religious insight and spiritual experience of the Prophet enabled him to enjoy some sorts of revelation from the Almighty Lord. Hazrat Ayesha said that often some idea was put into his mind and the Prophet believed that in such cases, the idea was put into his mind by Allah and that idea was not the result of his own knowledge or inference.

Ringing of the bell : The third method of revelation is expounded in the conversation between Harith bin Hisham and the Holy Prophet who said that revelation comes to the recipient sometimes as the ringing of the bells. In this method, the voice of the angel was heard only by the Prophet, not by others and he remembered what the angel said to him. This method was the most difficult and most taxing to the Prophet. Mostly verses of threats and punishment came by this way. In this case, the reception of the revelation was a severe experience, which made the Prophet perspire even on a cold day.

Appearance of the Angel: The simplest method of revelation was the appearance of angel Gabriel sent by God to deliver the Holy message in words. The angel used to come in the shape of a handsome companion of the Prophet—*Dahyatul Qalbi* and delivered the messages to him. Ibn al-Arabi and Imam Ghazzali agreed that the angel was the manifestation of the inner-self of the Prophet.

Compilation of the Quran

All the Surahs (chapters) and Ayats (verses) of the Quran were not revealed at a time. The Prophet Hazrat Muhammad (صلعم) received the revelations during the 23 years of his prophetical mission—thirteen years at Mecca, after the declaration of his mission and ten years at Medina since his migration. But it was not compiled during his life-time. Now the practice with the Holy Prophet was that whenever an Ayat or a Surah was revealed, a double process was employed to preserve it. There was a group of writers always at hand who recorded on palm leaves, leather, stones, and even on paper and others who committed it to memory.

No attempt was made by the Prophet to compile the Quran in the form of a single book. But according to some reports, the Surahs had taken their forms even in the life-time of the Prophet. Most of the Surahs were committed to memory by a large number of the Companions and some of them also, who could write, had gathered their own.

The following were the Katibs (scribes): Zaid bin Thabit, Abu Bakr, Umar, Usman, Ali, Zubair, Hanzalah, Abdullah ibn Sa'id, Abdullah ibn Rawahah, Ibn Masud, Khalid, Khadija and others. But the most important writer of the Quran was Zaid bin Thabit who wrote a greater portion of the Medinite Surahs. The compilation of the Quran could not be done during the life-time of the Prophet, because at any time a fresh verse might be revealed and a re-arrangement of the written pieces would accordingly become necessary. The collection and compilation of the Quran could only be done after his death, when the Quran had completely been revealed. Accordingly the collection of the Quran was done immediately after the death of the Prophet.

Shortly after the death of the Prophet, Hazrat Abu Bakr, the first pious Caliph of Islam, sent an expedition against Musailma, a false prophet. The battle took place at Yamama in 11 A.H. (632 A.D.) in which 70 of the Huffaz were killed. Therefore, Hazrat Umar advised Hazrat Abu Bakr that the written pieces of the Quran should immediately be collected and put into one volume, so that no portion of the Holy Book should be lost even if all the Huffaz lost their lives.

Hazrat Abu Bakr accepted the advice of Hazrat Umar and entrusted this task to Zaid bin Thabit, the chief scribe, who had written the greater portion of the Medinite Surahs. He was eminently qualified to carry out this task. Hazrat Abu Bakr asked Zaid to prepare a standard copy of the Holy Quran from the manuscripts written in the presence of the Holy Prophet, following the order and arrangement made under his direction. Zaid was also instructed to compare and verify every verse of the written manuscripts with the help of the reciters who had memorised the whole of the Quran.

Zaid bin Thabit carefully compared the recorded portions with that which he obtained from the memory of the Huffaz and prepared a standard copy. This volume was arranged in chapters and written on paper in a book form and was kept under the care of Hazrat Abu

Bakr. After his death, the Holy Book was in the charge of Hazrat Umar, after whose death, it passed into the custody of his daughter, Hazrat Hafsah, one of the widows of the Prophet. This standard copy was the first complete copy of the Holy Quran.

With the spread of Islam beyond Arabia, people of diverse nationalities and languages joined the fold. The people of Persia, Mesopotamia, Syria, and Egypt have their different tones and dialects. The difference of tone and dialect brought difference in the reading of the Quran. When this was reported to Hazrat Usman, the Caliph was alarmed at these variations of the modes of reading as well as writing of the Quran. In order to save the purity of the Holy Text, Hazrat Usman thought it better to make some copies of the Holy Quran and to send them to the different provincial governors of the Islamic world. Accordingly in 651 A.D. he appointed the aged Zaid bin Thabit as the Chairman of the Committee for copying the Quran. The other members of the Committee were Abdullah bin Zubair, Said bin al-As and Abdul Rahman bin Harith bin Hisham. They took the copy of Hazrat Hafsah and with assiduous care made out the required number of copies from the original one. These copies were sent to different provincial governors. The copies of the unofficial Quran, with discrepancies, were collected and destroyed.[1]

At the time of collection and compilation, the Quran was not provided with 'Harkat' or the vowel points. As a result, the people of non-Arab countries began to pronounce the Quran in different ways. In order to preserve the correct pronunciation of the Holy Quran, Hajjaj bin Yusuf, the Umayyad Governor of Iraq inserted the vowel points in the Quran and thus he rendered a great service to the cause of Islam.

1. Abu Abdullah Muhammad ibn Ismail al-Bukhari : *Al-Sahih al-Bukhari* (66 : 3).

Thus the Quran, revealed from Allah to Hazrat Muhammad (صلعم) through Gabriel, collected and compiled by Hazrat Abu Bakr and Usman and provided with vowel points by Hajjaj bin Yusuf has admittedly remained unaltered, unchanged, through more than 13 centuries that have since then passed.

Historical Value of the Quran

The historical value of the Quran is great. It is a record of the careers and activities of the great prophets of the past and also gives us information about various peoples of the pre-Islamic age. It narrates all the great events that took place in the world before the advent of the Holy Prophet. To the history and research scholars, it is a great source of information. As a political code, the place of Quran is very high. It deals with all questions that concern a king and his state—how the king will be elected, how he will run the administration and what are the rights and duties of the citizens. Above all the Holy Quran for the first time laid the principle of perfect democracy. The Quran is also considered a manual of science. It deals with the scientific truth regarding the earthly and heavenly elements. The astronomical facts which were established by the Quran testified to the importance of the Quran as a source of scientific studies. Long before the discovery by the European scientists that the earth moves round the sun or the earth is round, the Quran had established these facts. The Quran is a social and economic code too. It offers the most scientific, social and economic systems that are still unique in this world. The social and economic structures of the Muslims are based on the model laid down in the Quran. It deals with civil and criminal laws, regarding marriage and divorce, murder and theft, usury and inheritance. It lays down laws prohibiting wine, gambling, adultery, and other social vices. It is more read than any other book in the world. The Christian Bible may be a world's best seller, but nearly 250 million followers of the Prophet Muhammad (صلعم) read or recite long sections of Al-Quran five times a day, every day of their lives, from the time they can talk.[1]

Literary Value of the Quran

The Quran as a piece of literature is unique. It occupies such a place of eminence in Arabic language as has never been attained by any book. It was with the Quran that Arabic literature originated and it was through the Quran that Arabic became a powerful language to be spoken in many countries. "Without the Quran," remarks a modern critic, "the Arabic language would have been nowhere in the world. It transformed a dialect, spoken in a very limited area of a forgotten corner of the world, into a world-wide language which became the mother tongue of vast countries and mighty empires and produced a literature which is the basis of the culture of powerful nations from one end of the world to the other." Such is the unique achievement of the Quran.

Its language is rhythmical and rhetorical, but not poetical. Commenting on the style of the Quran, Sale says, "The style of the Quran is generally beautiful and fluent and in many places, especially where the majesty and attributes of God are described, sublime and magnificent."[2] According to Nicholson, the Quran is so pure in language and so beautiful in style that no human genius can either imitate or produce one like it. In the words of Palmer, "That the best of the Arab writers has never succeeded in producing anything equal in merit to the Quran itself is not surprising."

1. Charles Francis Potter : *The Faiths Men Live*, p. 81.
2. G. Sale : *The Koran : Peliminary Discourse*, p. 48.

"However often we turn to it, at first disgusting us each time afresh, it soon attracts, astounds, and in the end enforces our reverence . . . Its style, in accordance with its contents and aim, is stern, grand, terrible—ever and anon truly sublime . . . Thus this Book will go on exercising through all ages a most potent influence" (Goethe *vide* Hughe's *Dictionary of Islam*, p. 526).

Literature supplies material for writing history of a certain age. But the Quran is such a literature that it provides ample authentic materials to write history of different periods of the world. In literature generally the feeling of romance is created by fables and legends and those are imaginary. But in the Quran romance is created by real facts—the journey of the Prophet from earth towards the heaven, which is known as "Meraj".

The Holy Quran is the unique production in the world literature. The greatness and reasonableness of its ideas, sublimity in style, simplicity of its language and sincerity of its expression are still unsurpassed. No other book but the Quran has dealt with so many a subject : religious, social, economic, political, and judicial. The Quran is the charter and constitution of the Muslim faith which affords the most adequate means for securing the welfare of men in this world and ensuring their salvation in the next.

Arbuthnot opines : From the literary point of view, the Quran is regarded as a specimen of the purest Arabic, written in half poetry and half prose. It has been said that in some cases grammarians have adopted their rules to agree with certain phrases and expressions used in it, and that though several attempts have been made to produce a work equal to it, as far as elegant writing is concerned, none has as yet succeeded.[1]

1. F. F. Arbuthnot : *The Construction of the Bible and the Koran*, p. 5.

In fact, the Quran as a piece of literature stands pre-eminently above all. Its contribution to the development of Arabic language is incalculable. It is the mother of all the branches of Arabic literature.

CHAPTER II

HISTORY OF THE HADITH

What is Hadith?

Hadith or Sunnah is admittedly the second source and undoubtedly a secondary one, from which the teachings of Islam are drawn. The word 'Hadith' literally means 'Sayings' of the Prophet and Sunnah indicates the practice; but practically both cover the same ground and are applicable to his actions, practices and sayings. Hadith is the narration and record of the Sunnah, and also contains, in addition, some prophetical and historical elements. Each of the Hadith has two parts, the *Sanad* which means support and the *Matan* which means substance. And all the Hadith are divided into three kinds: it may be a *qaul, i.e.*, an utterance or a saying of the Holy Prophet which has a bearing on a religious question, a *fi'l, i.e.*, his action or practice, or a *taqrir, i e.*, his silent approval of the action or practice of another.

Canons of Testing Hadith

In the collection and compilation of Hadith the traditionists adopted certain methods to find out the genuine Hadith. After the death of the Prophet various parties and factions arose in Islam. Each party in order to support its own cause forged Hadith. Forgery and fabrication of Hadith became common under the Umayyads and the Abbasids. So in order to test its authenticity, the traditionists followed two methods, namely, *Rawayat* and *Darayat*. The methods of testing Hadith are given below:

(*a*) *Rawayat* (روایت) : It relates to transmission of a

Hadith. It also means verification of a report. It was a method which was applied to test the genuineness of the *Sanad* of each Hadith. Each narrator was examined with reference to his character, whether he was a liar, a man of weak memory, etc. Attempts were also made to find out that the report was traceable to the Holy Prophet through the various stages. The following are the principles of *Rawayat* :

(*i*) Each Hadith was authentically traced back to the Holy Prophet through a trustworthy chain of narrators and the name, nickname, title, parentage and occupation of each narrator were carefully examined.

(*ii*) The character of each reporter was studied with special reference to his truthfulness and veracity.

(*iii*) If the reporter was a man of excellent character but he had a weak memory, his report was disregarded.

(*iv*) If the reporter was said to have spoken a lie in relating any tradition, his report was discarded.

(*v*) If the reporter had been accused of any crime or carelessness in relating any tradition, his report was disapproved.

(*vi*) If the reporter had stated a tradition from imagination, or if he had held a peculiar religious view of his own, his report was discredited.

(*vii*) The narrator must state that he was present or he had heard a tradition uttered by the Prophet himself or he must give a complete chain of narrators from the last link up to the Prophet. It must also be proved by the historical evidence, otherwise the reporter was rejected.

(*viii*) It was to be proved that each of the narrators at the time he had heard the tradition he narrated, was of an age at which he was able to understand the full import of what he had heard.

(*ix*) The reporters must be men noted for learning, so that they may understand a tradition correctly and could deliver it faithfully to others.

(*x*) Lastly, books called *Asma-ul-Rijal* (lines of narrators) were compiled giving biographical details of all reporters and describing their character in detail. These books helped much in collection and compilation of genuine Hadith.

(*b*) *Darayat* (درایت) : In judging whether a certain Hadith was genuine or false, the collectors not only made a thorough investigation regarding the genuineness of the *Sanad* of that Hadith, but they also applied other rules of criticism, to prove the genuineness of its *Matan*. The method which was applied to test the *Matan* of a Hadith is called *Darayat*. *Darayat* means reasonableness. This method helped examine whether the Prophet could have uttered such a Hadith at all and whether it was in accordance with the moral principles of humanity, justice and equity, etc. The principles of *Darayat* are as follows :

(*i*) A report should be literally faithful. It must have been distinctly mentioned that such and such a thing was said or done by the Prophet.

(*ii*) If a Hadith was opposed to recognised historical facts, it was rejected.

(*iii*) If a Hadith was reported by the Shiites or the Kharijites with a view to supporting their doctrines, that Hadith should not be accepted.

(*iv*) If a Hadith was against reason, or against commonsense or against the chief doctrines of Islam or against the teachings of the Quran that Hadith was rejected.

(*v*) The description of a Hadith sanctioning a heavy punishment for ordinary sins or promising a high reward for slight good deeds was taken as untrue.

(*vi*) If a Hadith had non-Arabic style or ignoble sense of the words used or the subject matter was unbecoming the Prophet's dignity, that Hadith was rejected.

(*vii*) The Hadith which contradicted the universally accepted sayings of the Prophet was considered as incorrect.

(*viii*) In judging the veracity of a report, occasion and circumstances must also be considered.

Besides the principles of *Rawayat* and *Darayat*, the Quran was considered as the greatest test for judging the genuineness of Hadith. The Hadith which agreed with the Quran was accepted and that which contradicted the Quran was rejected. Thus we find that all the important collectors of Hadith, specially Imam Bukhari, applied all the principles of *Rawayat* and *Darayat* and above all the test of the Quran to each of the Hadith he had collected. But, from the above methods adopted to test its authenticity, the door of further criticism of Hadith is not closed. If possible, a hundred more canons of criticism may be laid down and applied to test each Hadith.

Sihah Sittah

Six collections of Hadith are recognised by Ahl-Sunnah as the *Sihah Sittah* or the six reliable collections. These are the collections made by Muhammad ibn Ismail, commonly known as Bukhari, Muslim, Abu Daud, Tirmizi, Ibn Majah and Nisai.

Among the *Sihah Sittah*, the *Sahih* of Bukhari holds the first place in several respects, while Muslim comes second. These two together are known as the *Sahihain* or the two reliable books. Bukhari has the unquestioned distinction of being first, because all the others modelled their writings on his.

Secondly, he is the most critical of all. "He did not accept any Hadith unless all its transmitters were reliable and until there was proof that the later transmitter had actually met the first, the mere fact that the two were contemporaries, did not satisfy him." Thirdly, in his *fiqh*, he surpasses all. Fourthly, he begins the more important of his chapters with a text from the Holy Quran. This shows that Hadith is not only an explanation of the Quran, but as such a secondary source of the teachings of Islam.

The works of the third and the last three are more generally known by the name of *Sunan*. These books classified reports under various sections and these made Hadith easy for reference. Such sort of arrangement was beneficial not only for the judge and the lawyer, but also for the ordinary and the research students, thus giving a further impetus to the study of Hadith.

THE SHIITE BOOKS

The Shiites had their own divines and their own compilers of Traditions. Four books hold the highest position in Shiite religious literature. They were written in the tenth and eleventh centuries. The first one is called *Al-Kafi fi ilm al-Din* and was written by the great scholar Muhammad ibn Yaqub al-Kulaini. It contains over sixteen thousand Shiite traditions. The second book is called *Kitab Man la Yadhuruh al-faqih* (Every man his own lawyer) and was written by Ibn Musa ibn Babuwaihi, popularly known as Ibn Babuya. This book contains 4,496 traditions. The third and the fourth books were written by the same learned scholar who was respected for his learning by both the Shiite and the Sunnis. He was Muhammad ibn Hasan al-Tusi. His books are called *Tahdhib al-*

Ahkam (Correcting of judgements) and the famous *Istibsar*.

Growth and Development of the Hadith Literature

The Quran is the fountain-head of Muslim laws and is absolute and final authority in all cases relating to the laws of Islam. But Hadith constitutes the secondary source of the laws of Islam. It is admitted by all the jurists that *Sunnah* completes and explains the Quran. The Muslims considered the Quran and the Hadith as two factors outwardly equal in importance, distinctly to fix the rules of religious life.

So long as the Prophet lived the Muslims felt no necessity of collecting the Hadith, because whenever any difficulty arose, they had the opportunity of meeting the Prophet and having his decision. There was no regular collection of Hadith during the lifetime of the Prophet. Different Hadith rested in the memory and writings of different Companions and there was none who knew all the sayings of the Prophet. The Holy Prophet is reported to have sometimes not liked the writing down of Hadith. Thus Abu Huraira is reported to have said : "The Prophet of God came to us while we were writing Hadith and said, 'What is this that you are writing ?' We said, 'Hadith which we hear from thee.' He said, 'What a book other than the Book of God ?'" Now the disapproval in this case clearly states that it was due to the fear of Hadith being mixed up with the Holy Quran. After the death of the Prophet there arose various circumstances which necessitated the collection of the Hadith. After the demise of the Prophet, his Companions spread abroad and they settled themselves in different parts of the Islamic world. As a result, the people of one place did not get the benefit of all the Hadith, because it rested piecemeal with different individuals then scattered in different places. Therefore, there arose the necessity of collecting all the Hadith from different traditionists so that the people of all corners might get the benefit of all the Hadith.

With the spread of the Muslim empire over different territories, there arose various problems regarding social, political, administrative, and judicial matters. In order to solve those problems the Muslims always tried to follow the dictates of the Quran and the Hadith. But the Quran deals only with the broad principles and there are many problems for which there is no reference in the Quran. The two most important religious institutions of Islam, for instance, are prayer and Zakat, but no details were supplied by the Quran. *Aqimu's-salata* (keep up prayer) is the Quranic injunction and it was the Prophet himself who by his own actions gave the details of the service. *Atu'l-zakata* (pay the alms) is again an injunction in the Quran, yet it was the Prophet who gave the rules and regulations for its payment and collection. To solve these problems, therefore, the Muslims wanted to follow the footsteps of the Prophet.

For the development of the Hadith literature, different centres came into existence. Among them the Hijazi and Iraqi Schools of Hadith have rendered valuable services to the development of Hadith literature. A Syrian School grew up at Damascus whose leader was Imam as-Sha'abi but it was the most unfamous and unpopular.

The Hadith is also considered as one of the most important sources of Islamic history. The study of Hadith and its methods of collection gave a great impetus to the growth and development of Muslim historiography. In fact, the study of the Hadith was the main foundation of the growth and development of Islamic history.

The writing of Islamic history began with the

study of the Hadith. To the Muslims the life and activity of the Holy Prophet were an ideal to be followed by each and every Muslim. Therefore, the Muslims were much anxious to know the details about the life of the Prophet and his Companions and a large number of Muslim scholars devoted themselves to the study of the life and activities of the Prophet and his gifted associates. Their sincere efforts resulted in the collection of the lives and activities not only of the Prophet and his Companions, but also of a large number of important Muslims who were connected with the transmission of Hadith. Thus they gave to the world, the richest store of biographical material which formed the foundation of Muslim historiography. They preserved the records of the lives and character of thousands of reporters and thus they laid the foundation of history in Islam.

Hadith is also a very important source of early history of Islam. It is not only the record of the life and teachings of the Prophet, but it has recorded all the activities of the Prophet—his wars and peace, his relations with the foreign powers, his administrative means and policy, his mode of warfare, his principles of government, etc.

The traditionists produced a new science called *Asma'ul-Rijal*, the biographies of the reporters, which is very important source of Islamic history. In the Hadith literature may be found a picture of life of the people of Arabia during the time of the Prophet.

The study of Hadith has influenced the methods of history writing. The 'Muhaddathin' devised various methods to ensure accuracy in their works and these methods were followed by the historians. The labour, sincerity and devotion exhibited by Muhaddathin in the study and collection of Hadith have no parallel in the entire history of human efforts to advance the cause of learning. The practice of dating the events by year, month and even the date which was adopted by Muhaddathin in the collection and compilation of Hadith was also followed by the historians. This method was not adopted in Europe until 1597. The historians also learned from Muhaddathin the methods of severe tests of criticism and scrutiny and applied them to the historical events. Hadith, on the one hand, formed the basis of Muslim historiography and on the other, supplied ample materials and various methods for history writing and thus it played an important role in the growth and development of Islamic history.

Eminent Muhaddathin

BUKHARI

Imam Bukhari—Abu Abdullah Muhammad ibn Ismail ibn al-Mughirah, known as al-Bukhari was born at Bukhara in 194 A.H. (810 A.D.) His father was a disciple of the famous Hammad ibn Zaid and Malik bin Anas. His father died while he was a mere boy. He was brought up under the care of his mother. His father, however, had left a small fortune which helped to bring up al-Bukhari and to afford him a good education without any undue strain on his widowed mother. He began the study of Hadith when only 11 years of age, and by the time that he was 16 had acquired a high reputation for his knowledge thereof. He had a wonderful memory, and the students of Hadith used to correct their manuscripts by comparing them with what he recited from memory. He performed Hajj with his mother and brother Ahmad and stayed at Hijaz for six years for study. When he reached the age of 18 he completed the book *Fadayal Sahaba wa al-Tabi'een*, and later the book *al-Tarikh al-Kabir*, which he wrote on moonlit nights while sitting by the grave of the Prophet Muhammad (صلعم). History was his favourite subject, and he used to say, "There is not a name in history about which I have not a story." Al-Bukhari then sought to meet the great scholars of the Hadith in various Muslim countries, and for this purpose he travelled to Damascus, Egypt, Basra and other Muslim countries. During his stay in Baghdad he frequently held discussions with Imam Ahmad ibn Hanbal (died July, 855), who is said to have been so highly impressed with his abilities that he urged him strongly to stay in Baghdad and relinquish Khurasan, his usual abode.

During all these extensive travels, al-Bukhari had one aim : to gather as much learning as possible and to make the greatest possible collection of reports of Sayings and Traditions of the Prophet Muhammad (صلعم). He possessed one of the most amazing memories, and his contribution to the science of Hadith was unequalled. His book *al-Jami al-Sahih* was the first written record in the history of Islam of genuine Hadith of the Prophet Muhammad (صلعم). He once said that he knew by heart some 100,000 Hadith which he knew were genuine and some 200,000 alleged sayings which he considered were false. To have gathered and memorized such a number of Hadith was indeed a great achievement.

He used to say that he never accepted a Hadith as genuine, unless he knew all there was to know about the life and death of these persons, and, after that, he checked up the accuracy of Hadith by reference to the surrounding circumstances and to other reports by other friends and companions of the Prophet Muhammad (صلعم). Many noble scholars of the days of Imam Bukhari gave testimony as to his unequalled repute and authoritative reports. His master Imam Abu Bakr ibn Khuzaimah once said of him, "There is no one on the face of the earth who knows more about the Hadith than Imam Muhammad ibn Ismail (al-Bukhari)." His colleague, Abdullah ibn Abdul Rahman al-Darimi, said of him, "I have seen and listened to the scholars of the Hijaz, Damascus and Iraq, but I came across no one who possessed more learning than Imam Muhammad ibn Ismail."

Imam al-Bukhari wrote several books on Hadith. His most notable achievement was *al-Jami al-Sahih*. This great work, which remains authoritative to this day, was the first book to be written by a Muslim scholar in which only those Sayings of the Prophet Muhammad (صلعم), the genuineness and accuracy of which had been established beyond the slightest doubt, were recorded. He used to take bath and perform two rak'ats of prayer before recording a Hadith and used to sit, while recording the Hadith, between the holy shrine of the Prophet and the pulpit or in the mosque of the Prophet at Medina, and between the Ka'ba and Maqam-i-Ibrahim in Mecca. In the compilation of his work, Imam Bukhari selected only 9,000 Hadith out of 60,000, which he had collected.

He was not content with merely recording the Sayings of the Prophet Muhammad (صلعم). He sought to deduce from them moral or justice principle and also to point out their application and significance in the field of fiqh (Jurisprudence). The Sayings of the Prophet Muhammad (صلعم) were classified in this book according to the subject-matter, and were grouped together in such a way as to illustrate a particular juristic point.

Throughout his life, he was strictly pious and honest and led a very pure and simple life. He was fairly wealthy, and spent a good deal of his money on encouraging students and those desirous of learning but prevented by lack of funds. He was extremely charitable in his remarks and opinions about men and scholars. He was conscious of the dignity of knowledge and learning and he refrained from debasing or dishonouring that high position by utilizing it as an instrument to serve the ends and wiles of rulers and other persons in authority.

According to the Sunnites, the collection of al-Bukhari is regarded as the most correct and authentic book after the Holy Quran. Hence *Sahih Bukhari* is the most critical of all.[1] He applied all the rules to test the authenticity of every Hadith. He died at Samarqand in 869 A.D. at the age of fifty-nine. Before his death he made the request that he should be buried in three sheets without either a shirt or head-dress.

MUSLIM

Muslim—Abul Hassan Muslim al-Nishapuri, better known as Imam Muslim, was born at Nishapur in 817 A.D. His father Hajjaj al-Quraishi was a traditionist of great repute. He got his early education in Hadith from his father. He began to study Hadith at the age of 18 and travelled in Iraq, Hijaz, Syria, Egypt and Baghdad in pursuit of knowledge and for the collection of Hadith. He devoted his whole life in the pursuit and study of Hadith.

Imam Muslim was a contemporary of Imam Bukhari. In the compilation of his work, Imam Muslim like Imam Bukhari applied the severest test of criticism. He selected only 9,200 Hadith out of 300,000 that he had collected. From the standpoint of classification, arrangement of the subject-matter and the authenticity of *Isnad* the *Sahih* of Muslim is peerless. The *Sahih* of Bukhari and that of Muslim together are known as

1. A modern writer, and one who has made a special study of Hadith, expresses the following opinion about Bukhari: "So far as one is able to judge, Bukhari published the result of his researches into the context of what he believed to be genuine tradition with all the painstaking accuracy of a modern editor. Thus he records even trifling variants in the Hadith, and whenever he feels that an explanatory gloss is necessary, either in *isnad* or *matan* it is clearly marked as his own."—*Traditions of Islam*, p. 29.

Sahihain or the two reliable books. Imam Muslim died at Nishapur in 874 at the age of 57.

ABU DAUD

Abu Daud—Abu Daud Sulaiman was born at Sistan in 202 A.H. (818 A.D.) He travelled all the important centres of Hadith and studied and collected wherever it was found. He was a contemporary of Imam Bukhari. He wrote many books on Hadith and Muslim Law. But his most important work is the *Sunan*. His work contains 4,800 Hadith selected out of 500,000 Hadith. It is the third authentic work on Hadith. According to Imam Ghazzali, the *Sunan* of Abu Daud alone is sufficient for a Mujtahid or jurist.

IBN MAJAH

Ibn Majah—Abu Abdullah Muhammad bin Yazid al-Majah was born in Iran in 209 A.H. (824 A.D.) He visited Iraq, Basra, Kufa, Syria, Egypt, Ray and Hijaz in quest of Hadith. He collected a large number of Hadith which he recorded in his *Sunan*. He was a great writer and wrote a commentary on the Holy Quran and a book on History. Eminent scholars on Hadith such as Ibn al-Jauzi, and Hafiz ibn Hajar have imputed the inclusion of some weak and apocryphal traditions in the *Sunan* of Ibn Majah. He died in 886 A.D.

TIRMIZI

Tirmizi—Abu Isa al-Tirmizi was born at Tirmiz in Transoxiana in 831 A.D. He was a great traditionist and in his search for Hadith travelled through Khurasan, Iraq and Hijaz. His *Jami-ul-Sahih* is one of the six canonical collections of Hadith. He collected 500,000 Hadith out of which he selected only 1,600 for his *Sunan*. He also wrote *Kitab-ul-Shamayel* on the life of the Prophet. He died in 892 A.D.

NISAI

Nisai—Abu Abdur Rahman al-Nisai was born in Nisa (Khurasan) in 215 A.H. (831 A.D.) He was a pupil of Qutaiba bin Sa'id Balkhi. He travelled all the important centres of Hadith and spared no pains in collecting authentic Hadith. The *Sunan* of Nisai contains 4,482 Hadith arranged under 15 heads sub-divided into 1,744 chapters. He died at Mecca in 303 A.H. (915 A.D.) at the age of eighty-eight.

CHAPTER III

THE SHARI'AT AND ITS SCHOOLS OF LAW

The Shari'at

The term 'Shari'at' literally means "the clear path to be followed", but technically 'the Law of Islam'. The Shari'at stipulates the Law of God and provides guidance for the regulation of life in the best interest of man. Its objective is to show the best way to man and provide him with the ways and means to fulfil his needs in the most successful and most beneficial way. The violation of this law is a sin as well as a social crime.

"The Shari'at, as an infallible doctrine of duties, comprises the whole of religious, social, political, domestic and private life of those who profess Islam." It is the right code for the whole life of a man ordained by Allah. According to a modern scholar, Shari'at is the "knowledge of the rights and duties, whereby man may fitly conduct his life in this world and prepare himself for the future life." Prof. Shushtery says that Shari'at distinguishes between what is *sahih* (lawful) and what is *batil* (forbidden).[1] Tabari interprets the Shari'at as the law of inheritance, the punishment, the commandments and the prohibtions.[2]

Shari'at deals with all aspects of life of a Muslim both religious and secular. The religious and secular rights and duties of a man have been divided into four classes. They are : (1) the rights of God, (2) the individual rights, (3) the rights of other men, and (4) the rights of all creatures. Now we shall briefly discuss

1. A. M. A. Shushtery : *Outlines of Islamic Culture*, (1954), p. 471.
2. *Shorter Encyclopaedia of Islam*, p. 524.

these rights and obligations so that an idea of life and its fundamental values may be formed.

(1) THE RIGHTS OF GOD

The foremost right of God is that man should have faith in Him alone. He should acknowledge His Authority and associate none with Him. This is epitomized in the Kalima : *La ilaha ill-Allah* (there is no god but Allah).

The second right of God is to accept Him wholeheartedly and follow His guidance.

The third right of God is that man should obey Him honestly and unreservedly.

Man must fulfil the needs of this right by following God's law as contained in the Quran and Sunnah.

The fourth right of God is to worship Him. This is rendered by offering of prayers and worshipping Him.

These rights and obligations precede all other rights and as such they are discharged even at the cost of some sacrifice of other rights and duties. For instance, in offering prayers and keeping fast one has to sacrifice many of one's personal rights and comforts. In the month of Ramazan, Muslims embrace hunger and inconvenience merely to please their Lord. By paying Zakat, they lose their wealth and demonstrate that the love of God is over and above everything else and that the love of wealth cannot come in their way. In the pilgrimage they undergo sacrifice of wealth and troubles of travel. And in Jehad they sacrifice money, material and all that they have—even their life.

(2) THE INDIVIDUAL RIGHTS

Among the individual rights are :

(*i*) Safety of person,
(*ii*) Safety of honour,

(*iii*) Safety of possession,
(*iv*) Safety of marital relations,
(*v*) Safety of Guardianship,
(*vi*) Safety of rights in inheritance,
(*vii*) Safety of freedom in all lawful actions.

(3) THE RIGHTS OF OHTER MEN

As Shari'at aims at the welfare of the whole humanity and foundation of an ideal society, it has enjoined along with the personal rights various obligations upon man which should be done for the welfare of the society, state and of the whole humanity at large. A man must not encroach upon the rights of other men. Shari'at has totally forbidden theft, robbery, bribery, forgery, cheating, interest, usury, for whatever man gains by these means is really obtained by causing loss and injury to others. Gambling, lottery, speculation and all games of chance have been prohibited, for in all of them one gains at the cost of losses to thousands of other people. Monopoly, hoarding, blackmarketing and all other forms of individual and social aggrandisement have been prohibited. Murder is not allowed, for a man has no right to take away the lives of others for his personal gain or gratification. Adultery, fornication and unnatural intercourse have been strictly prohibited for they impair the health, vitiate the society, spread corruption and immorality in the community, cause venereal diseases, give rise to public disorder and disturbance, and all abominable crimes should be eliminated.

Maulana Abul Ala Maududi says: "The first cradle of man is family. It is here that the primary character—traits of man are set. As such it is not only the cradle of man but also the cradle of civilization." A family consists of the husband, the wife and their children. Islam assigns to man the responsibility of earning and providing the necessities of his wife and children and to protect them. The wife has the duty of managing the household, training and bringing up the children and of providing to her husband and children the greatest possible comfort and contentment. The duty of the children is to respect and obey their parents and when they are grown up, to serve them and provide for their needs. The relatives of a man have also right upon him and he should try his best to make the tie closer and firmer. Islam enjoins a Muslim to treat his friends and neighbours honestly, truthfully, equitable and courteously. It is the duty of a man to attend to the sick to support the destitute, to sympathise with the trouble-stricken, to look after the orphans and the widows. According to Shari'at, no man should be allowed to squander upon himself a wealth that can maintain thousands of human beings. While using his money he should always keep in view the needs and requirements of his kith and kin, his near and far relations, his friends and associates, his neighbours and fellow-citizens.

A man is not merely member of a family, but he is also a member of the community of a nation. In order to safeguard the unity and solidarity of the nation and to achieve the welfare and well-being of the Muslim community, the Muslims must avoid hostility and social dissensions among themselves.

To preserve the moral life of the nation and to safeguard the evolution of society on healthy lines, free mingling of both the sexes has been prohibited. In dealing with the non-Muslims, Muslims should not be intolerant or narrow-minded. They have been enjoined by the Shari'at to win the hearts of people by their character and example.

(4) THE RIGHTS OF ALL CREATURES

God has honoured man with authority over His

creatures. Everything has been created for his service. He should make proper use of them. While using them for his service, he should not unnecessarily hurt them or harm them. To catch birds and imprison them in cages without any special purpose is considered abominable. "Islam does not approve even of the useless cutting of trees and bushes. Man can use their fruits and other produce, but he has no right to destroy them."

Fiqah

The term used to denote the whole of Islamic jurisprudence is called 'Fiqah' which literally means 'intelligence,' because it implies the independent exercise of intelligence in deciding a point of law, from the knowledge obtained by the study of the Quran or Hadith or any other reputed sources of law. It is narrower than the Shari'at and deals with what are commonly understood as 'legal acts' whereas the latter embraces in its orbit all human acts, ethical and non-ethical. "The path of Shari'at is laid down by Allah and his Prophet, the edifice of *Fiqah* is laid down by human endeavour," (Fayzee) in consonance of the tenets of the Shari'at.

Sources of Muslim Law

The following are the sources of Muslim Law :

(1) The Quran, (2) the Hadith, (3) Ijma, (4) Qiyas, and (5) Ijtehad.

The Quran and Hadith as sources of Muslim Law have been discussed in detail in Chapters I and II, and other sources of Law will be discussed now.

IJMA

Ijma is the third source of Muslim Law. The word *Ijma* is derived from *Jam'a* which means collecting or gathering together and *Ijma* carries the double significance of composing and settling a thing which has been unsettled and hence determining and resolving upon an affair, and also agreeing or uniting in opinion.[1] In the terminology of the Muslim Jurists, *Ijma* means a concensus of opinion of the Companions of the Prophet only, while some maintain that it is an agreement of the Muslim Jurists of a particular age on a point of law.[2]

Ijma is a principle of authority. It was meant to circumscribe the range of permissible beliefs and practices. It rests upon the conscience of the whole community. Beliefs and practices which have universal sanction are to be taken as valid. Purely personal views remain negligible unless and until they can secure the approval of the people at large.

Ijma is inferred in three ways : (1) by *Qaul* or word, *i.e.*, when the Mujtahids express their opinion on the point in question, (2) *Fi'l* or deed, *i.e.*, when there is unanimity in practice, and (3) by *Sukut* or silence, *i.e.*, when the Mujtahids do not disagree with the opinion expressed by one or more of them.

Ijma may be of two kinds, *Azimat* and *Rukhsat.* If all the worthy Mujtahids of an age give their direct consent in such a case it becomes *Ijma-i-Azimat.* Even if a single person disagrees it cannot be called *Azimat.* When a number of jurists agree upon a case and believe in its rightfulness it is the *Ijma-i-Rukhsat.* In the latter form initial *Ijma* may be made by three or two jurists. But in the cases where no original *Ijtehad* is required, as, for instance, the administrative affairs of a country, organisation of army, or a simple theological question that general Muslim masses can participate just like a referendum. Here unanimity is not necessary. The

1. Lane : *Lexicon,* (Arabic-English).
2. Muhammad Ali : *The Religion of Islam,* p. 106.

Caliph Abu Bakr consulted the companions about the compilation of the Quran. When he was convinced of its justification and the possible consent of the general masses he ordered its execution.

As regards *Ijma*, the Quran says: "Obey the Prophet and obey those who have authority among you." The Hadith says "that if anything comes to you for decision, decide according to the Quran; if anything comes to you which is not in the Quran, then look to the Sunnah of the Prophet; then look to what people unanimously agree upon." History furnishes facts that the first Caliph of Islam always followed the above principles, when a question came to him for decision. This is known *Ijma*. A large number of laws in the form of *Ijma* grew up in the hands of the four pious Caliphs, the companions and the jurists of the later ages and they form one of the important sources of Muslim Law.

Can *Ijma* be repealed? An *Ijma* may be of various characters. An *Ijma* that was made by the unanimous opinion of the Companions of the Prophet is called *Qati'e* or decisive. According to the majority of the jurists such an *Ijma* cannot be repealed. Fakhrul Islam Bazdavi says that such a decisive *Ijma* also may be repealed by another *Ijma*.

In fact, the spirit behind the *Ijma* has been to meet the ever-growing problems of progressive society and to keep pace with the time. Elasticity of law is the test of its benevolence and usefulness. And this is the merit of the Islamic Law. During the lifetime of the Prophet both the Holy Quran and the traditions had been dynamic. After him the institution of *Ijma* has been preserving this flexibility of *Fiqah*..

QIYAS

Qiyas or Analogical Deduction is another important source of Muslim Law. The literal meaning of *Qiyas* is 'composing with' or 'judging by comparing with a thing.' *Qiyas* may be defined as a process of deduction by which the law of a text is applied to those cases which, though not covered by the language of the text, are governed by the reason of the text. It is an analogical deduction from the three sources of law—Quran, Sunnah and *Ijma*. Abu Hanifa was the first jurist who addressed himself to *Qiyas* and this is why his followers were called the followers of *Qiyas* and *Rai*.

This was the principle which the Muslims adopted after the death of the Prophet to explain new problems of life. When any problem could not be interpreted with the help of the Quran, Sunnah or *Ijma*, they tried to derive a solution from an analysis of the old teachings. This involved *Rai* or decision. In taking a decision one should first depend on the Quran and the Hadith, then on analogy and lastly on personal judgment. In order to establish the validity of *Qiyas*, the jurists rely on those Hadith in which the Holy Prophet encourages the exercise of individual judgment. For instance, when the Prophet was sending Muaz bin Jabal to Yemen as a Governor, he asked him as to what he would do if a new problem arose. Muaz replied that he would follow the Quran ; if it was not clear in the Quran, he would follow the Sunnah of the Prophet and if this also failed to satisfy him, he would use his own judgment. This reply of Muaz was appreciated and encouraged by the Prophet.

Speaking of the exercise of *Qiyas* as allowed by the chief Sunni sects, Ibn Khaldum says, "The science of Jurisprudence forms two systems that of the followers of private judgment and analogy (*ahl-Rai, wa-ahl-al-Qiyas*) who were natives of Iraq, and that of the followers of tradition, who were natives of Hijaz. As the people of Iraq possessed but few traditions, they had recourse to analogical deductions, and attained great proficiency therein, for which reason they were called the followers of private judgment: Imam Abu Hanifa, who was their chief and had acquired a perfect knowledge of this system, taught it to his disciples. The people of Hijaz had Imam Malik and then al-Shafi." No jurist has ever claimed infallibility for analogical deduction or for decisions or laws which are based on *Qiyas*. It is a recognised principle of *Ijtehad* that the Mujtahid may err in his judgment. This is why *Qiyas* of one generation may be rejected by another generation. While *Ijma* is the concensus of opinion of the majority of the jurists, *Qiyas* may be done by a single jurist even, provided the majority of the jurists accept it.

Thus we find that besides the Quran and the Hadith *Ijma* and *Qiyas* are the most important sources of Muslim Law. Whenever any question arose for which there was no solution in the Quran and Sunnah, the Mujtahids adopted these two methods to find out the answer of that question, The basis of these two methods is the Quran, Sunnah and individual judgment. These two methods gave birth to many new laws and legislations which have not been dealt with in the Quran.

Important sections of Muslim Law are *Ijma* and *Qiyas*, such as, all apostolic laws, explanations, the rules regarding the caliphate, administrative measures, etc. Imam Abu Hanifa made an extensive use of *Qiyas* and many of his legal decisions are based on *Qiyas*. This grand principle gives the Muslim theologians an opportunity to adjust the laws according to the condition of the time.

IJTEHAD OR EXERCISE OF JUDGMENT

Ijtehad is one of the sources frcm which the laws of Islam are drawn. The word is derived from the root *Jahad* which means exerting one's self, *i.e.*, trying to discover the proper application of the teachings of the Quran and the Hadith to a particular situation, and *Ijtehad* which literally conveys the same significance, is technically applicable to a lawyer's exerting the faculties of mind to the utmost for the purpose of solving difficult legal problems.

Reasoning or the exercise of judgment plays a very important part in the religion of Islam and the value of reason is expressly recognised in the Holy Quran. "Those who do not use their reasoning faculty are compared to animals, and are spoken of as being deaf, dumb and blind." The Holy Quran does not recognise revelation as a source of knowledge higher than reason, but at the same time admits that the truth of the principles established by revelation may be judged by reason, and hence it is that it repeatedly appeals to reason and denounces those who do not use their reasoning faculty.[1] It also recognises the necessity of the exercise of judgment in order to arrive at a decision.

Ijtehad is expressly recognised in the Hadith as the means by which a decision may be arrived at when there is no direction in the Quran or the Hadith. The Hadith with regard to the appointment of Muaz bin Jabal as Governor of Yemen, as stated before, is regarded as the basis of *Ijtehad* in Islam. This Hadith shows not only that the Holy Prophet approved of the exercise of judgment, but also that his Companions were aware of the principle and that *Ijtehad* by others than the Prophet was freely resorted to when necessary, even in the Prophet's lifetime. The Prophet's immediate successors did not arrogate all authority to themselves in this respect but had a Legislative Council to which every important case was referred, and decisions were arrived at by the Caliph in consultation with the mem-

1. Muhammad Ali : *The Religion of Islam*, p. 97

bers of that Council in the light of the Quran and Sunnah.

In the second century of Hijrah came the great jurists who codified the Islamic Law according to the needs of their time. The first of these was Abu Hanifa an-Numan ibn Thabit. Other jurists were Imam Malik, Imam Shafi'i and Imam Ahmad ibn Hanbal. They are thus agreed in giving to *Ijtehad* a very important place in legislation, and the Shias attached to it an even greater importance. The sphere of *Ijtehad* is a very wide one, since it seeks to fulfil all the requirements of the Muslim community which are not expressly met with in the Holy Quran and the Hadith. The great Mujtahids of Islam have endeavoured to meet these demands by various methods, technically known as *qiyas* (analogical reasoning), *istehsan* (equity), *istislah* (public good), and *istidlal* (inference).

Is the door of *Ijtehad* closed today? Now the question arises whether the door of *Ijtehad* is closed for good or is still open to the Muslims? On this issue the Muslims are divided into two camps. One section holds that the door of *Ijtehad* is closed after the four orthodox Imams. But the progressive section including Allama Iqbal believe that the door of *Ijtehad* is still open. They contend that both the Quran and the Hadith allow the free exercise of judgment and neither of them has discarded it after a certain period. The Holy Prophet never ordered that the gate of *Ijtehad* would be closed after a certain period. "Ijtehad was a great blessing to the Muslim people; it was the only way through which the needs of the succeeding generations and the requirements of the different races merging into Islam could be met. Neither the Holy Prophet, nor any of his Companions, nor any of the great Mujtahids of Islam, ever said that the Muslims were forbidden to apply their own judgment to new circumstances and the ever-changing needs of a growing community after a certain time, nor has any one of them said, and in fact no one could say, that no new circumstances would arise after the second or third century."[1] Thus it is quite evident that Muslim community has the right to make any law for itself, the only condition being that such a law shall not contravene any principles laid down by the Quran and the Hadith.

In the present century Allama Iqbal realised the importance of *Ijtehad* and urged the Muslims to revive it. He writes in his book, *Reconstruction of Religious Thought in Islam* : "Equipped with penetrative thought and fresh experience the world of Islam should courageously proceed to the work of reconstruction before them." He further remarks, "Let the Muslim of today appreciate his position, reconstruct his social life in the light of ultimate principles and evolve, out of hitherto partially revealed purpose of Islam, that spiritual democracy which is the ultimate aim of Islam." Thus *Ijtehad* is the means through which the ever-changing needs and requirements of the Muslim community are satisfied.

Hanafite School

The Hanafi School is the earliest and the greatest orthodox School in Islam and it has undoubtedly the largest number of followers. This School was founded by Abu Hanifa an-Numan ibn Thabit. He was born in Iraq in 80 A.H. (699 A.D.) during the reign of Abdul Malik ibn Merwan. He received his first lesson in Jurisprudence from the great Shiite Imam Jafar as-Sadiq and heard traditions from Abu Abdullah ibn al-Mubarak. He is called by his followers the Imam ul-Azam (the great Imam). He died in 150 A.H. (769 A.D.) and was buried in Baghdad. The doctrines taught by him are in force among the majority of the Indo-

1. Muhammad Ali : *The Religion of Islam*, pp. 113-114.

Pakistan Muslims, the Afghans, the Turks, almost all Central Asian Muslims, and the Egyptians.

Abu Hanifa was a man of high moral principles and great kindliness of nature and was anxious to broaden the foundations of the religion. He set up "a system of spiritual and temporal laws, which has been developed by his disciples and which, to this day, commands the unreserved assent of the greatest majority of the East". Abu Hanifa laid the foundation of the Muslim constitutional law, "which has been the accepted basis for all later time". He is said to have composed a work on theology entitled *Fiqah-Akbar*.

Abu Hanifa rejected most of the traditions as untrue and relied solely on the Quran and by analogical deduction tried to make the simple Quranic utterances applicable to every variety of circumstances. He always resorted to the Holy Quran for his juristic views and said that the Quran was indeed the first and the primary source for deducing the form of rituals bearing on civil and criminal laws, or for deducing the moral principles which should govern a case. He accepted the Hadith only when he was fully satisfied with its authenticity. It is said that he was very cautious in relating the traditions of the Prophet, for forgery had become common even in his days. Ibn Khaldun writes that the Imam narrated only 17 traditions and preferred *Qiyas* or analogy, which means analogical deductions from the passages occurring in the Quran. He also recognised the authority of customs and usages and he advised his followers to take into account the prevailing circumstances when interpreting law. Abu Hanifa gave such an importance to the exercise of private judgment that he and his followers were called *Ahl-ul-Rai* or the upholders of private judgment.[1] Although he was not a judge himself he founded a school of law which, according to Von Kremer, is the

1. Muhammad Ali : *The Religion of Islam*, p. 101.

highest and the loftiest achievement of which Islam is capable. He was a speculative legist. He considered the recitation of the *namaz* and also of the *Khutba* or sermen, lawful and valid in any other language. The disciples of Abu Hanifa, Abu Yusuf and Muhammad, have accepted the doctrine of their master with a certain variation. They hold that when a person does not know Arabic, he may validly offer his devotion in any other language. Abu Hanifa is also noted for his principle of *Istehsan*, which means the law of preference or suitableness of an act. For example, take the rule that a thing which is washed must be squeezed. This can only apply to the case of a cloth and not to wooden or metal articles. When a man purchases a thing, he must see it, but in the case of an article to be manufactured, it is sold in advance. This, according to the law, is invalid. But•*Istehsan* permits a translation like this on the ground that it is needed by the buyer and practised among merchants and is not forbidden by the Quran. Thus a Muslim jurist could lean, besides the Quran and the traditions, upon the four principles of analogy and agreement, based upon the Quran and traditions and discretion and public welfare as ths circumstance of the age permitted.

The School of Theology and Jurisprudence which Imam Abu Hanifa founded became dominant in the court of the Abbasid Caliph and shortly after his death this school was officially recognised by Harun al-Rashid in the whole of the Abbasid empire. After his death, his disciple Abu Yusuf, who was the chief judge of Baghdad, expounded the Hanafi system of law in his famous book *Kitab-ul-Kharaj*. This is one of the greatest authorities of the Hanafi laws.

The Hanafi law is called the most liberal system of law. The founder of this system, Abu Hanifa, was the follower of the Murjite School, which was the most liberal and moderate sect in Islam. In this legal system he always tried to follow liberal and tolerant views. He is generally regarded as the champion of leniency, toleration, and mercy and that at a time of unbridled fanaticism. In the formulation of laws, he did not confine himself only to the Quran and the Hadith, but also leaned towards customs, usages, and prevailing circumstances. As a result of all these, his legal system has become broader, milder, more human and more reasonable than that of any other school.

Malikite School

The founder of the second school was Malik Ibn Anas. He was born in 713 A.D. in Medina and died in 795 A.D. in the caliphate of Harun al-Rashid. In his early life he studied the Quran and Fiqah. He was devoted to the family of the Prophet and was anxious to broaden the foundations of the religion. Medina was "the cradle of Islam, the adoptive home of Muhammad (صلعم) and the abode of his most zealous and devoted followers," and it was here that the heap of traditions was first and for all times, collected and codified by Imam Malik.

His work on Jurisprudence named *Kitab-ul-Muwatta* (The Beaten Path) was more acceptable to the simple Arabs and cognate races of Africa, being suited to their archaic forms of society than the speculative theories of Abu Hanifa. The object of this book was to give a survey of law of justice and rituals and practices of Islam. In this book, Malik codified the common law of Islam and thus paved the way for further studies and development of juridical systems.

Malik ibn Anas differed from Abu Hanifa in many respects. He excluded from his system all inferences and deductions. He based his system on traditions and Sunnah of usages of the Prophet, Thus Hanafites may be called rationalists and Malikites may be called traditionists.

Shafi'ite School

Imam Muhammad ibn Idris al-Shafi was the originator of the third school. He was born in Palestine in 150 A.H. (769 A.D.) and died in Egypt in 204 A.H. (819 A.D.) during the caliphate of Mamun. He was the disciple of Malik ibn Anas and thus became acquainted with the Malikite doctrines.

He was a great supporter of the Fatimids and, therefore, was arrested by the Abbasids and brought before Harun al-Rashid, but was pardoned by the Caliph. He was a contemporary of Fatimid Imam Ali ibn Musa ar-Qiza.

He was a voluminous writer and his works "form extremely valuable texts on law and tradition." Among them are: *Usul* or principles of the Muslim civil and canon law, *Sunnah* or traditions law, *Musnad* and on theology in 14 volumes. He adopted both the principle of *Ijma* of Abu Hanifa and *Istedlal* or the logical conclusion of Imam Malik. The school was based mainly on Hadith collected not from Medina alone, but from the different countries of the Muslim world.

The main difference between Hanafi and Shafi lies in the fact that while Abu Hanifia founded his system mainly on the Holy Quran and made very little use of the Hadith, Shafi was based chiefly on the Hadith. Shafi doctrines are generally followed by the people of north Africa, Egypt, South Arabia, and Ceylon. His followers are also to be found among Bohras of Bombay Presidency.

Hanbalite School

The last of the four orthodox schools is Hanbalite founded by Ahmad ibn Hanbal. He was born in Baghdad in 780 A.D. and died in 241 A.H. (855 A.D.) in Baghdad. He was the disciple of Imam Shafi. He flourished during the reign of Mamun and his successor Mu'tasim Billah. Ibn Hanbal's extreme orthodoxy inflamed the bigotry of the masses against the sovereign, and brought him into trouble with the rulers. As a result,he was put into prison by Caliph Mu'tasim, but was released by Mutawakkil. He never shrank from his orthodoxy and always denounced the Mutazilite doctrines.

Imam Ahmad bin Hanbal made a very extensive study of the Hadith and his monumental work on this subject was the *Musnad* containing nearly 30,000 Hadith. In this *Musnad*, the Hadith are not arranged according to the subject matter. Though Imam Ahmad collected a large number of Hadith, he had not applied those strict rules of criticism favoured byImam Bukhari and Muslim and therefore, he had to accept many weak Hadith as the bases of his discussion. He made the least possible use of reason and always tried to derive every possible law from the traditional sources.

Hanbalism is the most rigid orthodox school in Islam and it does not permit any free discussion and innovation in religious matters. This school came into being as a reaction against the innovations, distortions and corruption that had crept into Islam under the influence of various foreign agencies. The Hanbalites based their doctrines on blind dogmatic and uncritical acceptance of the teaching of the Holy Quran and they bitterly opposed the rationalistic views of the Mutazilite. As he represented the uncompromising attitude of the champion of 'Hadith' so it steadily lost ground and is today mainly in the interior of Arabia, chiefly among the Wahhabis.

CHAPTER IV

RELIGIO-POLITICAL PARTIES

The Shiism

Shiism was originally, and continued to be, a party of the discontented. It was started as a political movement, but ended as a theological sect. The word Shia means party derived from Shiat-i-Ali which means the party of Ali. The Shiite Movement was started by supporters and followers of Ali with the idea Muhammad (صلعم) had definitely "designated Ali" to be the leader of his people. Thus in the early period of Islam, there arose two antagonistic parties—the Sunnis (the people of the Path) and the Shias (the party of Ali). The Shias advanced the cause of Ali to be the immediate successor of Muhammad (صلعم). History furnishes fact that when Ali became the fourth Caliph of Islam, he was opposed by Muawiya, the governor of Syria. In the battle of Siffin (657), Ali was outwitted by Muawiya by proposing an arbitration. This arbitration led to the secession of a large number of his army with the slogan "La hukma illa lillah", *i.e.* judgment belongs to Allah alone. They were the first dissenters or Kharijites. Hence the cause of Ali was upheld by a group of people known as Shias. The battle of Karbala was the turning point in the history of Shi'ism and in the words of Prof. Hitti, ". . . the blood of al-Husayn, . . . proved to be the seed of the Shi'ite Church". Shi'ism was born on the tenth day of Muharram.

Shī'ite Doctrines

(1) Its essential dogma is political, the first three Caliphs were illegitimate, the fourth, Ali ought to have

assumed the Caliphate immediately after the death of the Prophet Muhammad (صلعم). They also consider all the Umayyad and Abbasid Caliphs as usurpers.[1] According to them, leadership of Islam belongs only to the descendants of Prophet Muhammad (صلعم) and therefore was limited to the children of Ali and his wife Fatima.

(2) To the fundamental creed of Islam that 'there is no god but Allah and Muhammad(صلعم) is the Apostle of Allah', the Shi'ites add' and Ali is the vicegerent of Allah'.

(3) The Shi'ites introduced the idea of Messiah or Mehdi. According to them, the twelfth Imam Muhammad al-Muntazar who disappeared at Samarra without leaving offspring would reappear in due time as the Mehdi, who will bring in the reign of justice and truth. They differed among themselves regarding the particular descendant of Ali to whom allegiance was due and who might be accepted as the leader. A section of the Shi'ites believe that Muhammad ibn al-Hanfiyah, a son of Ali who is kept alive in concealment by Allah, will reappear at the appointed time as the Mehdi to usher a new era in the domain of Islam before the end of all things. The idea of Imamate is the crux of the Shi'ite creed.

(4) The Shi'ites generally believe that there must be some law regulating the choice of Imam. They reject the authority of the people to elect the Imam, for their election might often be defective. According to them, the Imam must be divinely appointed. "He is the very embodiment of religion and morality and therefore to him was due blind, unquestioning obedience". They hold that "neither the vices, nor the tyranny of the Imam would justify his deposition, nor can the perversity or evil conduct of the Imam or those

1. D.M. Donaldson : *The Shi'ite Religion*, p. 41.

who preside over the public divine service, invalidate the prayers of the faithful." The Shi'ite Imam is a *masum* or immune from sin.

(5) According to Shi'ite opinion the Divine Light (*Nur*) which since Adam has been transmitted from prophet to prophet illuminated at the same time the fathers of Muhammad (صلعم) and of Ali, then fell on them and their descendants and consequently on the children of Ali and Fatima. The extremist Shi'ites consider the Imam as an incarnation of God. A later ultra-Shi'ite sect even hold that Gabriel mistook Muhammad (صلعم) for Ali, who was originally intended for the reception of the revelation.[1]

(6) The Imamate is indivisible and it is not lawful to have two Imams at one and the same time. The Shi'ite Imam had inherited from Muhammad (صلعم) not only his temporal sovereignty but the prerogative of interpreting laws. In that capacity, he is an infallible teacher.

(7) They believe in the revelation of the Quran, which is uncreated from eternity.

(8) The persecution of the Shias at the hands of the Umayyads and Abbasides compelled them to invent the doctrine of *taqiyya*, implying Secrecy. This doctrine taught them to hide their feelings and religious convictions quite contrary to Sunni Islam. The Shias paid homage to the illegitimate rule of the Umayyad and Abbasid Caliphs while concealing their inner religious convictions.

Difference between the Shia and the Sunni

The Shi'ite doctrine is distinguishable from Sunni-ism only in questions of detail the answers to which vary according to the sect :

1. P. K. Hitti : *History of the Arabs*, p. 248.

(1) The Shias maintain that the original text of the Quran has been mutilated. They charge the Sunnis for omitting passages relating to Ali and his family. The Sunnis hold that there is no corruption in the Quran and they charge the Shias with corrupting the Quran.

(2) The Sunnis believe that Hazrat Muhammad (صلعم) was a man like others, except that he was the best of men, and that Allah spoke to him through the revelations, that all Muslims are equal, that the man who fears and obeys Him most is the best in the eyes of Allah. The Shi'ites believe that Muhammad (صلعم) was 'appointed' and that his spiritual powers did not die with him. They think that he was sinless and possessed some semi-divine attributes. These spiritual powers and godly qualities were inherited by Ali, then by his sons and through them by his descendants who were called Imams. They were the real leaders of Islam and, since the Sunnis did not recognise them, they committed a great sin.

(3) While the Sunni world believe that Muhammad (صلعم) is the last of the Prophets and after him no Prophet will come to this world, a large portion of the Shi'ites, specially the Ismailis, believe that Imam Ismail was the last Prophet. The Shi'ites prefer Ali to Muhammad (صلعم) or at least esteem them both as equal. But the Sunnis admit neither Ali nor any Prophet equal to Muhammad (صلعم).

(4) The Shi'ites do not recognise the Imamate of the first three Caliphs after the Prophet. They hold briefly that the successor to the Prophet should be one like him divinely appointed, sinless and without any blemish, able to interpret and to explain ideas and give correct opinions on questions connected with religion, and that such a man was Ali, the cousin and son-in-law of the Prophet. He was, according to them, the only

right person to explain the meaning of the Quran and the teaching of Islam. But Sunnis recognise all the four Caliphs as legitimate Caliphs after the Prophet. The Shi'ites also consider the Ummayyad and the Abbasid Caliphs as usurpers and do not pay their due homage to them.

(5) The Shi'ites were opposed to the idea of an elected Imam, as leadership descended by divine appointment. Spiritual leadership cannot be entrusted to an elected Imam, as people with unaided faculties might make a wrong selection. They have other minor differences in liturgical (ceremonies, law of inheritance, marriage, etc.) matters. According to the Sunnis the Imam should be elected by the whole community of the Muslims from among the Quraishites, and may be vested with the power of nominating successor subject to the approval of the general body of the Muslims.

(6) The Mehdi of the Sunnis is an ill-defined personality and there is no theory that he must be a descendant of Fatima. But the Shi'ites believe in a particular person as the Imam Mehdi who is a descendant of Fatima, and who will reappear after centuries of absence. To them it is a cardinal principle of their faith.

(7) The Shi'ites reject all the Hadith and Sunna of the Sunnis. But this should not be taken to imply that the Shi'ites have no Sunna, or prophetic tradition. They have their own collections of Hadith, which differ from those of the Sunnis inasmuch as they admit only the testimony of the Alids, the Imams and their partisans.

(8) The practice of Shi'ism has certain peculiarities, in the call to prayer, in the Tarawih of Ramazan, etc. Shi'ites law has its own peculiar solutions. To take part in public prayers is not obligatory for the Shias. In the funeral prayer they add a fifth *Takbir*, to the four in use among the Sunnis. According to

Shi'ites the pilgrimage to Mecca may be performed by a hired substitute. The Shi'as are most zealous in the worship of the saints and in pilgrimage to their graves.

(9) In the celebration of religious festivals, the Shi'as differ from the Sunnis in many respects. They celebrate the "Nawroz", the new year of the old Persian Calendar. The Shi'ites make a slight variation in the laws of marriage and divorce. To a Shi'a, the temporary marriage (the *Muta*) is allowed, provided dowry is specified and the period is fixed.

(10) Lastly, the Sunnis observe the *Ashurah* or the tenth day of the Muharram. But the Shi'as perform the ceremony of the Muharram in commemoration of the grandsons of the Prophet.

SHI'ITE IMAMS

(1) Ali (d 661)

(2) Hassan (d. 669) — (3) Hussain (d. 680)

(4) Ali called Zain al-Abedin (d. 711)

Zaid — (5) Muhammad al-Bakir (d. 736)

(6) Jafar as-Sadiq (d. 765)

Ismail (d. 760)	(7) Musa al-Kazim (d. 799)
Muhammad al-Maktum	(8) Ali al-Reza (d. 818)
Ismail	(9) Muhammad al-Jawaid (d. 839)
Muhammad	(10) Ali al-Hadi (d. 868)
Ahmad	(11) Hassan al-Askari (d. 874)
Abdullah	(12) Muhammad al-Muntazar
Ahmad	(Disappeared at Samarra in 878)
Hussain	
Abdullah	
Obaidullah al-Mehdi	

SHI'ITE BRANCHES

Like all creed's Shi'ism has its gradation. There are moderates in it as well as extremists. Those nearest the Sunnis are the Zaidis who believe that the Imams were appointed to their high office by Allah, but were not semi-divine creatures. Next come the Imamis (who admit twelve Imams, the line ending with Mohammad bin al-Muntazar, they are also called *Ithna Ashariya* who believe in the Imams being appointed ; but also believe that the Imams were mortal like other men although the divine light and power (Nur) dwelt in them. Then come the extremists, among whom can be mentioned the Druzes, the Ismailis, the Qarmatians, the Batinis, and the Nusayrids who believe in the Imams as incarnation of Allah. The extremist Shi'ites, therefore, had little in common with other Muslims.

Ithna Ashariya (*The Twelvers*)

The Shi'ites differed among themselves regarding the particular descendant of Ali, to whom allegiance was due and who might be accepted as their leader. As a result of this, the Shi'ites were divided into two sub-sects—Twelvers and Seveners.

The Twelvers (Ithna Ashariya) believe in all the twelve Imams: (1) Ali, (2) Hassan, (3) Hussain, (4) Ali called Zain-ul-Abedin, (5) Muhammad al-Bakir, (6) Jafar as-Sadiq, (7) Musa al-Kazim, (8) Ali al-Reza, (9) Muhammad al-Jawaid, (10) Ali al-Hadi, (11) Hassan al-Askari, (12) Muhammad al-Muntazar and hold that the twelfth Imam who had disappeared in 878 A.D. in the cave of a great mosque at Samarra, would return to this world in due time before its destruction to establish the reign of justice. This twelfth Imam, though hidden, is regarded by the Shi'ites as the supreme authority over the spiritual and temporal power.

The theory of the Twelvers is followed by the Persian. Shah Ismail Safavi, the founder of Safavi dynasty in Iran, claimed the descent from Musa al-Kazim, the seventh Imam of the Shi'ites. He made the Ithna Asharism the state religion of Persia and established a great Shi'ite Empire in Persia. The Shah is only the political authority, who rules on earth until God restores the true Imam, who has been kept in concealment all the while. The Shah of Persia has no spiritual power; he is only the guardian of law and order. In spiritual matters authority rests with the learned doctors of law and religion.

The Twelvers believe that their Imams control the destiny of the world. The salvation of man depends on them. They hold special formula and special hours of prayers for their respective Imams. The prayer of Sunday is reserved for Hazrat Ali and Fatima. The second prayer of each day except Sunday is reserved for Hassan, the third for Hussain, the fourth for Zain-ul-Abedin and the fifth for Muhammad al-Bakir. Pilgrimage to tombs of the Imams brings special reward. According to them, the Imam must be sinless, a quality which their Imams alone possess, and that he must be the most excellent (*afzal*) of mankind.

Seveners

The Ismailis (Seveners) were one of the most important branches of the Shi'ites sect. After the death of Hussain there were three different lines of Alids—those descended from (1) Hassan and (2) Hussain, the two sons of Ali by his wife Fatima, and (3) the house of Muhammad, the son of Ali by his wife Hanfiyah. Among these three, the most important sect was the faction which recognised Hussain as the third Imam and his son Zain-ul-Abedin as the fourth. They regarded Muhammad al-Bakir, the second son of Zain-ul-Abedin, as the fourth Imam and his son Jafar as-Sadiq as the sixth. At Jafar's death the Alids were again divided into two lines, one following his first son Ismail and the other following his second son Musa al-Kazim. The first group which regarded Ismail is the seventh Imam was known as the Ismailis or the Seveners. They held Ismail as concealed Imam.

The Ismailis made a remarkable contribution to

the theology of Islam. The Ismailia doctrines were mainly devised and elaborated by Abdullah ibn Maimun. The leading tenets of Ismailia creed are as follows :

(1) To the Ismailis "every letter and word of the Quran has a double significance ; for all revelations must have an interpretation and everything visible has its counterpart in the invisible world".

(2) According to the Ismailia belief, the Shi'ites can conceal their real faith in case of danger and persecution. In the circumstances that threaten their lives, the Ismailis are allowed to deny their own faith and conform externally to the faith of the ruling people. The principle of dissimulation (*Taqiyya*) also helped the Ṣeveners to perform their Hajj, because unless they conformed to the Sunni faith they were not allowed to visit the Ka'ba.

(3) To them religion does not consist in external observance, but in an inner sense and feelings. It is a matter of the heart "so institutional religion should be replaced by a religion of inner experience and feeling".

(4) To them, Hazrat Muhammad (صلعم) was not the last of the Prophets, but Ismail ibn Jafar as-Sadiq was the last Prophet and Imam.

(5) According to them, the soul is reaching to reason, *i.e.*, perfection has to undergo a series of struggles against matter. But in the struggle the 'sanction' *i.e.*, the regulations of the Almighty and *Natiqs*, *i.e.*, the apostles who are the manifestation of the first principle became the helpers and guides of the soul.

(6) From the beginning of life to its end is the stage of action and from the end of the life to its amalgamation with infinity is the stage of perfection.

(7) According to the Ismailia doctrine, man cannot attain to the truth by his unaided endeavours but stands in the need of the teachings and instructions of the

Prophet or Imam. Every Prophet had a helper, such as Moses had Harun, Muhammad (صلعم) had Ali and Abdullah ibn Maimun was the helper of Muhammad al-Maktum bin Ismail.

(8) In the Ismailia doctrine the number seven assumed a sacred importance. They tried to explain everything with the number seven which had a mystic significance with them. There are seven planets in the universe, seven days in the week, etc. Seven is also the number of the Prophets who had been sent to purify the world. The seven Prophets are Adam, Noah, Ibrahim, Moses, Jesus, Muhammad (صلعم), Muhammad al-Maktum bin Ismail.

The difference between Ismailia and Ithna Ashariya

Though the Ismailia (Seveners) and Ithna Ashariya (the Twelvers) belong to the Shi'ite sect, they differ with each other in various points.

(1) The Ithna Ashariya believe in all the twelve Imams from Ali down to Muhammad al-Muntazar. The Ismailis, on the other hand, believe in the validity of only seven Imams from Ali down to Ismail. They denounce the validity of all other Imams.

(2) The Ithna Ashariya believe that the twelfth Imam, Muhammad al-Muntazar, will reappear as the Imam Mehdi while the Ismailis (Seveners) maintain that the seventh Imam will be the future Imam Mehdi.

(3) The Ithna Ashariya believe that their twelfth Imam though hidden is the master of the time. He guides the destiny of the world. During the absence of the hidden Imam the king, as his representative, maintains law and order and exercises temporal powers of the Imam. The Seveners, on the other hand, believe that their Imam is living and a greater part of the Seveners recognise the present Agha Khan XIV as their

Imam. According to them, the king is not the representative of the Imams.

(4) The Twelvers (Ithna Ashariya) give more importance to the external observance of their faith, the Ismailis maintain that religion does not consist in external observance, but in an inner sense and feelings. They give a greater importance to the secret worship.

Lastly, the Ithna Ashariya are more akin to Sunni Muslims, while the Ismailis have drifted far away from the pale of Islam and developed almost a distinct creed of their own.

Murjites

The word Murji (derived from Irja' or suspension) means 'one who postpones' (judgment until the last day when the secrets of all hearts shall be revealed). Those who believe in postponement of judgment are called the Murjites. This sect was formed in Islam as a reaction against the Kharijite extremists. This movement was a development of the moderate views of the persons like Abdullah bin Umar who may be regarded as the founder of the Murjite sect.

The Murjites had a political origin. They were men who refused to take life too seriously, arguing that they were in fact the rulers of the Muslim state and asked the Muslims not to revolt but to pay homage to them. The Murjites thus tried to justify the political claims of the Umayyads and opposed those of the Kharijites and the Shi'ites. At first the Murjites rose with a political motive but later on 'due to changed circumstances' they formed the theological sect.

Doctrines of the Murjites

(1) The chief article of their creed is that no Muslim who believes in one Allah and in His Apostle

should be called an infidel, whatever sins he commits, until Allah Himself pronounces judgment against him.

(2) According to them the doubtful questions such as disagreement among the early companions and the claims of several men for the office of Caliph, etc., must be left to Divine judgment. "Those companions whom the Muslim public consider sinners, may be forgiven by Allah or in truth, may not be guilty though misunderstood by others."

(3) To them all the first four Caliphs were good. They do not condemn Uthman and Ali outright, as the Kharijites do. Both Uthman and Ali were servants of Allah and they must be judged by Allah alone.

(4) Every Muslim, to whatever sect or school he belongs, is a member of Muslim community. A Muslim must not fight against a Muslim except in self-defence.

(5) The Murjites gave a new interpretation to the nature of faith. They put little stress on the outward performance of the rituals of religion but greater emphasis on the spiritual development of soul and private communion with Allah. They hold that if a man externally expresses himself as an infidel but internally works as a true Muslim, he will be treated as a Muslim. "Religion is more a matter of heart than of external conformity to rituals." But there are some moderate Murjites, who declare that a Muslim must be a Muslim in both action and heart. Religion to them is both a matter of heart and action.

(6) The Murjites have brought tolerant spirit into religion. They set faith above works, emphasised the love and goodness of God, and held that no Muslim would be damned everlastingly. The best representative of the Murjite view was Imam Abu Hanifa.

(7) The Murjites have made distinction between

the major (*kabira*) and the minor (*saghira*). They regard polytheism as a major sin and that can never save man from the punishment of Hell fire. According to them the major sins can be expiated by repentance and for which man will not be thrown into Hell.

Kharijites

The Kharijites formed one of the earliest religio-political sects in Islam. This movement was first stared by a group of fanatics, mostly the disciples of Abu Zarr, who were very eager to preserve the purity and simplicity of Islam from all sorts of worldly influence. They were so-called because they dissented from the Muslims guided by the pious Caliph Hazrat Ali and formed a party of their own. When the civil war began between Muawiyah and Hazrat Ali, the Muslims, divided into hostile camps, met at Siffin in July 657 A D. In the war Muawiyah saw his inevitable defeat and appealed for a peace treaty. Though Hazrat Ali and majority of his soldiers accepted the appeal of Muawiyah and it was decided that two arbitrators from each side would be appointed to decide the matter according to the principles of the Quran, yet a small band of warrior of Hazrat Ali strongly protested the setting up of a human tribunal and left his camp with a slogan : *La hukma illa lillah*, *i.e.*, judgment belongs to Allah alone. They were the first dissenters or Kharijites. They went to Harura near Kufa and elected Abdullah ibn Wahab as their leader.

The arbitration unfortunately ended in complete deceit and this gave the Kharijites a justification for their attitude. Many Muslims did not like the anti-Quranic decision of the arbitrators and requested Hazrat Ali to reject the verdict of the arbitration and declare war against Muawiyah. As Ali refused to accept their request, they left Ali and joined the Kharijites who were living along the bank of canal Nahrawan near Baghdad.

The Kharijites started propaganda against Ali and tried to stir up people against him. They took to plundering and began to disturb the peace of the country. At this Ali marched against Nahrawan. He defeated the Kharijites and killed a large number of them including their leader Abdullah ibn Wahab (658 A.D.)

The defeated Kharijites became more furious. They considered Hazrat Ali, Muawiyah and his war adviser Amr, the then governor of Syria, the enemies of Islam and decided to murder them. Cunning Muawiyah and Amr escaped. But Hazrat Ali lost his life at the hands of the Kharji assassin Abdur Rahman ibn Muljim, who had lost his relatives and parents at Nahrawan.

After the murder of Hazrat Ali, the Kharijites could not remain silent. They could not accept the Umayyad Caliphs as the well-wishers of Islam and waged a long drawn hostility against them. Though the powerful Umayyad Governors of the eastern provinces curbed their power, yet they associated themselves with the Abbasids and contributed to the downfall of the Umayyads.

But lastly they could not accept the Abbasids in good spirit. They revived their hostility against them and disturbed the peace of Mesopotamia, Eastern Arabia and eastern coast of North Africa.

At last the Fatimids of Egypt put an end to the power of the Kharijites who ultimately ceased to be a political party and turned into a religious sect.

THEIR RELIGIOUS AND POLITICAL DOCTRINES

The Kharijites had no uniform code of doctrines. Their teachings contained some views of a number of sub-sects and they sometimes represented both theology and politics and sometimes the different opinions of theologians on particular topics. Only in certain matters they maintained their uniformity.

(1) According to them a Muslim who does not regularly perform his prayer and observe fasting and other rituals is no better than a Kafir,[1] or he has become an apostate and can never re-enter the pale of Islam and he should be killed for his apostasy along with his wives and children.[2] If he be an Imam or a Caliph, his Caliphate or Imamate should be seized and he should be killed.

(2) According to them, the Muslims who had committed sins and died without severe repentance, deserved eternal punishment in Hell. To them a single false step inlvolves ex-communication from the pale of Islam. The true faith rests not only in lip service but also in the absolute avoidance of every sin. Thus they justified both the faith and action of the Muslims. Faith without actions has no value at all.

(3) Like faith and action, the Kharijites gave equal importance to the conscience. A man must maintain his purity of conscience, otherwise he would be a *Murtad* or dead from religious view point. His punishment would be like those who violated their morality in faith and action.

(4) According to the Kharijites, all those Muslims who did not agree with the Kharijites ought to be considered as infidels or apostates whom the Kharijites must fight and destroy. The attitude of the Kharijites towards the general Muslims was extremely hostile which had been the cause of innumerable strifes and revolts in Islam.

(5) The Kharijites were very lenient towards non-Muslims. If the Jews and the Christians recited *Shahadat*

1. A.M.A. Shustery : *An Outline of Islamic Culture* (1954), p. 417.
2. W.M. Watt : *Free will and Predestination in Early Islam*, p. 35.

with modification as "Muhammad (صلعم) is the apostle of Allah to the Arabs and not to us" they were shown tolerance. They had their tendency of levelling the Arab aristocracy down with the Mawalis. Even a Kharijite theologian Yazid bin Abi Anisa went further to declare that a new prophet with a new Quran would emerge from the Persians.

(6) The Kharijites also discouraged frivolity. On that ground they did not accept Sura "Yusuf" as a revealed chapter of the Quran as it is full of worldly affairs and declared it a later addition.[1]

(7) The Kharijites were extremely democratic. They were guided by the principle of absolute democracy. According to them, the Caliph must be elected by the whole Muslim community and be responsible to them. He need not belong to a particular family or tribe. Any Muslim, even a slave or a woman, provided he or she is a good Muslim, can be elected as Caliph.[2] He should remain in office so long as the people are satisfied with his rule, if not, he may be deposed or even killed. Some among them denied the very necessity of the Imam and held that the Muslim congregation can be ruled on by itself.[3] They accepted the Caliphate of only Abu Bakr and Umar.[4] They denounced Uthman and Ali because they had corrupted true Islam and abandoned the authority of the Holy Quran.

1. H. Lammans : *Islam, Beliefs and Institutions*, p. 38.

2. D.B. Macdonald : *Development of Muslim Theology and Jurisprudence*, p. 23.

3. Ibid., p. 24.

4. MacGregor : *Muslim Institutions* (Eng. Trans.), p. 37.

CHAPTER V

SCHOLASTIC MOVEMENTS

Rationalism

Rationalism is a term employed both in philosophy and in theology for any system which sets up human reason as the final criterion and chief source of knowledge. In Islam this science has been developed early because its origin lay with the Holy Book. Many a time the Quran says that among the main attributes of Allah, Rationalism or *Hikmat* is one. To develop the faculty of reason man has to acquire a high learning, because learning develops the faculty of reasoning. For this reason, the Prophet of Islam always encouraged his followers towards learning. Hadith records that the Prophet said, "The ink of the scholars is more holy than the blood of the martyrs." "He who leaves his house in search of knowledge, walks in the path of Allah." From what the Quran says and the sayings of the Prophet it is evident that from the very infant stage of Islam the Muslims were engaged in the development of *Hikmat*. The rationalists tested every question by the touchstone of reason; to them reason was the principal source of truth and they only admitted the verdict of reason.

Mutazilism

Though the School of Mutazilism like other schools and sects in Islam came into being in the later times of the Companions of the Holy Prophet, its origin can be traced back to an earlier date. Up to the Prophet's own lifetime Islam consisted of simple but broad principles. This simplicity of the creed continued for some time after him. The Prophet's death was closely followed by wars with the Romans and Persians.

These wars completely absorbed the mental and physical energies of the Arabs. Further, the Muslims in the beginning were so much occupied with the propagation of their faith that they had little time to indulge in abstract discussions about the dogmas. Even then there was a group of Companions who did not have much to do with the military campaigns, and thus had leisure enough to be busy with theological studies and other academic pursuits ; reference here is to those in particular who were known as "The people of the Bench." Though the people of this group generally did not allow reason a free traffic into matters religious yet where needed they did try to work out the practical ramifications of religious doctrines in the searchlight of reason. It may not be out of place to mention the names of Ali ibn Masud, Ayesha, Mu'adh bin Jabal along with them. These were the people who prepared the ground for the school of Mutazilism.

It was in the fitness of things that with the advance of Islamic creed and culture in the ever expanding empire, new and various issues should have cropped up and new schools of thought established. It is important to note, however, that only those schools and sects came into prominence which had some marked political bearings. The origin of the Kharijites is a point in hand and so is that of the Shiites. Later the School of Qadarites, the real founders of Mutazilism, also had its moorings in the then political developments of the day.

The evolution of the Mutazila School of thought was attributed to Wasil bin Ata, a man of profound learning and favourite disciple of the illustrious Hassan al-Basari, the then head of the Muslim religious community. One day when Hassan al-Basari was busy discussing some problems with his pupils, some one came to him with a question with regard to the conflicting standpoints of the Murjites and Kharijites[1]. The first held that

1. R. A. Nicholson : *A Literary History of the Arabs*, p. 222.

the perpetrator of a grave sin should be reckoned as a Muslim and not labelled as an unbeliever ; in fact his case should be left to God. The second laying more emphasis on the threats in the Quran, maintained that a committer of a moral sin having *ipso facto* deviated from the right path could not possibly be considered as one of the believers. Before Hassan al-Basari could give a reply, Wasil bin Ata broke out with the assertion of a *via media* position, *i.e.*, such a one would neither be a believer nor an unbeliever. Hassan al-Basari took it ill and said : *I'tazila anna*, *i.e.*, he has seceded from us. So Wasil left the circle of his master, went to another corner of the mosque of Basra and began teaching his own views. Those who gathered around him came to be known as the Mutazilites.

Most of the progress and advancement of the Mutazilites goes to the credit of Wasil bin Ata who carried an awful grandeur of scholarship and learning around them. Besides the doctrines of *Qadar* and *'Adl* they added many other important and subtle formulations in his creed. The prestige of the School was raised and it gained strength so much so that it attracted the attention of the Court. Yazid ibn Walid publicly proclaimed Mutazilism and during his reign, short-lived though it was, it got ascendancy over other schools of thought. After the fall of the Umayyad kingdom in 132 A.H. (749 A.D.) Mutazilism received very hospitable treatment at the hands of the Abbasids. The second Abbasid Caliph Mansur appreciated the piety, devoutness and scholarship of Amr ibn Ubaid, one of the disciples of Wasil bin Ata, so much so that he wrote an elegy over his death. Wasil bin Ata sent a number of missionaries to propagate the creed of Mutazilism in the various parts of the country. Having done with the establishment and security of his empire, Mansur applied himself to the propagation of Art and Sciences. Books on philosophy and science available in whatever language, Sanskrit, Persian, Syriac or Greek, he got translated into Arabic. These translations made under the royal patronage, very much encouraged the study of philosophy and Science. Mansur was too liberal and high-minded to suppress these incursions on Islam with the sword. He gave free allowance to argumentation and discussion. Jurists and traditionists came forward to have intellectual discussion with the non-Muslims; but the weapons of dogma could be of no avail in these contests, so they had to retreat honourably. At this critical juncture the Mutazilites came to the rescue of Islam, fully equipped with the weapons of reason and dialectics, they took the non-Muslims to task and gave them a losing game. This added to the prestige of the Mutazilites and some of the most distinguished scholars came to subscribe to their views.

Later the Mutazilites received great honours at the court of Mamun. The two great Mutazilites, namely, Abu al-Hudhail Allaf and Ibrahim bin Sayyar Nazzam were Mamun's own teachers, both of whom he held in great esteem and veneration. With regard to Abu al-Hudhail, Mamun used to say, "He spreads over the art of dialectics as a cloud spreads over the people."

Al-Mamun was very fond of listening to the debates between people belonging to different religions, allowing them complete liberty of thought and speech. In all such debates and religious contests it was the Mutazilites who would come out victorious and carry the day. Well night they proved themselves to be the very saviours of Islam.

The two Abbasids after al-Mamun, namely, al-Mutasim and al-Wasiq, lent their wholehearted support to the Mutazilites.

Mutazilism is essentially a movement to interpret the dogmas of religion in terms of reason. The Mutazilites are mostly independent thinkers, and have quite individual views with regard to various religious and philosophic problems. We shall consider here some of their fundamental doctrines overlooking the individual differences and minor details.

FUNDAMENTAL DOCTRINES

(1) Allah alone is eternal. No shadow of dualism or pluralism can attach to Him. He is the only Eternal Being, and Eternity is the distinguishing attribute of the Divine Being. The Attributes of Allah are not in His Essence (*Zat*), but identical with His Essence. He has no Attributes apart from His Essence. In order to discard the dualistic nature, the rationalists rejected 99 attributes of Allah. "He is omniscient and omnipotent, not because He has the qualities of omniscience and omnipotence apart from His Essence, but because His very Essence itself comprises all that is understood by those qualities." The words—face, hands and eyes of God and His sitting on the throne—must be taken in a metaphorical sense.

(2) The Mutazilites reject the orthodox view, that the Quran is eternal. They maintain that the Quran is the 'work' of Allah and so His creation and not the 'word' of Allah. The Quran is expressed in letters and sounds and revealed to the Prophet in time, in place, and in the local language. The miracle of the Quran is in its teaching and not in its language. If the eternity of the Quran is accepted, then there would be two eternal things, one Allah and the other the Quran. But this is against the laws of Islam. The acceptance of the eternity of the Quran is fundamentally opposed to the Quranic principle of Divine Unity, which is the cardinal principle of faith.

(3) The Mutazilites believe that the acts of man are free and that he receives the reward earned by him. His graver sins are contraventions of the prohibitions

of God, and the man who is guilty of them (*Fasiq*) is considered to be placed in a situation intermediary between the infidel (*Kafir*) and the true believer (*Mumin*). This view is based on the Quranic verses, such as "whoever acts virtually does so for himself, and whoever acts viciously, does so for himself." "Nothing belongs to man save what he strives for." "Whoever follows the right path, does so for his own good, and whoever goes astray bears on himself the responsibility (of going astray)." Evil cannot be referred to God. It is human. God is Just and justice is indispensable with Him. Towards man, justice is His animating principle. There are no eternal laws for human action.

(4) According to Mutazilites, knowledge is attained through reason, which gives man the ability to distinguish between good and bad, between the real and not real. If reason judges an action to be good, it is good, and if evil, it is evil. Distinction between good and bad is within the power of human reasoning. Revelation only confirms what Reason dictates. It is through Reason that the worth of Revelation is understood and the sanctity of the religion is believed. One must not obey the law of religion without reflecting and knowing its truth. Theology should be subject to investigation and based upon rationalistic foundations and logical conclusions. "The Quran only confirms the dictates of reason dispelling thereby any doubt or misgiving that might linger in the wavering mind." The Quran very often appeals to Reason, reflection and understanding, and emphatically declares that our Reason itself is the safe guide and sole arbitrator in respect of what is good and what is bad.

(5) Beatific vision: According to Mutazilites, Allah will not be seen by any of His creatures. The idea of the vision of Allah presupposes that He has some form. The Mutazilites strongly oppose anthropomorphic view of Allah and maintain that Allah has

not form and as such no vision of Him is possible. The Quranic promise that virtuous will be regarded with the vision of Allah, should be interpreted in an allegorical sense.

(6) Divine justice : Allah is Just and justice is indispensable with Him. He is Just, Wise and Merciful. He never overtaxes His creatures. He does not impose on man any obligation which he is unable to fulfil. The Quran says, "Allah does not impose any task on the soul, but to the extent of its capacity." Towards man, justice is His animating principle. He will reward the virtuous and punish the wicked. It is impossible to reward the vicious or punish the righteous. In the Holy Quran Allah has promised that He will favour the righteous with regards and blessings and punish the wicked. The Quran says, "Never think that Allah will violate the promises He made to His Prophet." "Verily Allah does not break His promises."

In order to maintain the theory of Divine Justice the Mutazilites, on the other hand, held that man has freedom of will and they reject the idea of intercession of the Prophet on behalf of guilty Muslims on the Day of Resurrection and considered that man does not stand in need of a mediator to reconcile him with Allah. Each man will be judged according to his deeds.

(7) Political views : The Mutazilites considered the accession of the first Caliph legitimate, but they did not base that view on any Divine revelation. He was superior in merit to the second Caliph and the second to the third, and the third to the fourth. But some of the Mutazilites gave preference to the fourth over the other three and some said that the fourth was superior to the third but not to the other two.

The Mutazilites differed among themselves as to the question of the Imamat. Some held that it descended by appointment, while others maintained that the Imam should be elected by the people. They admit that Muawiyah, the first Umayyad Caliph, including Talha and Zubair and other Companions of the Prophet, who rebelled against the fourth Caliph, were wrong in their action.

THEIR DIFFERENCES FROM ORTHODOX SUNNI BELIEF

(1) The Mutazilites reject the orthodox view that the Quran is eternel. They deny the eternity of the Quran.

(2) They did not agree with orthodox Muslims with exaltation of seven chief divine attributes of will, power, knowledge, life, hearing, seeing and speech, as separate qualities, because they considered such differentiation a sort of polytheism.

(3) The orthodox Muslims believe that Allah will be seen by the faithful in the next world. Only the faithful and not the infidels will see Him. The vision of Allah will be the most precious of the gifts lavished upon the blessed faithful. But the Mutazilites deny the vision of Allah.

(4) They reject the idea of the *Wali* (Sage), which involves belief in one Muslim enjoying special privilege by performing miracles and wonderful deeds, on the ground that if one Muslim can do this, the others must be able to do the same.

(5) They did not recognise the idea of intercession of the Prophet on behalf of guilty Muslims on the Day of Resurrection, as it is believed by the orthodox Muslims. The Mutazilites considered that man does not stand in need of a mediator to reconcile him with Allah and that each man will be judged according to his deeds.

Scholasticism

'Scholasticism was an attempt at the reconciliation

of religion with philosophy. It had to depend on both, but its essential object was the defence of religion. In advancing their theories, in some instances, the upholders of scholasticism had to seek the support of philosophy and in other instances, in order to refute philosophical conceptions they had to take shelter under religious commandments.'

This movement was started as a reaction against the Mutazilite innovations. At the end of the third century A.H. the position was such that the people refused to admit any innovation (*bid'at*). Malik ibn Anas held that all the anthropomorphic expression of the Quran and the Sunnah must be believed without questioning how (*bila kaifa*). Blind faith was thus the order of the day.

The theory of *bila kaifa* (believe without asking how) could not satisfy the inquisitiveness of the Muslim intelligentsia who wanted something more. To satisfy their spiritual demand, a new theological movement was soon started in Islam which hinted to bring about a compromise between the two extremists—the Mutazilites and the Qrthodox—and to find out a middle course between the two. This movement is known as the orthodox scholastic movement. The advocates of this movement were called *Mutakallemin*, for they used *Kalam* in defending their traditional belief against the heretical attack of the Mutazilites. '*Kalam* is a science of reason which aims at attaining truth in a compatible way with the laws of religion.' The real founder of the scholastic school in Islam was Abul Hassan al-Ashari[1] after whose name the school is better known as Asharism or Asharia school.

Asharism

The Asharism was started as a reactionary move-

1. Abul Hassan al-Ashari was a descendant of Abu Musa al-Ashari, the arbitrator who was appointed by the fourth Caliph, Hazrat Ali, to defend his legitimate claim to caliphate after the battle of Siffin.

ment against the Mutazilites. It was a reaction of Revelation against reason. Thus a new school of scholastics under the leadership of one Abul Hassan al-Ashari was formed and became known as Asharia, whose object was to satisfy the masses. They selected a middle path between philosophy and orthodoxy, and thus Muslim orthodox scholasticism succeeded the rational one, influenced by the Asharia doctrine. Abul Hassan al-Ashari was born at Basra in 260 A.H. He was a pupil of the Mutazilite master Al-Jabbai and a staunch believer of his master's faith. Ashari was a great master of tradition, logic, philosophy and science. On the point of Allah's predetermination, he disagreed with the view of his master and made a public renunciation of his old view in 300 A.H. from the pulpit of the mosque of Basra. He died in 324 A.H. in Baghdad.

THEIR DOCTRINE

Their doctrine, in brief, is: (1) God does whatever He pleases. His existence and essence are identical; (2) He is sovereign and Lord of existence; (3) Whatever He wishes and commands, is just: (4) What is obligatory is to be distinguished from what is necessary; (5) Secular knowledge may be gained by reason, but reason cannot point out the real good; (6) God's attributes are distinct from His essence, in a way that a similar comparison cannot be instituted between God and His creatures; (7) When he desires to do a certain thing, the power corresponding to his desire is granted by God. Thus, though apparently it is done by man, it really is subject to God's will. This action is called *Kasb* or acquiring, because it is acquired by a special creative act of God. The great Ashari scholar, Abu Bakr Baqilani says that the substance of action is the effect of the power of God, but its qualities or accidents proceed from creatives. Actions are created by God, but man may acquire the various forms of activity; (8)

God's vision is possible but not with physical eyes; (9) God is not in need of space or place; (10) Things are neither good nor bad in their essence, but become bad or good when fixed so by the law of religion; (11) God can command impossibilities; (12) God's justice is not in the sense adopted by man. He may punish man for good action and reward for bad deeds; (13) God may do whatever He pleases with His creatures. No law, including Justice, can limit His action; (14) He must be known through religion and not reflection or rational argument.

THEIR FUNDAMENTAL PRINCIPLES

The following are the fundamental principles of the Asharites :

(1) God has settled upon His throne as He says in the Quran : "The Beneficent God is firm upon His throne"; (2) He has knowledge; (3) He has power; (4) He has seeing and hearing; (5) His speech is uncreated; (6) He guides some towards right belief and leads astray others to be misguided; (7) He created the Universe by the word *kun* (be); (8) The Quran is the God's speech, uncreated and eternal; (9) God will be seen on the Day of Judgment by the believers, but not by the unbelievers, as in the Quran; (10) Those who believe in the unity of God and call themselves Muslims but commit sins and are indifferent to the laws of Islam, are not counted as unbelievers; (11) Through the intercession of the Prophet, God will release some from the punishment of hell; (12) Paradise and hell are created; (13) Man dies at the appointed hour as stated in the Quran: "And no one, whose life is lengthened has his life lengthened, nor is aught diminished of one's life, but it is all in a book" (Ch. 30 : 5-11; (14) Men are tempered by Satan as declared in the Quran: "But Satan made them both fall from

it and caused them to depart from that in which they were" (Ch. 11 : 36).

In short, the Asharites believe in the eternity of the Quran, revival of the life in the dead on the Day of Judgment and the appearance of Allah to human sight on the same day.

The Asharite school produced a large number of great scholars in the person of Abu Bakr Baqilani, Abu Mali, Imam Al-Razi, Muhammad al-Shahristani, Abu Mansur al-Matrudi, and others. But the greatest, the noblest and the most original thinker of the Asharite school was al-Ghazzali. He gave final shape to the Asharite teachings and is regarded as the highest authority of the Sunni school. Undoubtedly, with Ghazzali Asharism ceased to be a distinct theological school and merged with orthodox Islam and became a part and parcel of Sunni ideology.

DIFFRENCES BETWEEN THE SCHOLASTIC IDEAS OF THE MUTAZILITES AND ASHARITES

The Asharism was a reactionary movement against Mutazilism. It was a reaction of Revelation against Reason. Al-Ashari championed the cause of orthodoxy against the Mutazilite heresy. In order to save the purity of Islam he refuted the Mutazilite views and replaced them by those of his own. Some of the important differences between the scholastic ideas of the Mutazilites and Asharites are as follows :

(1) The Mutazilites emphasize that Allah possesses no attributes whatsoever. If there are attributes in Him, the unity of Allah is questioned and it implies plurality. But the Asharites upheld the traditional view that the attributes actually exist in Allah. They are in Allah, but not in the sense in which we possess them. Allah is an infinite being. Naturally His attri-

butes cannot be compared to those of finite things—the attributes possessed by His creation.

(2) The Mutazilites upheld the freedom of human will, but the Asharites maintain that man has got no freedom of will, no liberty of action. He cannot perform even a slightest possible thing without the power of Allah. Allah creates in man the power and does the action through him. If man is responsible for his actions in the next world, it is only because he possesses consciousness of freedom or self-determination which are also the creations of Allah.

(3) The Mutazilites reject the eternity of the Quran and maintain that the Quran is the work of Allah and so His creation. But the Asharites held that the Quran is eternal, hence uncreated. The Quran was first uttered to the angels long before the advent of the Prophet. It was communicated to him through the angel Gabriel. The Quran is the speech of Allah and uncreated, but the letters in which it is written are created. Here the Asharites fail to explain the Mutazilites' difficulty which implies plurality and limits the activity of Allah.

(4) The Mutazilites laid more emphasis on reasoning than on revelation. But the Asharites thought that reasoning cannot form the basis of religious thought always. The primary essentials of truth can be obtained only by revelation. Reasoning itself is no more than common sense and regulated thinking, which may be employed by men about religion or any other subject. At best it can act as a preservative against error in deduction and arguments. But the primary essential of these, so far as religion is concerned, can be furnished only by revelation.

(5) While the Mutazilites reject the orthodox view that Allah will be seen by the faithfuls on the Day of Resurrection, the Asharites support this view. The rationalistic view of the Mutazilites regarding *Qabr*

(grave), *Hashr* (Resurrection), *Mizan* (Balance). *Sirat-al-Mustaqim*, Hell and Heaven and the vision of Allah are denounced by Asharites. They believe in the physical nature of all these entities.

(6) As the Mutazilites believe in the doctrine of Divine justice and freedom of human will, they reject the theory of intercession of the Prophet on behalf of Muslims. The Asharites on the other hand confess the intercession of the Holy Prophet Hazrat Muhammad (صلعم). According to them every Muslim requires the intercession of the Prophet through whose intercession Allah will release many Muslims from the punishment of hell.

(7) The Mutazilites say that prayer is useless for the dead. This question is a matter of Divine justice. The Asharites on the other hand, approve prayer for evey departed Muslim.

(8) As regards the question of *Miraj* or the Ascension of the Prophet, the Mutazilites say that it took place not in a bodily way, the Asharites on the other hand, agree with the orthodox view that it took place in body.

Thus, according to Prof. Shustery, while the Mutazilite school created a rational theology and explained the Quran in the light of philosophy, the Ashariya took up the new standpoint :

(*i*) Refuting the Greek and Oriental philosophy on their own ground, *i.e.*, philosophical argument.

(*ii*) Refuting the older religions and the newly founded and developed sects of Kharijites, Shias, Ismailis. The task was no doubt difficult.

But the Ashariya leaders proved themselves equal to the task and made a good stand. On many points, they succeeded in defeating their rivals and introducing several new and independent theories unknown, perhaps, both to Greek and Eastern philosophers.

CHAPTER VI

CURRENT TENDENCIES

Ibn Taimiyya

Ibn Taimiyya was born in Harran in 1262. At the time of his birth, the Muslim East reeled under the iron heels of the marauding Mongol horsemen. He was soon taken by his father along with the rest of the family from his native place Harran to the safety of Damascus, then the capital of Syria. Here, young Ahmad, as he was called, devoted some fourteen years to a detailed and systematic study of the Quran, Hadith, Law, Theology and other Muslim sciences, and gained a remarkable mastery over them. Besides the lectures of his father who was himself an eminent doctor of Hanbali law, he attended the discourses given by the famous Zain al-Din Ahmad al-Muqddasi.

He succeeded his father as professor of Hanbali law in 1282. In this capacity, he expounded, each Friday, the Quran *ex cathedra* in the city's principal mosque. He occupied this post for 17 years. In the meantime, his polemics had, however, earned for him the hostility of the other orthodox schools. Finally, his reply to a question on the attributes of God implacably displeased the Shafi doctors, alienated public opinion against him, and, as a consequence, cost him his coveted post of professor. He was accused of anthropomorphism—that is to say, of attributing human characteristic to God, and was shut up in the fortress either at Cairo or at Alexandria. In 1311, he was released and was appointed professor in the school founded by the Sultan in Cairo.

Ibn Taimiyya was at last permitted to return to

Damascus in 1313 where he resumed his duties as a professor. Differences with the Sultan on a point of law soon cropped up and he was once again shut up in the fortress in 1320. He was, however, released after a few months when once again he resumed his duties. An iconoclast and a believer in the supremacy of the individual conscience that he was, he had made a host of enemies which were ever on the look out to cause him injury. One such cause they found in a *fatwa* he had issued some 16 years earlier on visitations of tombs of saints and the prophets, vows, offerings, and invocations. This brought a new wrath of the Sultan upon him and he was interned in the citadel of Damascus in 1326. Here, he devoted himself wholly to writing a commentary on the Quran. He died at the early age of 40. The vast crowds who attended his funeral, there were present 200,000 men and 15,000 women—bore witness to the profound respect which was universally felt for the intrepid reformer.[1]

His main objective was to inspire people to rediscover the original teachings of Islam and to apply individual judgment in the inerpretation of religious doctrines. Every one should try to know and understand the doctrines himself and must not accept the authority of others without rational proof. Himself a student of Hanbali school, yet he refused to own the principle of *taqlid bila kaif* on all counts. He rejected *taqlid* and even *Ijma*. Being an ardent Hanbalite, he believed in following the letter of the Quran and the Hadith to the last detail, nevertheless. he was not against employing *qiyas*. He was also a bitter enemy of innovations, *i.e. bid'at*. The cults of saints and the pilgrimages to tombs came in for bitter denunciation at his hands. It was from Ibn Taimiyya that Muhammad ibn Wahhab, the founder of Wahhabism took inspiration in this regard.

1. R. A. Nicholson : *A Literary History of the Arabs*, p. 463.

Orthodox that he was, he preached and wrote against almost all the Muslim sects. Philosophy, he believed, leads to unbelief and had largely caused the schisms in Islam.

In short, Ibn Taimiyya was upright, God-fearing, a man of great knowledge and rare excellence, a man of principle and daring spirit.

Abdul Wahhab

Muhammad ibn Abdul Wahhab (1703-1791) was the founder of puritanic reorientation movement of Islam in Arabia. He was born at Uyaynah, a desert settlement of Nejd. He completed his education at Madina about 1724 A.D., and then gathered experience in the academic centres of Baghdad, Basra, Hamadan and Damascus for eleven years. Thereafter, he is said to have revisited Hijaz (1735) and stayed at Mecca for a considerable time before he returned to his desert abode of Nejd. He was a man with new mission. Since the movement aimed at large to revive the faith in the true monotheistic origin of Islam the reformers claimed themselves "Al-Muwahhidun" or Unitarians to establish the supremacy or sovereignty of Almighty Allah on, earth. They called the community as 'al-Ikhwan', *i.e.*, Brethren; with regard to realize the equality and social justice word '*Salafe*' was also used in Arabia to denote the Wahhabi fraternity; the term *Salaf* means ancestry, automatically stands for Wahhabism since it calls for revival of purely religious traditions, cultural heritage and political hegemony of Islam as professed and practised by the Prophet and the pious Companions.

At the dawn of the eighteenth century, there arose the Wahhabi Movement in Arabia (Nejd) with a motto to free the body-creed of Islam from superstitions and foreign elements that it assimilated in its long race ever since its inception in 610 A.D. Imam Ahmad bin Hanbal and Ibn Taimiyya actually paved the way for Muhammad ibn Abdul Wahhab to establish a puritanic order. The time was high enough for a change, the faith wanted a restatement and the practice a reform. The timely epoch-making call of Muhammad ibn Abdul Wahhab for reform coincided with the spirit of the age and hence was soon universally responded to by the rank and file in Arabia.

The author of Wahhabi Movement aimed at the restoration of Islam to its original standard. In its initial stage, the movement was suspected to be an attempt to introduce a new religion. This school was based on the Sunnah. A Western scholar remarks: "It was the natural reaction against those adaptations of Islam to complicated and akin civilizations which had sapped the strength of its founder's thought and resulted in the too much secularisation of religion." This reaction was natural inasmuch as religion should not be based on the idea of human well-being in this world only. Wahhabism was thus a reaction against the tendency to recast Islam in the light of modern thought.

The worship of tombs and relics of saints is a great sin according to Wahhabism. Erection of minarets or *dargahs* on graves and the use of rosary are also condemned. They contend that prayer which is meant to purify and ennoble the heart may be said in the spoken language of the people. The meaning of prayer must be understood without which it degenerates into a mere physical movement accompanied with the meaningless utterance of Quranic verses. They refuse to accept as binding the decisions of the four orthodox schools. *Qiyas* (inference) as a source of religious code they also reject. The entire group of men can err and have erred. Only the arguments of Sahabas are binding upon them. It is the duty and right of every Muslim to draw his own conclusion from the Quran and the Hadith. Again, they explain the Quran in its literal sense. They also reject the possibility of intercession by *pirs* and saints before God. He proclaimed that all men are equal before God ; that even the most virtuous and devout cannot intercede with Him ; and that, consequently, it is a sin to invoke the saints and to adore their relics" (Dozy). In the same puritan spirit they forbade the smoking of tobacco, the wearing of gaudy robes, and praying over the rosary.

Muhammad ibn Abdul Wahhab revolutionized Islamic thought in Arabia and preached a truer observance of the spirit of the Quran and Sunnah. His teaching won over the chief of Dira'iyya in Nejd, Muhammad ibn Saud. The House of Saud also grew in importance with the movement. It was not long before the Saudis came into conflict with the Sharifs of Mecca, the hereditary governors of al-Hijaz. The Wahhabi tribesmen, influenced by this puritan creed, extended the domain of the Saudi rulers, and at the beginning of the nineteenth century occupied and purified Mecca and Medina. In 1801 the Wahhabis captured Karbala and pulled down the dome on the tomb of Imam Hussain. Prince Abdul Aziz, the Saudi ruler being killed by a Shiite fanatic at this time was succeeded by his son Saud ibn Abdul Aziz.

Jamaluddin Afghani

The greatest single force in the reconstruction of Islam in the 19th century was Syed Jamaluddin Afghani, who profoundly influenced the reform movement in all parts of Islamic world. He was born in Hamadan in Persia, but was taken as a boy to Afghanistan, where he grew up. A man of exceptional ability, extraordinary gifts and great personality, he became a friend of Amir Dost Muhammad Khan of Afghanistan. In 1870, some time after his friend's death, he moved to Istanbul, where his ideas made great impression. He was liberal in his ideas and thought that the Muslims must meet the challenge of the West, by adopting what was best in Western civilization and by bringing out the finest values in their own civilization. Muslims must realise that progress was not the birthright of Western nations only. Others could learn and take their place in the march of time. He was a great believer in *Ijtehad*, which has kept and can keep Islam a living force. He inspired the Muslims with the idea of pan-Islamic nationalism. He had two objectives—political and theological. As a politician his mission was to combine, consolidate and co-ordinate all the Muslim countries against foreign domination and exploitation. As a theologian his objective was still more radical. He tried to redeem Islam from the false doctrines and abuses which had brought about this degeneration. He advised people to purify Islam from un-Islamic practices that had crept into it in course of time. His programme was to recast and reinterpret the prevalent system.

He became very popular with the progressive element in Istanbul, and the Sultan was persuaded by the orthodox to send Jamaluddin away. From here, he went to Cairo and then to India, stimulating Muslim thought there also. In 1883 he left for Paris, where he published a paper with the assistance of Muhammad Abduh. This Muhammad Abduh became later a great force in Egypt. In Paris, Jamaluddin met Shah Nasiruddin Qachar of Persia, who brought him to Tehran but when he organised a Reform Party there he was asked to leave. Jamaluddin left for Baghdad and later went to London. He attracted followers wherever he went, for his personality was magnetic and his arguments stimulating. He returned to Istanbul where he lectured at the University till his death in 1897.

The influence of Jamaluddin was also felt in distant parts of the Muslim world, as, for example, in

Russia, where in the latter half of the 19th century arose the famous reformer Ismail Gasprinski, editor of the newspaper "Tarjuman" at Baghjisaria, in the Crimea, who proposed the convocation of a Universal Islamic Congress to discuss questions of general importance for the reformation of Islam.

Muhammad Abduh

He is one of the most outstanding figures in the modern history of Islam and finally he is the greatest Egyptian reformer and sociologist. He was a powerful thinker, a prolific writer and a great reformer. His programme of reformation has been classified by Prof. Gibb under four heads : (1) purification of Islam from all corrupt influences and bad practices ; (2) introduction of a new system of education adapted to the altered situation of life ; (3) reinterpretation of Islamic doctrines in the light of modern thought ; and (4) the defence of Islam against foreign criticism and influences.

In the first place, it is held almost unanimously that Muslims have deviated far from original Islam. The vices and bad practices which entered into Islam are to be eradicated by all means. This move to purify Islam enlisted the support of the orthodox section also. There has indeed been a widespread resentment against the activities of the *pirs* and other un-Islamic practices like the worship of graves (*mazar*) of saints and observance of festivals (*Urs*) in their honour. The legality of the cult of saints has been called to question.

In the second place, appointed a member of the Council of Administration of Al-Azhar, Muhammad Abduh began an indefatiguable activity in order to renew and to raise the cultural, moral and material level of this Islamic University. He held that living in a progressive world it was suicidal for Muslims to stick to the outmoded medieval interpretations. The need for remodelling was much emphasised by him. With this object in view, the educational system of Egypt was reconstructed. In 1895 A.C. the syllabus of the Al-Azhar University was revised and many modern subjects were introduced.

Thirdly, Muhammad Abduh tried to inspire people with the idea that real Islam admits of dynamic values as opposed to static ones. Accordingly, the primary duty of a Muslim is to reinterpret the old values in the light of new experiences and situations of life. So a dynamic and evolutionary view of religious values is the need of the hour.

In the fourth place, he advised Muslims to find out the rational basis of religion. To grasp the inner meaning they must have a clear conception of the Islamic doctrines. Reorientation of the teachings of Islam in the light of modern knowledge was strongly advocated by Muhammad Abduh, the Grand Mufti of Egypt (1899), in order to meet the criticism of non-Muslims. The orthodox Ulema are unaware of what others say about Islam ; and so far they have done nothing to develop any system of theology. In the West, missionaries have done a good deal to develop Christian theology. But in Islam this work has been done mostly by people receiving modern secular education and not by the orthodox Ulema.

Praising his services C. C. Adam writes that Muhammad Abduh was a great reformer of his age. He brought numerous reforms for the betterment of the Egyptian people. As ill-luck would have it, the great champion of liberty and fraternity could not see the fruition of his endeavour, because of his early death in 1905.

CHAPTER VII

RELIGIOUS INSTITUTIONS IN ISLAM

What is Islam ?

Islam is the religion revealed by Allah and preached by the Prophet Hazrat Muhammad (صلعم) who was born in Mecca in 570 A.D. It is the embodiment of the code of life which Allah has framed to serve as norm for mankind.

Islam is an Arabic word and denotes submission and obedience. As a religion, it stands for complete submission and obedience to the will of Allah and hat is why it is called Islam. The other literal meaning of the word Islam is "peace" and this signifies that one can achieve real peace of body and of mind only hrough submission to Allah. Such a life of submission eads to the peace of the soul and establishes real peace in human society at large.

Basic Principles of Islam

The basic Islamic concept is that the entire universe is created by Allah, Who is the sovereign of the Jniverse. He is one and has no associates. He is the Ruler of the Universe, its Sustainer and Maintainer. He created man and appointed for each human being a xed period which he is to spend upon the earth. Allah as prescribed a certain code of life for man. One who hooses to follow the code revealed by Allah becomes Muslim (believer) and one who refuses to follow it ecomes a *Kafir* (non-believer).

A man professes Islam by honestly believing in llah and the Prophethood of Muhammad (صلعم). Both hese beliefs are epitomised in the *Kalimah* : *'La ilaha ill-Allah Muhammad-ur-rasul-ullah.*' There is no god except Allah, Muhammad is His Prophet. The third basic postulate of Islam is belief in the life-after-death.

The world, according to Islam, is a place of trial and judgment for man. He will have to render an account of all that he does here. Life on the earth will, one day, come to an end, and after that a new world will come into being. It will be in this life-after-death that man will be rewarded or punished for his deeds and misdeeds.

Thus the basic articles of Islamic faith are three, *viz.*

(*a*) Belief in the Unity of God ;

(*b*) Belief in the Prophethood of Muhammad (صلعم) and in the guidance he gave ; and

(*c*) Belief in the life-after-death and in man's accountability before Allah on the Day of Judgment. Whoever professes these beliefs is a Muslim.

Simplicity and Practicability

Islam is a religion without any mythology. Its teachings are simple and intelligible. It is free from superstition and irrational beliefs. Unity of God, Prophethood of Muhammad (صلعم) and the concept of life-after-death are the basic articles of its faith. They are based on reason and sound logic. There is no hierarchy of priests, no complicated rites and rituals. Every body is to approach the Book of Allah directly and translate its dictates into practice.

Islam awakens in man the faculty of reason and exhorts him to use his intellect. It enjoins him to see things in the light of reality. This is how Islam brings man out of the world of superstition and darkness and initiates him into that of knowledge and light. Thus

Islam is a practical religion and does not indulge in empty and futile theorizings.

A Complete Code of Life

Islam is a complete code of life which covers every aspect of an individual's life from his birth to his death and from the grave to the other world. Islam provides guidance for all walks of life—individual and social life, material and moral, economic and political, legal and cultural, national and international. The Quran enjoins man to enter the fold of Islam without any reservation and to follow Allah's guidance in all walks of life.

Islam is a religion for all ages and all countries. It offers successful solutions to all the temporal and spiritual problems of humanity. It is the most progressive, most scientific, and most democratic religion of the world.

Universalism

The message of Islam is for the entire human race. God in Islam is the God of all the worlds and the Prophet is Messenger for the whole of mankind.

In Islam all men are equal and there is no distinction between man and man on account of birth or position. It appeals to the conscience of humanity and banishes all false barriers of race, status and wealth. Islam is cosmopolitan in its outlook and approach and does not admit barriers and distinctions. It wants to unite the entire humanity under one banner and it is a message of life and hope and of glorious future.

Political Aspects

Islam is an all comprehensive political code. It has enjoined all the rules and regulations that a man requires for the different spheres of his life.

In Islamic political theory, sovereignty belongs to Allah. The Islamic state must be founded upon the law laid down by Allah through his Prophet.

Islam preaches the idea of true Democracy. There is a great difference between the Western Democracy and Islamic Democracy. In Islamic Democracy, sovereignty belongs to Allah, while in Western Democracy, it ultimately rests with the people. "Islamic Democracy is the government of Allah conducted by the people, either elected or selected on the basis of competency and honesty, who will work for the welfare of the whole humanity." All the administrative matters should be conducted according to the laws of *Shari'at*, and those questions about which there are no explicit injunctions in the Quran and the Hadith, should be settled by the consensus of opinion among the Muslims themselves. In Islamic Democracy, every adult and sane Muslim, both male and female, have equal right to express his or her opinion.

The Pillars of Islam

Religion is not an end in itself. It is the means for the realisation of an ideal—the development and perfection of man. The function of religion is to guide and help man to attain the highest perfection. For the achievement of this end Islam has enjoined, among other things, certain beliefs and practices generally known as the five pillars (*Arkan*) of Islamic faith. These are the fundamental tenets of all the thoughts and deeds that lead man to perfection. These are : (1) *Iman* or Faith, (2) *Salat* or Prayer, (3) *Saum* or Fasting, (4) *Zakat* or Charity, and (5) *Hajj* or Pilgrimage.

(1) IMAN OR FAITH

Iman or Faith involves belief in (1) One God, (2) His Angels, (3) His revealed Books, (4) All Prophets, as the Quran states, "Each nation has its own Guide" of whom the last is Muhammad (صلعم) and (5) Day of Resurrection and Judgment The basis of faith rests upon these five principles. The first and important principle of *Iman* is the belief in '*La ilaha ill-Allah*,' there is no god but Allah. A possessor of *Iman* is called *Momin* or believer. He must believe in the above-mentioned fundamental principles of Islam. Those who believe and have faith in Islam but are indifferent to the rituals and commit unlawful acts, will be punished in Hell though they will be finally saved. Thus paradise is the final abode of all believers.

Thus all articles of faith are in reality principles of action. Allah is the Being who possesses all the perfect attributes and when a man is required to believe in Allah· he is really required to make himself possessor of the highest moral qualities. He must set before himself the highest and purest ideal which the heart of man can conceive, and make his conduct conform to that ideal. Belief in the angels means that the believer should have the good impulses which are inherent in him, for the angel is the being associated with a good impulse. Belief in the Books of God signifies that we should follow the directions contained in them for the development of our inner faculties. Belief in messengers means that we are to model ourselves on their noble example and sacrifice our lives for humanity as they did. Belief in the Last Day tells us that physical or material advancement is not the end or good of life, but that its real purpose is an infinitely higher one, of which the Resurrection of the Last Day, is but the beginning.

(2) SALAT OR PRAYER

Prayer is the second pillar of Islam. Among the five pillars of Islam prayer occupies the most important position and is given the greatest prominence in the

Holy Quran. It is the obligatory duty of every Muslim to perform prayer. Unless a man performs his prayer regularly he cannot be a true Muslim. 'Islam considers prayer,' says Dr. Khalifa Abdul Hakim, 'to be the dividing line between believer and unbeliever. Islamic prayer is purified of all low and irrational elements and prescribed as a great help in the building up of a character by remembering God.'

Prayer is no doubt an institution which Islam has in common with all other religious systems, though it should be regularly performed by Muslims five times a day and at regular intervals, facing towards *Qibla* (Ka'ba) although the Quran clearly states that in the "East and the West everywhere is Allah, therefore whither you turn, thither is Allah's countenance, surely Allah is all-embracing and all-knowing". (Ch. II, 115). Therefore the object of facing Mecca is to bring uniformity among Muslims while they pray. The form and detail of the prayer is not mentioned in the Quran, but the Holy Prophet has given the details of this institution.

The fixation of prayer to five times a day has got a religious background. It is connected with the Prophet's Mi'raj or ascension to heaven. When he went there he received the order from Allah to prescribe fifty times of daily prayers. On his return journey he passes by Moses (Musa) who points out that the number of prayers is too much for his followers and asks him to go back and get it reduced. He makes five rounds between Allah and Musa. In each of the first four times of his approach to Allah, a concession of ten times of prayer is made. Now remain ten times of daily prayers which Musa tells him, are still burdensome to his followers. Under his instruction Muhammad (صلعم) approaches Allah once more and five times of daily prayers are finally ordained for the Muslims (Bukhari). Regarding the fixation of prayer to five times a day,

Muslim, Abu Daud and others are of opinion that Gabriel came out five times in one day and performed Salat in Muhammad's (صلعم) presence and the latter on each occasion imitated the angel (*Shorter Encyclopaedia of Islam*, p. 492).

The prayer is offered five times a day, and each prayer has two parts, the congregational, which is called *Farz* (obligatory), and the individual, which is called *sunnah* (the Prophet's practice). Each is made up of a number of *rak'ats* varying from two to four. The word *rak'at* is derived from *raka'a* meaning bowing down, and literally the *rak'at* is an act of bowing down before Allah. But technically it indicates standing, bowing down, prostrating and sitting reverentially, and is thus a kind of unity in the Divine service as inculcated by Islam. The order in which these different postures are adopted is a natural order. The worshipper first stands reverentially and offers certain prayers ; then he bows down and glorifies God ; then he stands up again praising God ; then falls prostrate placing his forehead on the ground and glorifying God ; then he sits down in a reverential position and makes a petition ; then again falls down in prostration. The congregational parts which are called *Farz* (obligatory) contain the following number of *rak'ats* :

1. *Fajr* or morning prayer .... 2 *rak'ats.*
2. *Zuhr* or early afternoon prayer ... 4 *rak'ats.*
3. *Asr* or late afternoon prayer .... 4 *rak'ats.*
4. *Maghrib* or sunset prayer .... 3 *rak'ats.*
5. *Isha* or night prayer ... 4 *rak'ats.*

The individual parts which are called Sunnah (Prophet's practice) contain the following number of *rak'ats* :

1. *Fajr* : 2 *rak'ats* said before the congregational prayer.

2. *Zuhr* : 4 *rak'ats* before the congregational prayer and 2 *rak'ats* after it.

3. *Asr* : 4 *rak'ats* before the congregational prayer.

4. *Maghrib* : 2 *rak'ats* after the congregational prayer.

5. *Isha* : 2 *rak'ats* after the congregational prayer followed by 3 *rak'ats* called *Witr*.[1] The 3 *rak'ats* of *Witr* are really part of the voluntary prayer called *Tahajjud*[2] which consists of 2 *rak'ats* said successively four times, followed by three *rak'ats*.

Every *rak'at* consists of the following parts :

1. *Qiyam* or the standing position.
2. *Ruku* or bowing down,
3. *Sajdah* or prostration,
4. *Qa'dah* or sitting.

In every mosque there is a semi-circular recess called the *Mihrab* which the worshipper must face, because he is then facing Mecca. He stands and says inaudibly that he intends to recite so many *rak'ats* or bowings. Then opening his hands and touching the lobes of his ears with his thumbs he says '*Allahu-Akbar*' and then proceeds to recite the prayers that go with the bowings. Lowering his hands and folding them, the left hand within the right, he recites the Surah *Fatiha*, the first chapter of the Quran. A few other verses follow. He then bows from the hips with hands on knees, says '*Subhana Rabbi al-Azim*' Glory be to my Lord, the Great), assumes an upright position with the words '*Sami Allahu-li-man Hamidah*' (Allah listens to him who

1. *Witr* odd number of rak'ats 3, 5, 7 which may be said after Isha prayer.

2. The word *tahajjud* is derived from *hujud* which means sleep and *tahajjud* literally signifies the given up of sleep. This prayer consists of 8 rak'ats.

praises Him), then, sinking gently to his knees, he places his hands on the ground and his nose and face also to the ground During this prostration (Sajdah) he recites '*Subhana Rabbi-al-Ala*' (Glory be to my Lord, the most High). He then rises to his knees, sitting on his heels, and performs a second prostration, reciting the same words. The prayer of one *rak'a* is then completed. At the end of the last *rak'a* he pronounces the credo, then looking over his right shoulder he says '*As-salamu-'alaikum-wa rahmatu-llah*' (peace be on you and the mercy of Allah) and then says the same words over his left shoulder. Besides the daily prayers, the following are performed on specified times :

1. Friday, or congregational prayer (Salat-ul-Juma), performed about one o'clock, when people, before prayer, listen to *khutba* or address, delivered usually by the one who leads the prayer. The *Zuhr* prayer of that day is not held. Salat-ul-Juma is not incumbent on a traveller, a sick person, a slave, a woman, a young child, a blind or a lame person.

2. Festival prayers : (for example on the occasion of Id-ul-Fitr and Id-ul-Azha). People are assembled in large numbers in an open place or mosque and perform two *rak'at* prayers and listen to *khutba* or sermon delivered by the Imam after the prayer.

3. Eclipse prayer (Salat-ul-Khusuf) consists of two *rak'ats.* This eclipse occurred on the day of the death of Ibrahim, the Holy Prophet's 18 months old son.

4. Prayer for the dead (Salat-ul-Janaza) : A Divine service is held over the dead body of every Muslim, young or old, even of infants who have lived only for minutes or seconds. It is called Salat-ul-Janaza. Technically, taking part in Divine service is called *Farz Kifayah,* which means that it is sufficient that some Muslims should take part in it.

During the journey or when at war, the prayers are shortened from four to two *rak'ats*, but two *rak'at* and three *rak'at* prayers of the early morning and after sunset are performed as usual. Women, during the menses, are exempted from performing prayers. If a mistake is made in prayer, or the worshipper is doubtful about the number of *rak'ats*, he adds, what is called *sajda sahw*, at the close of the prayer, just before the *Taslim*. The *sajda sahw* consists in performing a double prostration like the ordinary prostration in prayer. If the Imam has made a similar mistake he, along with the whole congregation, adds a *sajda sahw*.

Each prayer time is preceded by *Azan* or call to prayer. *Azan* was first introduced after Hijrat, at the suggestion of Umar. The Holy Prophet adopted the system of calling out to prayer at the fixed hours by a certain man. Bilal was first appointed to this noble job.

Before the prayer, the worshipper must be in a state of legal purity and must be free of every defilement, great or small and he should wear clean dress. The purification of body can be done by '*Wazu*' or ablution or "*Tayammum*' or when necessary by a bath.

RELIGIOUS AND SOCIAL SIGNIFICANCE OR PRAYER

In prayer, a Muslim is expected to observe the external form as well as the internal devotion and attention. His innerself must be absorbed in Allah so that for the moment his soul must enjoy perfect peace and calmness. It must be detached from all worldly cares and remain attached in concentration on the Supreme Being.

Prayer is the means of spiritual illumination and its aim is to know Allah and seek His help in man's attempt to attain his spiritual perfection. Prayer keeps man away from evil. Prayer in Islam gives man an opportunity for self-development and moral greatness. The Quran says, "Successful indeed are the believers who are humble in their prayers," (23 : 1, 2). In the institution of prayer, mankind has been made responsible for his deeds to the Ultimate Reality.

The fixation of a direction for prayers fosters the unity of purpose and discipline. Prayer teaches equality and fraternity among the worshippers. Congregational prayer imparts punctuality and concentration of the self to the ultimate Ego. It gives ample scope for social, religious and cultural symposiums after prayer. In short, prayer is the means of levelling all differences of rank, colour and nationality and the means of bringing about a cohesion and unity among men which is necessary basis of a living civilization. Ibn Sina says that a man at prayer is in intimate coverage with his Lord. Prayer is the plight of the alone to the Alone.

(3) SAUM OR FASTING

Fasting is the third pillar of Islamic faith. The fasting is obligatory on every Muslim, who is grown up and physically fit. The word Saum means 'abstaining' or 'to be at rest'. The institution of fasting in Islam clearly signifies abstaining from food and drink and sexual intercourse from dawn till sunset.

Fasting is common among many nations and with the exception of Zoroastrianism, it has been commended by all religions, but its modes and motives vary considerably in different religions. Fasting was practised by the Jews as an act of mourning Jesus Christ fasted for forty days before starting his ministry. Islam has introduced the highly organised institution of fasting as a means of developing the inner faculties of man. The reasan assigned in the Quran for fasting is that it is intended to prevent evil tendency and to purify one's soul. 'The institution of fasting in Islam,' says Amir Ali, 'has legitimate object of restraining the passions, by diurnal abstinence for a limited and definite period, from all the gratifications of senses and directing the overflow of the animal spirits into a healthy channel.' The institution of the fast of Ramazan was set up by the Prophet in the second years of the Hijra.

The month of Ramazan is specified for the purpose of fasting. The word 'ramz' literally means 'to burn'. In the month of Ramazan a man burns his evil propensities. The Quran says: "The month of Ramazan is that in which the Quran was revealed, a guidance to men and clear proofs of guidance and destination, therefore, whoever of you witness the coming of this month, he shall fast therein.' The fast of Ramazan lasts for one whole month during which a Muslim must eat light food before the daybreak and remain withoult food, including water, till sunset. He must abstain during these hours from all vicious actions, such as abusing, back-biting, anger, jealousy, sexual intercourse. Vomiting does not break the fast if the matter vomited is not mouthful. Kissing of wife does not break fast.[1] Thus, fasting among the Muslims does not mean remaining hungry for certain hours but to abstain from all evils and restrain one's eyes, tongue, ears and all other senses of the body from lust and passionate activity. The fast must be broken only after sunset, after which Muslims go to the mosque and join in the prayer known as *Tarawih* which is in addition to the usual prayer, in 20 *rak'ats*. One of the last ten nights of the month of Ramazan is called *Lailat al-Qadr*. The word *Lail* or *Lailah* means night and *Qadr* means originally, measuring. But *Lailat al-Qadr* is also translated as meaning the night of grandeur or majesty. *Lailat al-Qadr* is better than a thousand months. The angels and the inspiration (*al-ruh*) descend

1. Bukhari mentioned that the Prophet would kiss his wife when fasting (30 : 23).

in it by the permission of their Lord for every commandment. Here this night is spoken of as the night in which the Quran was revealed. It is also called the night of measure because on it was laid the basis of a new revelation to the world which contains every commandment (*amr*) full of wisdom and knowledge, for the same reason, it is called a blessed night or the grand night. The *Lailat al-Qadr* is, therefore, the anniversary of the revelation of the Holy Quran. Again according to some other traditions the twenty-seventh night of Ramazan is the *Lailat al-Qadr*. In most of the Islamic countries the 27th night of Ramazan is generally observed as *Lailat al-Qadr*, and on that night the Muslims pass the whole night in prayer and recitation of the Holy Quran.

The fasting is obligatory upon every Muslim, male and female, who is physically fit (*qadir*) and who is mature (*baligh*). The fasting must be preceded by '*Niyyat*' which means intention or purpose in doing a thing. For the weak, the sickly, the traveller, the student (who is engaged in the pursuit of knowledge), the soldier engaged in *Jehad* against the assailants of the faith, and women in their ailments, it is disallowed. Fasting is forbidden (*haràm*) on the days of the two great festivals: Id-ul-Fitr and Id-ul-Azha, (Bukhari 30 : 66). Fasting is a means of spiritual discipline. The ultimate aim of fasting is the seeking of Divine pleasure. According to the Holy Prophet, fasting is a shield which protects from all kinds of evils. While fasting a man refrains not only from food, drink and other desires, but also from all kinds of evils. But fasting is not starvation. Though food and water are in his possession, he does not take them, because it is the commandment of Allah that he should not take them and he also believes that Allah is with him and sees him. Thus the underlying spirit of fasting is to awaken the spiritual discipline.

The 'breaking' of the fast, which occurs on the first of the month of Shawwal, is the occasion of a feast, called Id-ul-Fitr. This involves a solemn prayer, called *Salat al-Id*, consisting of two raka'ts performed in the morning after day-break.

In a nutshell, fasting plays the double role of (*a*) teaching self-discipline and self-control in the way of Allah, and (*b*) acquainting the rich with the feeling of hunger as experienced by the poor. It also teaches us to conquer our passions and selfish desires.

(4) ZAKAT

One of the five foundations of religion, incumbent upon all adult Muslims who are sane, free and possess *Nisab* (property) is to give Zakat or charily.[1] "No religion of the world prior to Islam has consecrated charity, the support of the widow, the orphan, and the helpless poor, by enrolling its principles among the positive enactments of the system." (Ameer Ali)

Zakat or charity is an institutionalized way of translating the thus created sentiments of compassion, and craving to help the poor, into practical action. It tends to counteract the trend towards the accumulation and concentration of wealth, and to reduce the gulf between the rich and the poor. Muslims are enjoined to express their gratefulness to the Creator by helping the created out of what He has given them.

Zakat was a sort of compulsory poor-tax, levied on definite forms of property, and collected only from Muslims who had attained their maturity and were in full possession of their faculties. The Prophet framed some rules in regard to it, which were strictly followed

1. The word for charity is *infaq* which means spending benevolently; *ihsan* means the doing of good: *zakat* means growth or purification, and *sadaqah* which is derived from the root *sidq*, meaning truth and comes to signify a charitable deed.

by his successors. It was levied on (*a*) grain of the field, fruits, dates, grapes, etc., (*b*) animals, *i.e.*, camels, cattle, and other domestic quadrupeds, (*c*) gold and silver, and (*d*) merchandise.

The word zakat has been derived from the root '*zāka*, which means 'it grew or it purified'. Zakat has been described as 'wealth which is taken from the rich and returned to the poor' (Bukhari 24 : 1). It is so called because the giving away of wealth to the poor and needy increased the wealth of the community as a whole and at the same time, 'it purifies the giver's heart of the inordinate love of wealth which brings numerous sins in its train'.

The zakat is a religious tax which is levied on the various categories of possession according to a definite rule. It affects the productions of the soil, cattle, precious metals (gold and silver) and merchandise. Those things are liable to tax only if they reach a certain minimum value called *Nisab* which varies for each item. It is Rs. 40 in the case of cash money, 52½ tolas in case of silver and 7½ tolas in the case of gold. In the case of merchandise of all kinds, the value is calculated and the *Nisab* is judged by the silver standard. The tax is generally paid in kind. On land produce, it was levied at the rate of 10% or 5% according to whether the land was watered by rain or stream or by buckets to be paid immediately after the harvest. It was payable only when the produce exceeded a certain quantity fixed by the Quran. For instance, in the case of wheat, zakat was levied only when five *wasuq* (1 *wasuq* = 323 lbs. approximately or 26 maunds 10 seers) were produced in a season. 'Precious stones are,' says Mohammad Ali, 'also exempted from zakat. because in taking a part in this case, the whole would have to be destroyed.' But in the case of animals the rate of zakat differs for different kinds of animals, but in the main the general rate of 2½ per cent seems to have been kept in view. Though the rate has been fixed at $2\frac{1}{2}$ per cent, the rich can give away in Allah's name more than the fixed proportion ; it is a good act and it deserves more merit.

The distribution of zakat money was made among the following categories :

(1) To the poor and the needy (*Fuqara* and *Masakin*) ;

(2) To the tax collectors (*Amala*) ;

(3) To those whose hearts one desired to win (the new converts to Islam) ;

(4) To assisting slaves to purchase their freedom from their masters ;

(5) To those who were in debt ;

(6) To the arming of the volunteers to the Holy Wars and to the military expenses incurred in the fight against the infidels ;

(7) To incur the expenses for the maintenance of an establishment and office for the collection and distribution of zakat ; and

(8) To give aid to poor travellers.

Charity is of two kinds—obligatory and voluntary. The obligatory charity is called zakat and the voluntary is called *sadaqah.*[1] *Fitrah* after Id is a *sadaqah*. At the end of the fasts of Ramazan, every Muslim is obliged to give in *fitrah* for himself, and for every member of his family. *Sadaqah* can be given by any Muslim at any time. There is no fixed rate of *sadaqah* ; it may be given as much as a man can give in private and it should be given purely out of love for Allah.

1. To remove from the road anything which may cause hurt is called a *sadaqah* or a charitable deed, (Bukhari 46 : 24)

Religious and Social Value of Zakat

Islam is a religion of humanity. With this object in view, Islam has enjoined the institution of zakat. It is the most benevolent institution in Islam. It serves as a purifying substance in the sphere of morality, social status and economic strata. It is said that the benevolence is one of the two mainstays of religion. The combination of salat and zakat is of frequent occurrence in the Quran. Prayer becomes meaningless if it does not lead to acts of benevolence. Love of Allah should be the motive in all charitable deeds, so that the very doing fosters the feeling that all mankind is but a single family. "And they give food out of love for Him to the poor and the orphan and the captive." (76 : 8) Only good things and well-earned wealth should be given in charity. The Holy Prophet himself has described zakat as wealth "which is taken from the rich and returned to the poor." (Bukhari)

The institution of zakat in Islam has not only provided the solution of wealth problem, but also showed the way to "develop higher sentiments and character-building, on which alone can be laid down the foundation of a lasting civilization for the human race." Zakat, therefore, acts not only as a levelling influence, but also as a means of developing the higher sentiments of man, the sentiments of love and sympathy towards his fellowmen. In other words, like the blood circulating in a living organism, wealth is made to circulate in the body-politic of Islam. The object behind the imposition of zakat is to give economic security to the Muslim community and to prevent the accumulation of wealth in a few hands. It is the duty of the rich to give zakat for the maintenance of the poor or needy and it is the right of the poor to receive it. Zakat brings harmony and perfection in the society and thus leads to the achievement of the universal brotherhood of man.

The institution of zakat regulates the conduct of the individual Muslim as a member of the society or community and develops his social consciousness. It teaches that no Muslim should be selfish ; he should spend a part of his wealth for the welfare of the Muslim society. The institution of zakat instills fellow-feeling among them and thus strengthens the unity of the Muslim community as a whole. The institution of zakat discourages capitalism and attempts to solve the problem of disparity in wealth.

(5) HAJJ

Hajj or pilgrimage is the fifth institution of Islam. The word Hajj literally means "repairing to a thing for the sake of a visit" and technically it means "repairing to Bait-Allah to observe the necessary devotions." It is one of the obligatory duties in Islam, at least once in lifetime. It is obligatory upon those who are adult, in good health and have enough money to meet the expenses of their journey to Mecca and maintain their family during their absence.

The pilgrimage is not a new institution. It is a revival of ancient rites common throughout the Semitic East. Mecca had been the centre of pilgrimage from the time immemorial. According to the Quran, Ibrahim was the founder of Hajj. Pilgrimage is the only real bound that unites the different Muslim communities, and the only opportunity for a pan-Islamic reunion.

The Prophet after removing all idols and signs of idolatry from Ka'ba and making certain modifications in the rituals observed by the Hajis (pilgrims), permitted the pilgrimage to his followers. The annual pilgrimage of the Muslims to the Ka'ba at the fixed time in the month of Dhul-Hijja is called Hajj. The man who performs this is called a Haji. But there is also a lesser or minor pilgrimage to Mecca called '*Umra*' or visitation. The Umra can be performed at any time of the year and the rites pertaining to it are fewer in number.

The ceremonies begin at the last stage of the journey, near Mecca, in the following manner :

(1) The pilgrim, after taking a bath and performing two *rak'at* prayers, removes his dress and wears two pieces of cloth, one of which covers the lower extremities of his body and the other his chest and shoulders. The head remains uncovered. None is exempted from this rule and all Muslims, from a king to the poorest peasant, has to observe it. This is called *Ihram*. When this is done, one must not shave, remove his nail or kill any living being. The women are allowed to put on their ordinary dress, but their faces are kept open. Veil is forbidden while in *Ihram*.

(2) The pilgrim must take a vow to abstain from worldly affairs and continuously call on and recite *Talbiah*, *i.e.*, say : *Labbaik Allahumma Labbaik*, *i.e.*, I stand in thy service, O Allah, I stand in thy service.

(3) The pilgrim must next perform *Tawaf*, *i.e.*, make circuit round the Ka'ba thrice at a quick pace and four times at a slow pace. Men and women are allowed to perform *Tawaf* together, the women keeping apart from men. *Tawaf* may be performed while one is riding on an animal. Menstruating women are not allowed to perform *Tawaf*.

(4) The pilgrim must next kiss the Black Stone[1] (*Hajr-Al-Aswad*) which is embedded in the wall of the Ka'ba at a height of about 5 feet and it is nearer the door of the House.

(5) The pilgrim must then perform two *rak'at* prayers at a place known as *Maqam-i-Ibrahim*.[2]

1. The original colour of this stone is not known but the Arabs think that it was white, but it grew black by the touch of sinful men.

2. The *Maqam-i-Ibrahim* is a very old sacred stone on which Ibrahim stood up at the time of building the Ka'ba.

(6) The pilgrim must next perform *Sayee i.e.*, run from mount Safa to mount Marwah seven times on the 6th of Dhul-Hijja.

(7) The pilgrim next listens to the *Khutbà* in the great mosque at Mecca (this being done on the 7th day of Dhul-Hijja). This *Khutba*, which immediately follows the *Salat* (prayer) of *Zuhr*, gives counsel to the pilgrims and supplies a kind of programme of the ceremonies in which they are about to take part.

(8) The following day, the eighth, is called the day of slaking of thirst (*Yaum-al-Tarwiyah*) because it is said, the pilgrim must lay in a supply of water for himself and his mount. In imitation of the Prophet, the pilgrim performs at Mina (which is about 4 miles from the city of Mecca) the prayer of *Zuhr* and remains there the whole night.

(9) On the 9th Dhul-Hijja, the pilgrims move to the plain of Arafat (which is situated to the east of Mecca at a distance of about 9 miles) to perform *Zuhr* and *Asr* prayers combined, after which the Imam delivers a *Khutba* from the pulpit on the Jabal al-Rahmah. The pilgrim's stay in Arafat lasts only from afternoon till sunset and is known as *Waquf* (meaning halting or standing still), but so important is the place it occupies in the devotional acts that Hajj is considered to have been performed if the pilgrim reaches Arafat in time on the 9th Dhul-Hijja, but if he is unable to join in the *Waquf*, the Hajj is not deemed to have been performed.

(10) After sunset the pilgrims leave Arafat and stop at Muzdalifah (from 'Zalf' meaning nearness). On reaching Muzdalifah, the pilgrims say their *Maghrib* and *Isha* prayers, combining the two. There the night is passed, and then after saying the morning prayer at an early hour the pilgrims leave for Mina.

(11) Thus the pilgrims again reach Mina on the morning of 10th Dhul-Hijja, which is called *Yaum al-Nahr* (the day of sacrifices), being the day which is celebrated as the Id al-Azha all over the Muslim world. At Mina, the animals are sacrificed, the pilgrims then return and perform the *Tawaf* of Ka'ba. This is called the *Tawaf al-ifazah*, and with it, the pilgrim emerges from the state of *ihram*, by having his head shaven or his hair clipped. The pilgrims then return to Mecca and again after going round the Ka'ba once again, complete the Hajj. The 11th, 12th, and 13th days of Hajj are called *Ayyam al-Tashriq*, the moonlit nights.

The minor rituals connected with the Hajj are: Drinking of water from the well of Zamzam near the Ka'ba, fasting and the throwing of pebbles at sacred pillars and visiting the tomb of the Prophet at Medina.

Religious and Social Significance of Hajj

Hajj or pilgrimage to Mecca, has been taken over from the pre-Islamic customs of the Arabs, aud strengthens the sense of trans-national unity in the Islamic world. The visit to Mecca, which is associated with the life and activities of the Holy Prophet, has a strong reaction on the mind of the pilgrims. Hajj is a higher spiritual experience. They pray to Allah to pardon them and grant them strength for obedience to Him in future. They give up all sorts of evils and sins and seek the mercy of Allah. To get closer attainment of Allah, man has to satisfy Him and this is only possible by the silent performance and observance of His orders and rituals. In Hajj there are many rituals, as going round the Ka'ba, kissing the Black Stone (Hajr al-Aswad), running between Safa and Marwa and the throwing of stones, and the pilgrims perform these deeds very earnestly and without question. These actions of the pilgrims are sure to satisfy Allah. Imam Abu Hanifa calls Hajj the best of all *Ibadat* (worship) saying that here one takes a risk of life in the way of Allah, spends in His way and thus exhibits his love towards Him. Love towards the Creator is amply exhibited here, according to al-Ghazali, for the pilgrim does even apparently irrational things, such as the throwing of stones or going round the Ka'ba. The very purpose of these acts is purposelessness, and the objective test of love.

Social Solidarity

Hajj has a great social importance. Hajj strengthens the tie of unity among the Muslims. During the days of Hajj Mecca becomes the centre of Muslim World Congress. "No other institution in the world has the wonderful influence of Hajj in levelling all distinctions of race, colour and rank. Not only do the people of all races and all countries meet together before the House of Allah as His servants, but they also clad in one dress—in two white sheets—and there remains nothing to distinguish the high from the low". Hajj gives an opportunity to remove all misunderstandings among the Muslims themselves. Moreover each pilgrim has the keen sense of fellow-feeling, love and affection. Dr. Laner in his book 'Religious Systems of the World' says, "The demonstration of equality furnished on the occasion of Hajj is so complete that it is well-nigh impossible to distinguish a servant from a master. The whole of humanity assumes one aspect and one attitude and thus the noblest sight of equality and brotherhood is witnessed in the Hajj. There is in this city a force which transcends the littleness and division of mankind." Thus the unity of dress, feeling and one common place of annual meeting hasten the idea and spirit of universal brotherhood among the Muslims. Hajj affords a greater opportunity for mutual help and develops the spirit of benevolence. Hajj also gives opportunities to the Muslims to acquire knowledge of different lands, climates, regions, etc. Regarding the socialistic influence of Hajj, Prof. Hitti says, "Down through the ages this institution has continued to serve as the major unifying influence in Islam and the most effective common bond among the diverse believers. . . The socializing influence of such a gathering of the brotherhood of believers from the four quarters of the earth is hard to over-estimate. It afforded opportunity for Negroes, Berbers, Chinese, Persians, Syrians, Turks, Arabs—rich and poor, high and low—to fraternize and meet together on the common ground of faith. Of all world religions Islam seems to have attained the largest measure of success in demolishing the barriers of race, colour and nationality—at least within the confines of its own community. The line is drawn only between believers and the rest of mankind. These Hajj gatherings have undoubtedly contributed their share towards the achievement of that result."[1] Thus all these enrich the knowledge of the pilgrims and give an impetus to the social and cultural progress of the Muslim world.

1. P. K. Hitti : *History of the Arabs*, p. 136.

CHAPTER VIII

IMAN AND ISLAM

The religion of Islam may be broadly divided into two parts—the theoretical or what may be called its articles of faith or its doctrines—and the practical, which includes all that a Muslim is required to do, that is to say, the practical course to which he must conform his life. The former is called *Iman* or Faith and the latter *amal* or deeds. The former is also called *aqaid* (pl. of *aqidah*) or beliefs, and the latter *ahkam* (pl. of *hukam*) or the ordinances and regulations of Islam.

Iman

"Iman," according to Raghib, the famous lexicologist, "is sometimes nothing more than a confession with the tongue that one believes in Muhammad صلعم." Further he says, "*Iman* also implies the condition in which a confession with the tongue is accompanied by an assent of the heart, *tasdiqun-bil-qalb*, and the carrying into practice of what is believed, *amalun-bil-jawarih* (lit. doing of deeds with limbs)." Thus the word *Iman* as used in the Holy Quran, signifies either simply an assent of the heart or a fixed conviction of the truth brought by the Holy Prophet or the doing of good deeds and carrying into practice of the principle accepted or it may signify a combination of the three.

The first and the greatest principle of *Iman* is the belief in *La ilaha ill-Allah*, 'there is no god but Allah.' A possessor of *Iman* is called *Momin*,—believer. He must believe in all the fundamental principles of Islam. Those who believe and have faith in Islam but are indifferent to the rituals and commit unlawful acts, will be punished in Hell though they will be finally saved. Thus paradise is the final abode of all believers.

Islam

Islam means submission and obedience. Islam is called by this name because it is submission and obedience to the will of Allah. Islam aslo signifies *Salamti* and thus stands for peace. More comprehensive meaning will be 'striving after righteousness.' There is absolutely no difference between the "submission and obedience to the will of Allah," and "striving after righteousness." Righteousness is nothing but the path shown by Allah. Islam is a complete code of life which covers every aspect of an individual life from his birth to his death and from the grave to the yonder world. Islam is a body of doctrines and a code of practices. Islam puts forth a philosophy of life concerning the individual's conception, his Allah, his messenger of God, Hazrat Muhammad (صلعم), and the universe, that is all around him. Islam is thus a philosophy of action and a way of life. It is a transformation of the individual, of the family, of the society, of the state and of humanity ; it is a revival, moral and intellectual, and the attainment of the highest pinnacle of civilization both spiritually and materially.

Islam and Iman

The word *Iman* signifies originally connection of the heart, while the word 'Islam' signifies originally submission and hence relates primarily to action. The difference in the original meaning finds expression both in the Quran and the Hadith, though in ordinary use they both convey the same significance, and the word *Mumin* and Muslim are generally used interchangeably. A man is said to have believed when he simply declares his faith in the Unity of God (*Tauhid*) and the Prophethood of Muhammad (صلعم), which in fact is the first stage of belief, because it is only by declaration of the acceptance of a principle that one makes a start, and a man is also said to have believed when he carries into practice to his utmost extent the principles in which he declared his faith. The only difference is that in the first use, belief of *Iman* is, in its first stage, a confession of the tongue—a declaration of the principle ; and in the second, *Iman* has been perfected and indicates the last stage of faith—which has entered into the depths of the heart, and brought the change required. The same is the case with the use of the word Islam. In its first stage it is simply a willingness to submit, in its last it is entire submission. Thus both *Iman* and Islam are the same in their first and last stages—from a simple declaration they have developed into perfection and cover all the intermediate stages. They have both a starting point and a goal ; and the man who is at the starting point, a mere novice, and the man who has attained the goal are both called *Mumin* and Muslim, as are also those who are on their way, at different stages of the journey.

Allah

Of the principal beliefs of Islam, the belief in Allah comes first. The Holy Quran says, "There is no god but Allah. He is Self-subsisting, the Eternal. Neither sleep nor slumber can overpower Him. All that is in heaven and earth belong to Him. None can intercede before Him except with His permission. He knows the past and the future. None can compass His knowledge. His throne extends over the heavens and the earth, whose care and preservation cause no fatigue to Him. He is the most Exalted and the most Glorious." He creates things and brings them to perfection. He makes things according to a measure and shows them the ways whereby they may attain to perfection : He is the Nourisher of all creatures. His worshipper must do his utmost to serve the cause of humanity, and exercise care even for creatures that are dumb. Allah is loving and affectionate to His creatures, so the one who believes in Him will be moved by the impulse of love and affection towards His creation. Allah is merciful and forgiving.

Allah has created everything out of nothing by the sheer act of will. He created the universe and the angels before He created man. He made universe in six days and did not rest on the seventh. Out of a vapour that filled all space Allah created the water, the earth, the mountains, then living creatures and finally on Friday, Adam. There are seven heavens and seven earths, as there are seven regions in paradise and seven divisions of Hell.

The Surah *Ikhlas* gives a clear conception of Allah. "Say, He is One. Allah is He on Whom all depend. He begets not, nor is He begotten. And none is like Him." Hundreds of verses can be cited from the Holy Book to testify to the power, glory, knowledge, mercy and love of Allah.

Conception of God

In all religious books the existence of God is taken almost as an axiomatic truth. The Holy Quran, however, advances numerous arguments to prove the existence of a Supreme Being who is the Creator and Controller of this universe. The Holy Quran chiefly deals with three main kinds of arguments. These are : First, the arguments drawn from creation, which may be called the lower or material experience of humanity ; secondly, the evidence of human nature, which may be called the inner experience of humanity ; and thirdly, the arguments based on Divine revelation to man, which may be called the higher and spiritual experience of humanity.

The argument from creation simply shows that there must be a creator of this universe, who is also the controller. The testimony of human nature proceeds a step further, since there is in it a consciousness which may differ in different nature commensurate with the brightness or dimness of the inner light. It is only revelation that discloses God in the full splendour of His light, and shows the sublime attributes which man must emulate if he is to attain perfection, together with the means whereby he can hold communion with the Divine Being.

The Law of Evolution

The first argument, that is drawn from creation, centres round the word *Rabb*. Though the world *Rabb* is generally translated as 'Lord' yet it conveys really quite a different significance. According to Raghib, *Rabb* signifies the fostering of a thing in such a manner as to make it attain one condition after another until it reaches its goal of perfection. There is thus, in the use of the word *Rabb*, an indication that everything created by God bears the impress of Divine creation, in the characteristics of moving on from lower to higher stages until it reaches completion. It thus appears that the creative force is not a blind force but one possessing wisdom and acting with a purpose. Even to the ordinary eye, wisdom and purpose are observable throughout the whole of the Divine creation, from the tiniest particle of dust moving in the universe on their appointed courses, because everyone of them is travelling on along a certain line to its appointed goal of completion.

Guidance afforded by Human Nature

The second class of argument for the existence of God relates to human soul. In the human soul there is the consciousness of the existence of God. There is an inner light within each man telling him that there is a Higher Being, a God, a Creator. Here two things must be borne in mind. In the first place the inner light, within each man, which makes him conscious of the existence of God is not equally clear in all cases. It differs according to the spiritual development of each man ; with some, as with the great divines, that light shines forth in its full glory and their consciousness of the Divine presence is very strong. In the case of ordinary men, consciousness is generally weaker and the inner light more dim ; there may even be cases in which that consciousness is only in a state of inertia, and the inner light has almost gone out. Secondly, even the atheist or the agnostic recognizes a First Cause, or a Higher Power, even though he may deny the existence of a God with particular attributes ; and occasionally that consciousness is awakened in him, and the inner light asserts itself especially in times of distress or affliction.

There is in man's soul something more than mere consciousness of the existence of God, there is in it a yearning after its Maker—the instinct to turn to God for help; there is implanted in it the love of God for whose sake it is ready to make every sacrifice. Finally, it cannot find contentment without God.

Guidance afforded by Divine Revelation

The Divine revelation affords the clearest evidence of the existence of God. In the Holy Quran there are hundreds of proofs of the existence of the Divine Being. The Quran also contains many prophecies which had been foretold when the whole circumstances were against them and when none could imagine that those prophecies would come true. But all those prophecies came in reality in time and thus testify to the truth that there is a Great Power, who knows the past, present and future and who controls the destiny of man.

The Divine revelation thus affords the clearest and surest testimony of the existence of the Divine Being. Besides, the existence of Allah can also be perceived through the career and activities of the Holy Prophet Muhammad (صلعم) and various other messengers of God. The success of Hazrat Muhammad (صلعم) and other Prophets bear testimony of the existence of the All-Powerful, All-loving Allah.

A belief in God possessing the perfect attributes made known by Divine revelation, is the highest ideal which a man can place before himself; and without this ideal there is a void in man's life which drains it of all earnestness and every noble aspiration.

THE ONENESS OF ALLAH (TAUHID)

Oneness is the key-note to the conception of the Divine Being in Islam. It denies the plurality of godhead and any participation of any being in the affairs of the world. The Quran also has laid a great stress on the Oneness of Allah (Tauhid). The first and foremost principle in Islam is the belief in the Oneness of the Divine Being. Unless a man believes in the Oneness of Allah, he cannot be a Muslim. The belief in Tauhid is the cardinal-stone of the faith of Islam. The doctrine of Divine Unity is a standing protest against polytheism, dualism, atheism and idolatry and it generally means that God is One in His person (*zat*), One in His attributes (*sifat*), and One in His works (*af'al*).

The best known expression of the Divine Unity is that contained in '*La-ilaha ill-Allah*'. It is made up of four words *La* (no), *ilah* (that which is worshipped), *illa* (except), and *Allah* (the proper name of the Divine Being). Thus these words which are commonly rendered into English as meaning 'there is no god but Allah', convey the significance that there is nothing which deserves to be worshipped except Allah.

By Oneness of Allah ordinarily we understand His uniqueness in essence, quality and action. He is One, the only Eternal Being, Pure and Simple. The Quran emphasizes the doctrine of unity. The whole teaching of Islam is based on this conception. Matter, time, space and every spirit have no independent existence. The Quran draws our attention to nature, its laws and phenomena—the gathering of clouds, the fall of rain, the growth of plants, the existence of animal and human life, the movement of the stars, the rise and fall of nations, the change of seasons, life, death, historical events and mythical wonders. In all these we can detect the same law prevalent. In all apparent diversity there is a unity of purpose and therefore the unity of the originator.

It would not be out of place to mention that the doctrine of Divine Unity had been preached by every Prophet who appeared in any part of the world. But in course of time the doctrine of polytheism was introduced in almost every religion, and thus all the religions became corrupt. ' Corruption had spread in land and sea." The Quran has restored the doctrine of Divine Unity to its original purity. It emphatically says that there is no god but Allah and invokes the people to worship the One and only One Allah.

The doctrine of Oneness of Allah is a reply to all kinds of Polytheism. Though the doctrine had been preached by each and every Prophet it was made perfect by the Holy Quran. The Surah *Ikhlas* clearly negatives the four kinds of Polytheism that prevailed in the world before Islam. There was a belief in the plurality of God or the plurality of persons in godhead, a belief that other things possess the perfect attributes of the Divine Being, a belief that any one may be related to Him as son or father and a belief that others may do what is possible only for the Divine Being. These four kinds of Polytheism have been discarded by the Quran which has established strict monotheism.

The doctrine of Oneness of Allah is a principle of moral elevation. It denounces *shirk* (associating anything with Allah) which demoralises and degrades man and makes him unfit for the high place for which he has been created. Man is called the *Khalifa* or the vicegerent of Allah on earth (2 : 30) and he is gifted with the power of controlling the rest of the creation which has been made subordinate to him. If such a man, who has been created to control the universe and who has the power and capacity to subdue everything and to turn it to his use, bows his head before anything other than Allah, certainly he degrades himself. It is the doctrine of Divine Unity that rescues him from the evils of *shirk* and guides him to the path of moral elevation.

This doctrine has freed man not only from the slavery of nature but also from the slavery of man. This doctrine establishes the fact that all men are equal. Man should not bow his head before any man whatever may be his position or rank or dignity, not even to Prophet Muhammad (صلعم), the greatest of men.

Thus the doctrine of Oneness of Allah is a great force of bringing about the unity of the human race. All the people of the world are the creation of one creator, who has created them alike, and who takes equal care of all.

Allah is the '*Rabb-ul-Alamin*', the Lord of all nations and the Creator of all the worlds. He is the Lord of all, the Lord of the heavens and the earth, the Lord of the East and the West and the Lord of the Muslims and non-Muslims. Men and nations may differ but they are the children of one common Father and they have one Lord, one God and therefore they are brethren.

Thus the idea of universal brotherhood underlies the doctrine of the Oneness of Allah.

Prophets

One of the cardinal principles of Islam is the belief in the Prophets who were sent to this world to preach the religion of Allah. The Arabic word for Prophet is *nabi*, which is derived from *naba*, meaning an announcement of great utility imparting knowledge of a thing. One lexicologist explains the word *nabi* as meaning an ambassador between God and rational beings from among His creatures. According to another, a *nabi* is the man who gives information about God, and this is further explained as the man to whom God gives information concerning His unity and to whom He reveals secrets of the future and imparts the knowledge that he is His Prophet.

NABI AND RASUL

A *Nabi* is called a *Rasul*[1] which means an apostle or messenger. But there is a distinction between *nabi* and *rasul* or between prophet and apostle. The *rasuls* are those persons who introduce a new law including religious, social and legal ordinances, while those who repeated the messages of their predecessors are called *nabi* or prophets. Both *nabi* and *rasul* are prophets but not apostles. All the *rasuls* or apostles are *nabis*, but not all *nabis* are *rasuls*. Only a small number of the prophets were *nabi*. They are Adam, Abraham, Noah, Moses, Jesus, David and Muhammad (صلعم). The other Prophets were *rasuls*.

FAITH IN PROPHETS

The faith in Divine messengers is one of the essen-

1. The literal meaning of *rasul* is one sent.

tials of Islam. The Prophet is not only the bearer of the Divine message, but he also shows now that message is to be interpreted in practical life and therefore he is the model to be followed by humanity. It is the Prophet's example that inspires a living faith in the hearts of his followers and brings about a real transformation in their lives. This is why the Holy Quran lays special stress on the fact that the Prophet must be a man. The reformation or transformation of man can only be accomplished through a man—Prophet.

The Muslims must have faith not only in Prophet Muhammad (صلعم) alone, but also in all other Prophets who appeared in all ages before Muhammad (صلعم). The Holy Quran says, "Believe in that which has been revealed to thee and that which was revealed before thee." Again the Holy Quran says, "Righteousness is this that one should believe in Allah and the last day and the angels and the Books and the Prophets." A belief in all the Prophets of the world is thus an essential principle of the religion of Islam. Thus Islam claims a universality to which no other religion can aspire, and lays the foundation of a brotherhood as vast as humanity itself.

Prophets were sent to every nation, but their messages were limited to a particular nation and in some cases to one or a few generations. All these Prophets were, so to say, national Prophets, and their work was limited to the moral uplift and spiritual regeneration of one nation only. But while national growth was a necessity of the first condition of the human race, when each nation lived almost an exclusive life and the means of communication between different races were wanting, the grand aim which the Divine Scheme had in view was the uplift and unification of the whole human race. So the final step in the institution of prophethood was the raising up of one Prophet for all the nations. The day of national Prophets was ended and the day of the world

Prophet dawned upon the earth in the person of the Holy Prophet Muhammad (صلعم) to lead humanity to the grand idea of the oneness of man and of the whole human race.

FUNCTIONS AND NECESSITY OF THE PROPHETS

The Prophets are sent by Allah for the uplift of humanity and for freeing men from the bondage of sin and for guiding them to the right path. Undoubtedly, man is subject to temptation of the devil who exercises a great hindrance in the moral and spiritual progress of man. In order to overcome the temptation of devil, man always requires the help of Divine revelation which comes to him through the Prophets. Again every Prophet brings the message of Unity of Allah.

The Prophets are the givers of good news (*mubashir*) relating to his advancement and elevation and they are also the warners (*munzir*) to the sinners who are not following the religion. The Prophets were sent to establish the religion of Islam and Adam was made the first Prophet. The religion of Islam was not first founded by Muhammad (صلعم) but by Adam, the first Prophet and it was Muhammad (صلعم) who finalised it. The Prophets will intercede on behalf of the believers on the Day of Resurrection.

The doctrine preached by all the Prophets is essentially one and the same, but their methods of teachings and the laws regulating life were different according to the people among whom the Prophets were raised. The methods of teaching were determined by the degree of ignorance which was to be dispelled. When the people were in the primitive stages of society, their instructions and laws were simple and as the people made progress, they were modified and improved. In the messages of the Prophets, there had been a gradual evolution towards the final and perfect Revelation which came with Muhammad (صلعم), the Last Prophet.

Intercession

The Arabic word for intercession is *shafa'ah* which is derived from *shaf* meaning making a thing to be one of a pair and *shafa'ah* signifies the joining of a man with another assisting him, especially when a man who enjoys a high rank and honour joins a man of a lower position.

In the Quran the Prophets are spoken of as intercessors. They will intercede on behalf of the believers on the Day of Resurrection. Divine mercy will be manifested through the Prophets. The *shafa'ah* of the Holy Prophet Muhammad (صلعم) on the Day of Resurrection will be given the greatest prominence. On that day the Holy Prophet Muhammad (صلعم) will prostrate himself before Allah, praise Him with the most earnest prayer. It is then that Allah will say to him, "O Muhammad (صلعم)! Raise the head, and speak and thou shalt be granted the desire, and intercede and thy intercession shall be accepted."

FINALITY OF PROPHETHOOD

In the Holy Quran, the Holy Prophet Muhammad (صلعم) is spoken of as the last of the Prophets. Before the last Prophet Allah sent 124,000 Prophets among whom 313 were apostles or messengers, who tried to guide the humanity to the right path. The Prophets were sent to every nation of the world. They preached the religion of Allah. But Muhammad (صلعم) is called the "seal of the Prophets." After him, no Prophet will come in this world. The Quran says, "Muhammad (صلعم) is not the father of any of your men, but he is the messenger of Allah and the last of the Prophets (*Khatam al-Nabiyyin*) and Allah is cognizant of all things" (33 : 40). The Hadith speaks of him as the corner-stone of prophethood and the last of the Prophets.

Angels

The Arabic word for angel is *malak*, of which the plural form is *malaik*. The root from which the word is derived is *alk* or *alukah* meaning *risalah* or the bearing of messages. The angels are creatures of Allah, are without sex and free from sin. They are made of light (*nur*) and are generally ranked below the Prophets. The Quran states, "The angels are bidden by Allah to prostrate themselves before Adam ; this they did except Iblis."[1] Iblis pleads that whereas man was created of clay, he and the Jinns are created of fire (نار). The Quran speaks of the form of the Satan (شیطان) and Jinn as nar (نار) but does not reflect on the form of angels. The angels have no particular shape and form and as such they cannot be seen by human beings. As regards their shape and form, the Quran is silent on this point. Of course it is believed that the angels can take any form and it is related that archangel Gabriel came to the Prophet several times in human form. They are the chosen creatures of Allah and are always engaged in His worship or in carrying out His orders. They surround men from all sides and are always in their company. They keep record of every action of man in this world and they will producc it on the Day of Resurrection.

FUNCTION OF ANGELS

The function of angels in the spiritual world is the same as in the physical world—to serve as intermediaries in carrying out the Divine will which, in the latter case, is to bring about the evolution of creation, and in the former, the evolution of man. According to the teachings of Islam, angels have a close connection with the

1. Sura ii, 32, vii, 10.

life of man from his birth, even from the time he is in the mother's womb till his death, and even after his death, in his spiritual progress in paradise and his spiritual treatment in Hell. Thus the law of nature find expression through them.

At the head of the angelic band there are four archangels (*Karubiyan*), the Gabriel or Jibril, the messenger of Allah who brought revelations to the Prophet, Michael or Mikail who watches over the order and the life of nature ; Israfil, who will sound the trumpet on the Day of the Last Judgment, and Izrail, the angel of death, who takes the life of the dying. There are several other important angels, *viz. Hafizayn* (the two guardians) and *Kiraman-Katibin* (two honourable recorders) who take note of good and evil actions ; *Munkar* and *Nakir*, the angels of grave (*Qabr*) who ask questions from the dead ; *Rizwan*, the gate-keeper of the Paradise ; *Malik*, the gate-keeper of the Hell.

The most important function of the angels is to communicate the Divine messages to the Prophets. This function was generally done by archangel Gabriel who came down not only to the Holy Prophet Muhammad (صلعم) but also to various other Prophets and delivered the Divine messages. He is called *Namus al-Akbar* or the great angel who is entrusted with secret messages. Through this angel Allah speaks to his Prophets.

Another very important function of the angels is that of intercession and prayers for men. The Hadith also speaks of the intercession of the angels (Bukhari). Now, intercession is really a prayer to Allah on behalf of the sinners on the Day of Judgment but we are also told that the angels pray for men in this life. "The angels celebrate the praises of their Lord and ask forgiveness for those on earth."

The angels inspire men to noble deeds. Every man is said to have two associates—an associate angel (*shahid*) leading man to a good and noble life aiming at the development of the human faculties; and the associate devil (*saiq* or driver) leading man to a wicked life. The angel's suggestion is for good and acceptance of truth.

Faith in angels is one of the principles of Islam. The different functions of angels in the spiritual world are thus connected, in one way or another, either with the awakening of the spiritual life in man or its advancement and progress. Herein lies the reason why faith in angels is required along with a faith in God: "Righteousness is that one should believe in Allah and the Last Day and the Angels and the Books and the Prophets."

Thus the faith in angels only means that every good suggestion must be accepted, because it leads to the spiritual development of man.

The Day of Judgment

Belief in *yaum al-qiyamah* or the day of the great rising, is one of the articles of Muslim faith. It has also been enjoined by the Holy Prophet that every Muslim must have his faith in the *qiyamat*. The resurrection is spoken of under various names such as *al-sa'ah* (which means the hour, and occurs forty times); *yaum al-akhir* (the last day, occurs twenty-six times); *yaum al-din* (which means the day of requital); *yaum al-fasl* (the day of decision); *yaum al-hisab* (the day of reckoning); *yaum al-fath* (the day of judgment); *yaum al-jam* (the day of gathering together); *yaum al-talaq* (the day of meeting); *yaum al-hasrat* (the day of regret), etc.

The Day of Destruction

The faith in the Day of Judgment implies that one day Allah will destroy the whole world with all the creatures in it. This day is called the Day of Destruction or the Last Day. The date of the Last Day is not mentioned in any of the Divine Books. It is known only to Allah. According to Muslim traditions the *qiyamat* will be preceded by several signs which will announce the coming of the Day. They are the rising of chaos and confusion in human society, the disappearance of the House of Ka'ba and the Holy Quran, the rising of the sun in the west, the appearance of *Yajuj* and *Majuj* and *Dajjal* and lastly the descent of Imam Mehdi. The latter will reign for about forty years and after his death, the world will be once again in chaos and confusion, when Allah will ask Israfil to sound the trumpet. As soon as Israfil will blow on the trumpet, the earth will be broken up, the solar system will be totally dislocated; and lives will be destroyed, and in short every vestige of creation will disappear. Only Allah will remain. He will ask, "Whose is the sovereignty today?" And as none would answer as everything being destroyed, He Himself would answer, "For Allah, the One, the Supreme."

The Day of Judgment

Forty years after the bowing of the first trumpet, Israfil will again be brought to life and asked to blow the trumpet for the second time. The second blast of the trumpet will restore all beings to life, and they will be taken to the presence of Allah. This event is called the Resurrection or '*Hashr*.' God will appear on His Throne. The Great Book will be opened, and a list of his deeds, both good and bad, done in this world, will be given to every man. It will be placed on the right hand of the blessed and on the left hand of the damned. A balance (*Mizan*) will be used to weigh the deeds. The righteous will then obtain eternal peace and enjoy in Heaven (*Jannat*) and the wicked will be damned to Hell (*Jahannam*).

It is at this moment that the Holy Prophet will

intervene, and his intercession in favour of the Muslim community will be accepted by Allah. Then Allah will pronounce His Judgment. After the pronouncement of Divine Judgment all will have to pass over a bridge called "*Pul-Sirat*" which is finer than a hair and sharper than a sword. This bridge will be placed over the Hell and the blessed will cross it very easily and enter the Paradise but the wicked will not be able to cross it and they will fall down into Hell.

The Life Hereafter

A faith in the life hereafter is the last of the basic principles of Islam. The word generally used in the Holy Quran to indicate this life is *'al-Akhirah.'* Death, in the light of the plain teaching of the Quran, is not the end of life. Another kind of life will began for man after his death. The life after death is, therefore, not a new life but only a continuation of this life, bringing its hidden realities to light.

The Holy Quran accords to faith in the future life an importance which is next only to faith in Allah. Very often all the doctrines of faith are summed up as amounting to belief in Allah and the future life. Physical death only releases it from its earthly existence and opens for it the door of a higher life and a wide vista of progress, a new world of advancement. The present happiness and the misery of a man are not the be-all and end-all of his existence, there will be another life after death, in Heaven (*jannat*) or Hell (*jahannam*), where he will be happy or miserable in accordance with the consequence of his actions in this world.

QURANIC CONCEPTION

Hazrat Muhammad (صلعم) confirmed the idea of future existence then prevalent among various peoples. The Quranic conception of future existence is based on the belief that on the Day of Judgment every man will have to give an account of his deeds in past life, how he used or misused his qualities and possessions, whether he lived a life in accordance with the commandments of God, which were useful for the human beings, or whether he was living for himself and his own comforts and pleasure and wasting his health and wealth. Those whose good deeds are greater than their sins will be pardoned and sent to paradise which is a place where man will have peace of mind and the sight of his Maker. But those whose evil deeds are greater than their good deeds will receive punishment from God and will be sent to Hell which is a place of misery and unhappiness where they will suffer from many troubles until God pardons them and takes them to paradise. This is in short the Quranic conception of future existence.

Barzakh

The state between death and Resurrection is called *Barzakh* which literally means a thing that intervenes between two things or an obstacle or a hindrance. The reward or punishment of a man will be decided on the Day of Judgment. The intervening state between death and Resurrection is known by the name of *qabr*, which means grave, but has also been used in the wider sense of the state which follows death. Thus the three states, death, the grave and Resurrection are spoken of, where the grave undoubtedly stands for *Barzakh*.

EXPERIENCE IN BARZAKH STATE

It should be noted that in the Holy Quran the guilty persons are spoken of as receiving chastisement in the state of *Barzakh* and in the Hadith it is described as '*azab-ul-qabr*' or the punishment in the grave. Similarly the virtuous are spoken of as tasting the fruits of their good deeds immediately after death.

DURATION OF BARZAKH

All questions connected with the life of the other world are of an intricate nature, inasmuch as they are not things that can be perceived by these senses, they are 'secrets' that shall be made known only after death. The very ideas of time and space as relating to the next world are different from those here, and therefore, we cannot conceive of the duration of *Barzakh* in terms of this world.

Heaven

The life after death takes two forms : a life in paradise for those in whom the good preponderates over the evil, and a life in hell for those in whom the evil preponderates over the good. The word *Firdaus* occurs twice in the Holy Quran. It is the word '*Jannat*' that is generally used to indicate the abiding place of the righteous. '*Jannat*' is derived from *Jann* which signifies the concealing of a thing so that it is not perceived by the senses, It also means a garden with trees luxuriant in growth. Every piece of land sown with various seeds is a garden in embryo while all the seeds remain hidden. It is *Jannat* in the first meaning of the word. But, when the seeds come up and trees grow, it becomes *Jannat* in other sense. Even here, those who do not dissolute lives and hold themselves aloof from any sort of dissipation, enjoy a form of heavenly life by reason of their good beliefs and righteous actions. The blessings of the heaven are such as that "no eye did ever see, no ear did ever hear, and that never occurred in human mind."

In paradise the righteous will be accompanied by ever-youthful '*Hurs*' whose beauty is free from all defects. Some commentators of the Quran take these *Hurs* to mean our own wives, mothers and sisters, but others regard them as belonging to some heavenly order where beautiful damsels and boys have been called *Hur* and *Ghilman*. The Holy Quran speaks, on one occasion, of the presence in paradise of *Ghilman* (plural of *ghulam* meaning a boy), and on two occasions of *Wildan* (pl. of *walad* meaning a son or a child) : "And round about them shall go boys (*ghilman*) of theirs as if they were hidden pearls. " (58 : 24).

The Holy Quran describes the paradise as "Allah has promised to the believing men and the believing women gardens in which rivers flow, to abide in them, and goodly dwellings in gardens of perpetual abode ; and greatest of all is Allah's goodly pleasure, that is the grand achievement" (9 : 72).

In short, Heaven is a spiritual experience of the best type whereby all desires will be more than satisfied. Everything will be of an honourable character with no ignoble feature of any kind. The Quran suggests this idea in the clearest terms when it gives us the list of those who are entitled to enter into the heavenly abode. Their very character shows that it would not be a place for licentiousness. Here are some of them :

1. Those who hold good beliefs and translate them into actions.

2. Those who lead a pious life.

3. Those who on earth kept their promises and fulfilled their covenants.

4. Those who are righteous and not only remain in prayer, but translate the demands of their prayers into actions.

5. Those who have become cleansed of all their wrong desires and whose hearts are pure of every error. In short, good deeds of all kinds—piety, righteousness, patience, chastity, charity, almsgiving, regard for bounds, truthfulness, abstention from vanity, and giving

good advice to others are the chief qualities of those who will enter into the paradise of the Lord. In paradise, peace will reign supreme there so much so that Heaven has also been named *Dar-us-Salam* (the House of Peace) and *Dar-un-Naim* (the House of Good Gifts).

Hell

Hell is a natural sequence to men's evil actions. Hidden Truths will then become revealed at the day of judgment. "Hell is the fire kindled by Allah which rises above the hearts. Now the fire which rises above the hearts, is the heartburning caused by inordinate passion".[1] In Hell pains of body and souls are united. The evil-doers will undergo severe chastisement according to the degree and gravity of the evil deeds in this world. The sinners,—some will be thrown into the blazing fire, some in the scorching heat of the sun, some will be entertained with the stinking, bitter and deadly fruit and so on and so forth. Blackness of the face is again mentioned as the chastisement of Hell: "On the day when some faces shall turn white and some faces shall turn black, then as to those whose faces turn black; 'did you disbelieve after your believing?' taste therefore the chastisement because you disbelieved" (3 : 105).

Hell is described by several different names in the Holy Quran. It helps to explain its nature. *Sa'ir* (from *Sa'r* which means the kindling of fire), *Jahim* (derived from *Jahm* signifying the burning or blazing of fire), *Jahannam* means something in the nature of fire, *Laza* (which means the flame of the fire) explains the nature of its function meaning anything that stupefies the brain. But *Hutamah* (which is derived from *hatam* which means the breaking of a thing—while *hutmah* means a vehement fire) is very suggestive. It

1. Muhammad Ali, *The Religion of Islam*, p. 305.

means remorse, a feeling of shame and disgrace, because abasement and intense remorse are some of the chastisements administered to the denizens of Hell which they may in no way escape. It shows that Hell is a mental torture: that its agonies are agonies of the mind.

The Quran makes mention of some seven gates of Hell meant for different classes of sinners. The doors would lead to seven spiritual evils.

REMEDIAL NATURE OF HELL

Hell, therefore, only represents the evil consequences of evil deeds, but still it is not a place merely for undergoing the consequences of what has been done; it is also a purgatory. In other words, its chastisement is not for the purpose of torture, it is for purification in order to make a man fit for spiritual advancement. The aim of human life in this world is to attain a higher life after death. If the life of a man has been well-spent and his faculties have been fully developed in the short span of his existence in this world, he will be granted a higher spiritual life in Paradise. But the man who has wasted his opportunities in this world or who has corrupted his soul by evil deeds, will be required to undergo the ordeal of Hell in order to purify his soul, so that he may attain spiritual advancement. The punishment in Hell is a remedial measure. Hell is a temporary place for the sinner, whether Muslim or non-Muslim. Hell, as it appears from the Quran, is purgatory for moral and spiritual cure. It is the general orthodox Muslim belief that no unbeliever or idolator will ever be released. Neither the Holy Quran nor the Hadith upholds this view. On the other hand, there is a tradition of the Prophet that the sinners will be released from chastisement when they are fit for new life and when Allah pleases. "He shall say, the fire is your abode, to abide in it, except as Allah pleases, for thy Lord is Wise, Knowing" (6 : 129). The believers who have sinned will undergo purgatory stage until they are permitted into Paradise.

CHAPTER IX

AL-GHAZZALI

Early Life and Education

Abu Hamid Muhammad al-Ghazzali surnamed Hujjat al-Islam (the Argument of Islam) was born in 450 A.H./1058 A.D. at Tus in Khurasan. His father was a pious *dervish.* He very often visited and sat in the company of *fuqaha.* And when he listened to their sermons, he wept and prayed to Allah to grant him a son who would be a *faqih.* "God granted," says al-Subki, "the prayer of his father and al-Ghazzali was born who became the most learned of all the *fuqaha,* and rose to the eminence of becoming the Imam of his age."

His father died when he was a small child. A Sufi friend of his father took care of him. He received his primary education from the same Sufi. Then al-Ghazzali entered a school in his native town and studied fiqh under Ahmad bin Muhammad Razkani. Thereafter he went to Gurgan and studied under Imam Abu Nasr Ismaili.

After completing his study with Abu Nasr Ismaili, he moved out of his native town and went to the Nizamiyya (a college established by the great Nizam al-Mulk, Prime Minister of the Saljuqs) at Nishapur. The principal of the Nizamiyya was Imam al-Haramayn. Under him al-Ghazzali studied theology, fiqh, science, philosophy, logic and mysticism, and soon became the most distinguished of his pupils. The teacher called him a "Plentious Ocean." After completing his studies al-Ghazzali served under his master as his assistant and remained there till his (master's) death in 1085 A. D. When he left Nishapur, at the age of 28, he had no equal in erudition in the entire Muslim world.

After leaving Nishapur he plunged himself headlong into *munazras* (religious discussions) for about six years. It was during these duels that Nizam al-Mulk, the celebrated Prime Minister, came to know his worth. He appointed him President of the Nizamiyya Academy of Baghdad.

His lectures at the Nizamiyya were attended by three hundred scholars and one hundred dignitaries of other walks of life. Four years of teaching placed Baghdad at his feet. His reputation spread far and wide and he earned the honorific title of Imam al-Khurasan wal-Iraq. He was equally honoured in the courts of Isfahan and Baghdad.

His Inner Development

In Baghdad at that time there were a horde of religious and pseudo-religious sects, each fighting the other and making high claims regarding 'Truth' and 'Salvation.' Being inherently inquisitive he investigated into the beliefs and practices of each sect. For this purpose he met and discussed with the representatives of all the sects and creeds in Baghdad. Confronted with multiple of falsehood, contradictions and heresies he was disturbed profoundly. "Struck with contradictions which I encountered in endeavouring to disentangle the truth and falsehood of these opinions, I was led to make the following reflections. The search after truth being the aim I set before myself, I ought to ascertain in the first instance, the foundations of certitude. In the next place I recognized that certitude was the clear and complete knowledge of things, such knowledge as left no room for doubt and no possibility of error and mere conjecture, so that there remained no scope in the mind through which falsehood might find an entrance."

A very important and revolutionary development in his thought had already taken place. "No sooner had I emerged from boyhood than I had already broken the fetters of tradition and freed myself from hereditary beliefs."

After establishing the foundations of certitude he proceeded to examine the sum-total of knowledge that he himself possessed, "I then examined what knowledge I possessed, and discovered that in none of it, with the exception of sense-perceptions and necessary principles, did I enjoy that degree of certitude which I just described . . . I then set myself earnestly to examine the notions we derive from the evidence of the senses and from that of the sight in order to see if they could be called in question. The result of a careful examination was that my confidence in them was shaken."

"Then I reflected in myself : 'Since I cannot trust to the evidence of my senses, I must rely only on intellectual conceptions based on fundamental principles.' But the notions I derived from senses made the following objections : 'Who can guarantee that you can trust to the evidence of reason more than that of the causes?' Perhaps there is above reason another judge who, if he appeared, would convict reason of falsehood, just as reason has confuted (the senses)."

Now, who can be thus 'another judge' superior to reason ? Al-Ghazzali explains that notions derived from reason may be real in relation to the thinker's present state. But it is possible that he may enter upon another state of existence which bears the same relation to his present state as the present one does to his condition when asleep: In this new sphere he will perhaps realize that the conclusions of reason arrived at formerly are only delusion. The ecstasy of the Sufis, al-Ghazzali says, may furnish an example of this new sphere. Or, the whole world may be but a dream and man may wake up to the consciousness of reality only after death. It seemed as if all the ground had been cut from under al-Ghazzali's feet. "This unhappy state lasted about two months during which I was . . . morally and essentially a thorough-going sceptic."

God alone rescued him from this precipice. It (light) brought him peace and reassurance from within that life was not a dream but a reality and the light of reason was not to be dismissed as possibly a mere hallucination. He, however, did not return to *Taqlid* for now it had dawned on him positively that *Taqlid* would not lead him to the convincing ground of Truth.

When he emerged from the state of scepticism he resumed his study and research into the beliefs and practices of the prevailing sects and creeds. He divided them into four broad groups :

(1) the Scholastic Theologians,

(2) the Philosophers,

(3) the Talimites or the Ismailians, and

(4) the Mystics.

His method of study was very scientific and objective. He even practised the precepts of various schools in order to observe and determine for himself the practical learnings of their doctrines. In course of his study of Sufism he arrived at a very difficult stage, which indeed transformed his entire life and thinking. Sufism is not merely a theoretical discipline. It is primarily based on mystical practices, such as, experience (*dhawq*), state (*hal*) etc., which could not be attained without the purification of the heart and the transformation of character, which demanded a complete renunciation of this material world. Al-Ghazzali being deeply attached to a life of pomp and splendour was, for a long while, torn between the opposite forces of earthly passions and religious yearnings for about six months . . . at the close of which he lost his will and gave himself up to destiny. "Finally," says al-Ghazzali, "I took refuge in God like one who has exhausted himself and is denied all means . . . He made easy for me to sacrifice honours, wealth and family."

Travels

He left Baghdad in 488 A. H./1095 A. D. and visited holy places in the lands of Islam.

He first came to Damascus and stayed there for two years. From there he went to Jerusalem where at the tomb of Prophet Ibrahim he took three following vows :

(1) He would not visit the court of any king.

(2) He would not accept gifts from any king.

(3) He would abstain from religious disputations, *i.e.*, *Munazras.*

Then he went to Egypt and visited Alexandria where he stayed for a long time. From there he went on the pilgrimage to Mecca and Medina. At Mecca too he stayed for a pretty long time. It was during this journey that he wrote his masterpiece "Ihya al-Uloom ad-Din" (Revival of the Religious Sciences).

When he returned from his journey in 494 A.H./ 1106 A.D. he found that philosophy had taken hold of the people's mind and the spread of irreligious doctrines and the increasing indifferences of masses to religion had shaken the very foundations of faith. At first he was very hesitant to stand up against the mounting tide of heresies. He was finally prevailed upon by his enlightened friends and associates to come out of his seclusion. The Fakhr al-Mulk, the eldest son of Nizam al-Mulk and Premier to Sanjar son of Malik Shah the Saljuq, himself travelled to Nishapur and urged him to assume the headship of the Nizamiyya Academy at Nishapur. After teaching there for two years he retired to his birthplace (Tus) where he lived until his death in 505 A.H./1111 A.D.

His Works

Al-Ghazzali was a prolific writer. In spite of his busy life that he led, he wrote hundreds of books covering all range of subjects under the sun. Much of his works are lost and untraceable now. His average writing per day is estimated to be 16 pages. Some of his books are monumental and epoch-making. They have held sway for centuries revolutionising the life and ideas of the peoples of the East and the West alike.

Al-Subki and other writers have mentioned 78 of his extant works. But the most important and popular among them are *Maqasid al-Falasifa*, *Mizan al-Amal*, *Al-Munqiz min az-Zalal* (Saviour from error) and *Tahafut al-Falasifa* (Incoherence of Philosophers) and *Ihya. al Uloom ad-Din*. The last named, of course, being the most comprehensive treatise on Islamic theology—a masterpiece of al-Ghazzali. It is ranked next to the Holy Quran and the sayings of the Prophet. In the West it attracted the attention of the medieval scholars, especially the clergymen who translated it in many European languages and wrote commentaries on it. Men like Raymund Martin, Thomas Aquina, Bar Hebraeus, and Pascal were profoundly influenced by al-Ghazzali.

Time and Environment : Historical background :

In order to make an impartial and correct appreciation of al-Ghazzali's thought and views it is necessary to go into the history and development of various trends—religious and political—which constitute the background of his thought. For he took the spiritual and cultural heritage of the past, subjected it to critical analysis and evaluation and then passed on to the posterity in pressing on it the stamp of his unique personality. And this makes up the greatness of al-Ghazzali.

In Islam religious and philosophical movements were closely associted with the political movements. If we take a deeper look at any of the movements in Islam, apparently religious in character, we will find that its rcots really lie in politics.

Emergence of Theo-Political Parties

After Hazrat Muhammad (صلعم) Abu Bakr (632-634 A.D.) took up the reins of the Khilafat. The most important event during his reign was the movement called Ridda or 'apostasy'. This, however, did not create any breach in the ranks and files of Islam. Abu Bakr successfully crushed the rebellious and restored the supremacy of Islam in Arabia. Under Caliph Umar (634-644 A.D.) Islam was on the move. It spread beyond the limits of the Arabian Peninsula. Lands of once glorious civilization like Iraq, Persia, Syria, Palestine and Egypt were conquered. During Usman's Caliphate (644-656 A.D.) there were wide-spread resentment and discontent among the non-Arab population of Egypt and Palestine on account of the tyranny and despotism perpetrated by the Umayyad governors appointed by Usman. The upsurge culminated in the murder of the Caliph himself. The tragedy itself being of purely political significance it, nevertheless, caused the polarization of forces into distinct parties and groups.

The first real schism that made its appearance in

Islam was the birth of the Kharijite party. During the battle between Ali and Muawiya at Siffin, a section of the Ali's army camprising 12,000 strong refused to accept arbitration between the contenders to the Khilafat and seceded from the main body. They were called 'Khawarij' (the seceders). Those who remained with Ali called themselves Shi'at-i-Ali (partisans of Ali).

The Khilafat, however, passed on to the House of Umayya in 661 A.D. Their rule was of great sociopolitical and cultural significance. Muawiya (661-680 A.D.) the first Umayyad caliph, converted the democratic Khilafat into a dynastic rule—a monarchy; Arabic became the *lingua franca* of the new empire; and Medina no longer remained the metropolis of Islam.

During the reign of Yazid bin Muawiya (680-683 A.D.) a number of tragic events took place which alienated the sympathy of all good pious Muslims from the House of Umayya. For instance, the Tragedy of Kerbala took place in 680 A.D.; Medina was sacked in 681 A.D. during which 80 Companions of the Prophet and 700 huffaz of the Quran were slain Ka'ba was attacked in 682 A D. Again Ka'ba was attacked, desecrated and burned by Hajjaj bin Yusuf during the reign of Abdul Malik (685-705 A.D.). These misdeeds of the Umayyads provoked open revolts by the Muslims who divided themselves into the following groups :—

(1) The orthodox Muslims (the Sunnis), which comprised an overwhelming majority of the people, including the Companions of the Prophet who resided at the holy cities of Mecca and Medina. They were orthodox in their beliefs and refrained from giving peculiar and mischievous interpretation to the verses of the Quran. They adopted middle of the road in every matter—religious or political. To them, however, the Umayyads were ungodly creatures who indulged in

all imaginable vices. The hostile feelings of this group were openly expressed in the rebellion of Abdullah bin Zubair who held the holy cities for full nine years (683-692 A.D.).

(2) The Khawarij were originally a political party that gradually turned into a religious sect. They were fanatics and over-zealous about Islam, and wanted to enforce their doctrines at the point of sword. They admitted neither the claims of Ali nor of Muawiya to Khilafat and declared "there is no rule but the Rule of Allah." They preached equality and refused to submit to the rule of man, for obedience was due to Allah alone. Hence they could not conceive of any organized state and of responsible society. Rebelion and anarchy were the key-note of their philosophy. The Kharijite ferment was thus one of the potent factors that dismembered the Islamic Empire. The movement produced a number of learned men who wrote remarkable books in support of their ideology and doctrines.

(3) The Mawalis were the subject races who were Muslims but not Arabs. In oppositing the Umayyads they made a common cause with the Shias, since they were not treated as equals, as enjoined by Islam, and were compelled to pay the Jizya, contrary to the law of Islam. Only in the reign of Umar bin Abdul Aziz, did the subject races experience some relief.

With the passage of time opposition to the Umayyads spread from political to non-political fields. The Mawali movement formerly stood for equality among all Muslim peoples. Now it joined hands with the Syrians, the Egyptians and the Persians to prove the superiority of the non-Arab peoples over the Arabs. This new combination came to be known as "the Shu'ubiya". Since the Persians were in the vanguard of this movement it ultimately aimed at proving the superiority of the Persians over the Arabs. The movement produced numerous books on this theme.

(4) The Shia: The Shi'ism began as a purely Arab and a purely political faction grouped around the claims of Ali and his descendants to the Khilafat. The movement was founded and organized by Abdullah bin Saba, a native of Sana and of Jewisn origin. He came to Hejaz during the Khilafat of Usman and outwardly embraced Islam. His actions and views created rift and misunderstanding among early Muslims. He formed secret societies to spread his malicious propaganda against Islam. He introduced doctrines alien to Islam and misinterpreted the verses of the Quran to support his doctrines. He was the first man to attribute divinity to Ali for which the latter rebuked him. He regarded Ali a divinely appointed Caliph and Imam. Hence Ali had exclusive right to the Khilafat while the first three Caliphs were illegitimate and the so-called Caliphs of the Umayyad and Abbasid houses were usurpers.

The first achievement of this party was the assassination of Chaliph Usman. Later it took prominent part in the battles of Jamal (battle of Camel) in 656 A.D. and Siffin (657 A.D.). It was, however, after the Tragedy of Kerbala (680 A.D.) that this movement took a definite shape and developed itself into a separate theo-political creed. They intermittently fought to bring down the rule of the Umayyads and that of the Abbasids.

The first Shia rebellion against the Umayyads was organized and led by Mukhtar who avenged the Tragedy of Kerbala in 686 A. D. by putting to death thousands of people who owed fealty to the Umayyads. One thing of interest here is that the rebellion was carried out in the name of Muhammad ibn al-Hanifiyah, step-brother of Hasan and Husain, and who was universally accepted as the 'Imam' It was only after his death that the Shias were divided into various sects. Those who accepted his son Abu Hashim as the 'Imam' were called Hashimiyya and those who sided with Ali, the Zain al-Abedin, son of Imam Husain, were called Imamiyya.

The Hashimiyyas, being far stronger than the Imamiyyas, kept alive the spirit of revolution and rebellion against the Umayyads and carried out an incessant propaganda in support of Ali's descendants to the Khilafat. On his death-bed (716 A. D.) Abu Hashim bequeathed his rights to Muhammad bin Ali bin Abdullah b. Abbas, the uncle of the Prophet. Imamiyya's support for the Abbasids was secured by appealing to them in the name of Hashim, the common ancestor of the Abbasids and the Alids. Henceforth all the opponents of the Umayyads were united on one platform in supporting the Abbasids. By now the Persians in large number had joined this movement which spread from one corner to the other of the Islamic Empire. A popular revolt broke out under Abu Muslim Khurasani, a man of rare genius, which overthrew the Umayyad yoke and established the Abbasid rule. Abul Abbas was proclaimed the first Abbasid Caliph in 747 A. D.

Anti-Islamic Trends

The Abbasid era, the Golden Age of Islam, is remarkable not for its many-sided developments but for the trends which underlie these developments. Since the forces which established the new regime were opposed to Arabism, they strove to stress and prove the superiority of every thing non-Arab over every thing Arab. Its characteristic manifestation was found in a new movement called 'Shu'ubiya'. Persians had been in the vanguard of the revolution which overthrew the Umayyads. Hence the new order was entirely dominated by them, their ways and manners. The Shu'ubiya movement too gradually formed into a purely Persian movement stressing the superiority of the Persians over the Arabs.

The first step towards an organized and planned development of science and learning was the foundation of 'Bait-ul-Hikmat' by Mansur, the second Abbasid Caliph, where thousands of books from different languages were rendered into Arabic. It was there that the foundation of Muslim philosophy was laid by Al-Kindi, the Director of the Academy. Authorised translations of philosophical and scientific works of Greek philosophers like Plato and Aristotle were for the first time made available to the Arabic reading public. The emphasis being greatly on 'reason'. Muslim philosophers tried to reconcile 'Reason' (philosophy) with 'Faith' (religion). This rationalistic temperament of the age had already given rise to an independent school of Rationalism known as 'Mutazila' which forcibly made a canon of faith by Mamun.

It was during this time that Shi'ism got divided into two great factions—Twelvers (the Imamiyyas) and Seveners (the Ismailiyyas). The latter introduced the doctrine of *Tawil*, *i.e.*, allegorical interpretation of the Quran, emphasising the significance of the so-called hidden meaning of its verses. Hence they were called Talimyyas or Batinyyas. The Shia concept of Mehdi, *i.e.*, the hidden Imam or Messiah was also given a peculiar twist by them. They also evolved certain heretical doctrines like *Hulul* (Incarnation), *Tanasukh* (metempsychosis), and the raj'at (return).

Furthermore, toleration of free thought caused the emergence of many hereticals like Bih Afridi, Sinbadh, Ibn al-Muqaffa, Al-Muqanna, Babek Khurmi, etc., who introduced many heretical doctrines of local origin in Islam. Thus it can be easily perceived that the period preceding the rise of al-Ghazzali was assailed by a mighty wave of un-Islamic tendencies which shocked the religious foundations of the Muslims.

According to al-Ghazzali all the movements of his time were extremely biased, uncompromising and exclusive in character.[1] Greek science and theology had intoxicated the later Mutazilites and the philosophers, and the Shi'ism and the Sufis, were enamoured by the Persian subtleties. These heretical and un-Islamic ideas sowed the seeds of scepticism and disbelief and debased the traditional faith of the Muslims. The Asharites attempted to revive Islamic religion by purging it from heterodoxy. Although Asharism succeeded in destroying Mutazilaism under the inspiring guidance of Al-Ashari yet they were incapable of reinvigorating the benumbed spirit of Islam. This work was most successfully completed by Al-Ghazzali who analysed threadbare all the current thoughts prevalent in Muslim world with a view to weed out the true, original and orthodox spirit of Islam. Al-Ghazzali has been regarded as the final shaper of the Asharite theology.

Starting his career as an Ashari, Al-Ghazzali ended his life as a Sufi or a mystic. He was not a critic of religion but a renowned reformer of religion Islam every witnessed. It was at Baghdad that he got spiritual consolation in Sufism. Intellectual pursuits could not satisfy his hungry soul and he sought to know some spiritual illumination. He underwent 20 years of regorous saintly life, roaming from place to place until he settled at Baghdad to preach his doctrines. He mystified the Asharite theology. His teachings stood in sharp contrast to the system of philosophers. He preferred revelation to reason. His system has been regarded as the greatest and the perfect exposition of Muslim theology.

Al-Ghazzali's Contribution to Muslim Theology

The contribution made by al-Ghazzali to the

1. M. Umaruddin : *The Ethical Philosophy of Al-Ghazzali.* p. 41.

rise and development of Muslim scholastic theology and Islamic mysticism can never be exaggerated. He made his mark by leading Islam back to its fundamental and historical facts and by giving the place in its system to the emotional religious life. He rendered philosophy subordinate to theology and introduced the elements of fears in his teachings. It was under his influence that Sufism attained a firm position in the church of Islam. He brought philosophy within the range of ordinary minds. He is reckoned not only as a great restorer of the faith but also the Mujtahi or renewer of his century. The final triumph of Asharism over scholasticism was the work of al-Ghazzali. He has been regarded as an Asharite with the Asharites, a Sufi with the Sufis and a philosopher with the philosophers.

Nationalism and Sufism

The trends of nationalism and Sufism contributed much to the general anti-Islamic trend of the Abbasid era. The Umayyads had ruled over the then entire Muslim empire while the Abbasids succeeded to it without the State of Spain, where the only Umayyad survivor, Abdur Rahman, had established his rule in 756 A. D. Soon thereafter many independent and semi-independent states cropped up in North Africa, Palestine, Syria and Persia. By the end of the 10th century the authority of the Caliph had shrunk so much that it hardly extended beyond the precincts of Baghdad. This was the logical outcome of the policy of general toleration practised by the Abbasids. The Fatimids were not only an independent and rival power to the Abbasids, they aided and directed the Ismailian uprisings in the Abbasid realm and encouraged local aspirations for independence.

Asceticism, a life of purity and piety led by the Prophet and some of his Companions, later attracted many people. This way of life developed into a full-fledged ideology which came to be known as *Tassawuff, i.e.*, Islamic mysticism. There was nothing un-Islamic in it so long it remained confined in the Arab environment. Later Greek and Persian heresies crept into it through the writings and pronouncements of Bayazid Bistami (d. 876 A. D.) and Mansur Hallaj (d. 921 A. D.). They were the first to introduce pantheistic elements in Sufism. With al-Ghazzali, Sufism, an ethical self-culture began to take place in the orthodox Islam. He systematized Eastern Sufism. D. M. Macdonald has summarised the contributions made by al-Ghazzali to Islam :

(1) Al-Ghazzali reintroduced the element of fear in his moral teachings. He laid emphasis on the need of such fear which went into oblivion. The fear of hell-fire put a hindrance to the immoral conduct of life.

(2) He brought men from scholastic speculations on religious dogmas and diverted them to the study and exegesis of the Quran.

(3) Sufism attained a firm and systematic footing through his predominant influence.

(4) He did not condemn the study of philosophy but only subordinated it to theology.

CHAPTER X

SUFISM (ISLAMIC MYSTICISM)

Origin

The Muslims are of opinion that Sufism had its rise in Muhammad (صلعم) himself, and that all the religious orders trace their lines of succession back to him. He is said to have been the recipient of a two-fold revelation, the one embodied in the contents of the Quran, the other within his heart. The former was meant for all and is binding on all ; the latter was to be transmitted to the chosen few through these lines of succession. Hence it is that Muhammad's (صلعم) knowledge in popular language is described as being 'ilm-i-Safina' (book knowledge), and 'ilm-i-Sina' (heart knowledge). Von Kremer, Dozy and O'leary[1] traces the origin of Sufism from Indian Vedanta and Brown from Aryanism, Nicholson derives it from Neo-Platonism.[2] H. A. R. Gibb is also of opinion that Christianity made solid contributions to the origin of Sufism.[3] But Prof. Massignon, in his monumental work on Muslim mysticism has attempted to prove that mystical movement was the direct outcome of the Quran and the Traditions of the Prophet. Dr. Iqbal has mentioned political, social, intellectual conditions of Islamic world about the end of the eighth and the first half of the ninth century which led to the evolution of Sufism.[4]

The Derivation of Sufism

A variety of opinions exist among scholars as to

1. O Leary : *Arabic Thought and its place in History,* p. 191.
2. R. A. Nicholson : *Mystics of Islam*—1914.
3. H. A. R. Gibb : *Muhammadanism,* p. 130.
4. Dr. Iqbal : *The Development of Metaphysics in Persia,* pp. 98-101.

the meaning and derivation of the word Sufi. Some derive the word Sufi from '*Suf*' meaning wool. A woollen garment was a symbol of simplicity of life and renunciation of luxury. Some sought the origin from "Ahl us-Suffa" or the people of the bench. They spent their time in worship, imitation of the Prophet and searching the Quran and Hadith. They did not engage in a worldly business ; men who married were expelled from their company ; they wore little dress and were devoted to poverty ; for a living they gathered sticks and they often fed on fallen dates ; Muhammad (صلعم) fed them and Commanded his Companions to do like-wise.[1] Some derive it from '*Saf*' meaning line or rank. Jami and several other scholars derive it from '*Safa*' or purity. According to Nicholson, each term of the Sufism illustrates certain aspects and character of this mystic movement in Islam. It will not be out of place to mention here that Sufism means striving to know the real and neglecting the un-real. According to Abul Hussain Nuri of Khurasan, "Sufism is neither performing religious rituals, nor is it knowledge of science and philosophy. It means moral perfection and purification. It means freedom, manliness, non-attachment (to worldly desires) and generosity (self-sacrifice). Sufism means enmity to world and friendship to God."

Development of Sufism

It is generally assumed that Sufism came into being towards the close of the second or the beginning of the third century of Hijra era. But it is not true. In fact Sufism is as old as Islam itself. It was brought into being as soon as the verses of mystical cult were revealed to the Prophet. It cannot be denied that the Quran is often allegorical with a mystical touch.

1. Bukhari : *Sahih Book*, Ch. 8, p. 58.

The Prophet himself displayed mystical inclinations, and not infrequently restored to some hidden place (cave Hira) for meditation and devotion. He was often found in the state of complete absorption in his Lord. His intimate associates did not fail to imitate their leader. A section of the Companions from their acceptance of the Faith, had been mystical in tendency and ascetic in practice. They had cut themselves off from wordly affairs and passed their time in a portico of the mosque of the Prophet in meditation, prayer and devotion. They are known as "Ahl us-Suffa", from which the word Sufi was sought to be derived by the early Muslims.

The early Caliphs occasionally indulged in mystical expressions, denying existence to things other than God, and ascribing every action of the universe to the Divine Hands. The outstanding figure in this early ascetic movement was Imam Hasan of Basra (728 A.D.). It is said that the fear of God seized him so mightily. that "it seemed as though hell-fire had been created for him alone." He combined in himself the qualifications of a philosopher and a mystic.

In the words of John A. Subhan, "The early Sufis, however, were orthodox Muslims in regard to their beliefs and practices. They laid great emphasis on certain points in the teachings of the Quran and Traditions. They had not yet begun to indulge in metaphysical and theosophical speculations, but cofined their thoughts to matters bearing on practical theology. The distinctive features of their creed consisted in self-abandonment, self-mortification, fervent piety, and quietism carried to the extreme."

The outstanding figures during this period were Abu Ishaq Ibrahim bin Adham of Balkh (d. 777 A.D.), Fudayal bin Iyad (d. 801 A.D.) and Rabia al-Adwiyya (d. 776 A.D.). The last one is regarded as one of the greatest saints and Sufis the world has ever produced. Her utterances. fell of mystical ideas, are still fresh in the minds of the spiritualists. Needless to say these saints had nothing to do with Greek or Aryan philosophy.

In the course of the third century A.H., Sufism assumed a new character. Side by side with the quietistic and devotional mysticism of the early period there now sprang up a speculative and pantheistic movement which brought the Sufis in conflict with the orthodox Ulama.

Maruf Karkhi : He was a disciple of Imam Ali Musa al-Reza. He was a saint, pure and simple. He is reported to have said that Sufism is "the apprehension of divine realities and renunciation of human possessions." Another of his sayings runs as follows : "The saints of God are known by three signs. Their thought is of God, their dwelling is with God, their business is in God."[1]

Abu Sulayman al-Darani : He was a native of Wasit, but afterwards emigrated to Syria and settled at Daraya (near Damascus), whence he is called al-Darani. He developed the doctrine of 'ma'rifat' (gnosis).

Dhul-Nun al-Misri : He was a great scholar—both as a mystic and a philosopher. The key-note of his mystical ideas is : "The man that knows God best is the one most lost in Him." To him is ascribed the authorship of the mystical theories and doctrines.

The early Sufis are particularly interested in the theory of mystical union (*fana wa baqa*). Bayazid (or Abu Yazid) Bistami made some improvements on the existing condition of mysticism by introducing the doctrine of self-effacement and self-annihilation. This is the final stage in the spiritual development of man

1. See *Tadhkiratu'l-Awliya.*

when the individual self is absorbed in Universal soul. Thus in a frantic stage of ecstasy, Mansur al-Hallaj declared. "I am the Truth" (*Ana'l Haqq*).[1]

Sufi Orders

The twelfth century of the Christian era saw Sufis split up into several orders. Broadly, they are divided into the following major orders of fraternities :

(1) Qadiriyya : Abdul Qadir of Gilan (Iran), known for his piety and religious devotion, developed the order from the school founded by Junayd of Baghdad.

(2) Naqshbandiyya : Khwaja Bahauddin Mohammad founded the school. Its followers are in Indo-Pakistan, China, Turkey and Java.

(3) Shattariya : Abdulla Shattar founded the school in 1415 A.D. Its chief centres are in Sumatra, Java and Indo-Pakistan.

(4) Chishtiyya : Founded by Moinuddin Hasan Chishti. Its followers are mostly in Indo-Pakistan.

(5) Sanusiyya : It was founded by Shaikh Mohammad bin Ali as-Sanusi. It is a branch of the Qadiriyya. Its followers are found in North Africa.

(6) Moulvi : Founded by Jalaluddin Rumi, noted for its whirling dervishes. Its followers are in Turkey.

Sufi Theme

"Mysticism," according to Margaret Smith, "is not theoretical but practical teaching way of life."[2] The theme and paths of Sufism are enumerated as follows :

1. R. A. Nicholson : *The Idea of Personality in Sufism*, p. 27.
2. M. Smith : *Readings from the Mystics of Islam*, p. 2.

(1) Submission or Resignation : A Sufi novice must treat his spiritual teacher with great respect and obey him 'like the corpse in the hands of the corpse-bearers.' In the same manner and more completely, he must submit himself to the will of Allah and live in perfect harmony with the Divine will.

(2) *Ikhlas* or Sincerity and Devotion : This indicates the effort of moving towards the Divine Being and keeping this ideal of movement above all desires. It is opposite to *riya* or hypocrisy. *Ikhlas* demands self-sacrifice and indifference to all other ideas. When Ikhlas becomes perfect, self-consciousness also is lost.

(3) *Tauba* or Repentance : This indicates the return or conversion from the world to Allah. It is not only renunciation of the evil but a change from a tendency towards the world to a tendency towards Allah. The human soul being pure in its essence, when polluted, becomes restless and asserts its true nature by feeling repentance for its unnatural tendency.

(4) Fear of Allah : The fear of Allah is the deep consciousness of His sublimity and grandeur—a man in the presence of a king may not fear him, but the feeling of respect is so deep that the balance of mind is lost.

(5) *Tawukkul* or Trust : A Sufi must trust in Allah. Some extremists went to the extent of neither working, nor even begging and of expecting that their daily necessities would reach them without labouring to obtain them. The idea led to quietism and degenerated into laziness.

(6) *Kashf* or Unveiling of the Spiritual Mysteries : This is classified into (*a*) *Mazaherah*, in which intellect is the means of reaching to a conclusion, and (*b*) *Mushaheda*, in which personal knowledge is a proof of ecstasy (*wajd*) and the condition attained (*hal*).

The state of *wajd* is higher than prayer when the Divine will is revealed. A constant state of *wajd* leads to comply submission to the Divine will.

(7) Supernatural Knowledge : This is of three kinds : (*a*) Normal (*Ilm ul-Yaqin*), reach to a proof by intellectual reasoning, (*b*) Abnormal (*Ainul-Yaqin*), loss of worldly consciousness in a state of *wajd*, or knowing a spiritual secret by perceiving it, and (*c*) Supernormal (*Haq ul-Yaqin*), union with the truth or seeing and feeling the quality of a thing. These three stages of knowledge are illustrated by saying that a fruit may be known by its correct description, and better known by seeing it and perfectly known by seeing and tasting it.

(8) *Hal* or Condition : This is a mental state gifted momentarily by divine grace. In this state, one is either in the form of Cast, of expansion of heart or by *Qabz* (depression of the same). When it is gifted continuously it is called *Milk* or possession and when it becomes permanent it is named *Maqam* or station.

(9) Renunciation is of two kinds—external and internal. It stands for detachment from worldly pleasures. A Sufi must minimise his worldly needs and thus become harmless to other creatures. Next, he should try to free the soul from attachment to sensible objects. A Sufi values this life as a source of training himself for a true life.

(10) Music: As a Sufi must train his mind to appreciate beauty and by some means to stir up his inner spiritual feeling and music is considered to be beauty and harmony the sound, a large number of Sufi leaders, particularly Chishtis and Moulvis, approve of the hearing of songs and the playing on musical instruments on condition that the purpose must be to stimulate spiritual emotion. Music is called 'Sama' or

spiritual concerts, in which, one or several singers, sing and play.

(11) *Zikr* or Recitation or Meditation : Each order has its own method of reciting a sacred word or formula. In a general sense, it is divided into : (*i*) *Jali* (loud muttering adopted by the Chishti and Qadiriyya orders ; and (*ii*) *Khafi* (mental muttering, preferred by Naqshbandiyya order). Both are based on text of the Holy Quran.

(12) *Fana* (annihilation) and *Baqa* (affirmation) are the highest stages of spiritual development. By *Fana*, the Sufi means self-negation or negation of earthly tendency and *Baqa*, retention of spiritual existence or extraction of evil qualities and retention of virtue or permanency of mind from sensible objects to spiritual reality, the extinction of material desires and the loss of self-consciousness.

Tenets of Sufism

The Sufis agree that the Quran is the uncreated words of Allah. It is not an innovation. They are of opinion that the believers and not the unbelievers will be able to see Allah with the eyes in the world hereafter.

The Sufis agree in the pre-destination and say that all the acts of His servants either good or bad, is in accordance with Allah's decrees.

They believe in the intercession of the Prophet Muhammad (صلعم), in the Balance, in the Bridge of A'rafat. Allah will deliver from hell every man who has atoms of faith in their heart. They believe in the eternal hell and heaven and consider punishment and reward as eternal.

The Sufis consider the Prophets as superior to

ordinary beings and respect Muhammad (صلعم) as the most excellent of the Prophets.

According to Sufis, faith consists of speech, act and intention.

Sufi and Orthodox Muslims

The difference between the Sufi and the orthodox Muslims' views may be briefly set down here :—

(1) The orthodox Muslims depend upon external conduct while the Sufis seek inner purity.

(2) The orthodox believe in blind obedience to or observance of religious rituals while the Sufis think love to be the only means of reaching God ; and

(3) The orthodox say that good deeds are a sign of inner goodness but the Sufis assert that without a pure heart, the apparent good deeds have no value.

PART II

CULTURAL HISTORY

CHAPTER XI

CULTURAL HISTORY OF THE UMAYYADS

The "sons of the desert" were not advanced in arts and architecture, painting and music, science and arts. It was due to their economic backwardness and geographical environments, Before the rise of Islam, they were uncivilized and barbarous. They lived in small huts and most of them were nomads. But Islam changed their lives. Arabia which was a mere geographical expression was turned into a mighty state a few centuries after the demise of the Prophet. The Prophet changed their lives by giving religious education and creating a thirst for learning of arts and science.

With the expansion of Islamic empire, the Muslims came into contact with the ancient seat of civilization such as Mesopotamia, Persia and Egypt. The contact of the Muslims with the ancient civilization was a boon to them. They learnt their arts and science and carried on further research in that direction. By this time, they became masters of the vast wealth of Persia, Iraq, Syria, Egypt and other parts of the world such as India and Spain. It is natural that with the unlimited wealth, luxurious life will develop. During the rule of early caliphate, the life of the Caliphs was simple and honest. Hence, neither any Royal Palace was constructed, nor any beautiful court was established. The only art that was favoured was the learning of theology. Schools and Maktabs were established, and patronised, but that also did not reach any high standard.

But all things changed with the establishment of the Umayyad rule. In the early caliphate, painting, music and dancing, were hated at anti-Islamic arts. But the Umayyad caliphs were luxurious. The income of the State became their paternal property and hence with that money they established palaces, gardens, mosques and patronised fair arts as painting, dancing and music to amuse themselves. Besides, alchemy, medicine, poetry, the study of theology also progressed.

In those days, the royal patronage was an essential factor for the development of any art. The Umayyad caliphs' contribution to the development of art and science, however insignificant, may be compared with modern art and science, and it should be taken into consideration. All the Umayyad caliphs were not worthless drunkards; some of them were refined, cultured and enthusiastic patrons of art and science. But the progress was slow and the development was in a rudimentary state owing to the fact that most of the Umayyad rulers were busy in war and the life of the empire was short. Hence, no great achievement was possible. Nevertheless whatever improvement we find is remarkable for the "sons of the desert". On the foundation of the Umayyad art and architecture, the latter Umayyads and Abbasids created a new history. It inspired them with an idea, an inspiration and an ambition.

In the words of Hitti, "Muawiya was not only the first but also one of the best Arab kings." Nevertheless, he freed himself from the corrupt court life, characteristic of the age. But Yazid introduced the Byzantine system of court life and it continued up to the end of the Umayyad rule with increasing rapidity. Hence, centring the court which was the centre of amusement and enjoyment, painting, music and dancing developed as an art. Famous musicians and dancers were patronised and large sums of money were spent. Greek and Persian ladies were imported in the Harem for singing and dancing.

Painting as an art was developed to decorate the

royal palace and bathrooms of the caliphs. Human pictures were not drawn as they were prohibited in Islam. The pictures drawn were mostly scenery, birds, flowers and fruits.

Education

The Umayyad period witnessed little progress in literature and learning. But the period cannot be considered as barren: it sowed the seed of learning which blossomed under the Abbasids. The Umayyad caliphs had taken interest in education. It is a historical fact that under the Umayyads, the Arabs began to study history, geography and astronomy, besides tradition, philosophy and theology. The common people desiring to secure education, patronised the mosques where classes on the Quran and Hadith were taken. The earliest teachers in Islam were therefore the readers of the Quran. Most of the schools were attached to mosques and endowed with property. "The system of teaching was based upon free lectures. A famous lecturer could find hundreds of pupils and thousands of people for his audience. Admission, generally, was free and without any restriction whatever."[1]

The Umayyad caliphs patronised arts and literature and built schools and hospitals in different parts of the empire. Muawiyah, the first caliph of the Umayyad dynasty, was fond of hearing legendary stories.[2] He had a large heart and liberal mind for learning. He invited the Christian physician named Ibn Athal to his court who translated for him several medical books into Arabic. "Himself a poet of no small merit, Yazid bin Muawiyah patronised the learned and the learning." Khalid bin Yazid was a devotee of learning. He was a philosopher and is said

1 A. M. A. Shustery : *Outlines of Islamic Culture*, p. 122.
2. Ibid., p. 121.

to have been the first in Islam to translate Greek and Coptic books on alchemy, medicine and astrology. Omar II is said to have transferred the schools of medicine from Alexandria to Antioch. Many savants and scholars enjoyed the patronage of Walid I and Hisham. The Umayyad caliphs thus nursed and nourished learning in its infancy. Mr. Chenery says, "It is impossible to doubt the service of these caliphs, particularly in preserving the compositions of the past which were in danger of being lost through the fall of so many of the recitors in the ceaseless wars." So the Umayyads cannot be charged according to Khuda Bakhsh with having been indifferent to the advancement of learning.

Medina, Basra and Kufa as Centres of Intellectual Activity

Medina, Basra and Kufa were the chief centres of intellectual activity in the Muslim world. The students from different parts of the Muslim world gathered for the purpose of learning Arabic pronunciation and recitation of poems.

Medina was not only the seat of Islam during the lifetime of the Prophet, but three of his successors—Abu Bakr, Umar, and Uthman made it the metropolis of the Caliphate. Medina was the most important cultural centre of Islam, because of the historical developments which led to the migration and the subsequent founding of the Islamic state in this city. It was here that the vast majority of the Companions were available for imparting education to the people. Umar and Ali were the authorities in their own field. Zaid bin Thabit and Abdullah ibn Umar were famous for their devotion to learning. Zaid bin Thabit, the chief scribe of the Quran, was the authority on Jurisprudence, the Quran and the Sunnah during the days of Umar, Uthman and Ali.

It was here that the seekers of knowledge flocked to gather the wisdom of the new cultural movement whose most authentic exponents lived in Medina. Most of the learned scholars were graduates of schools in Medina which attracted students of history, Hadith and Jurisprudence from all over the Muslim world. Mohammad bin Ishaq and al-Waqidi, the main authorities on biography of the Holy Prophet and the history of the Muslim campaigns, were both brought up in this city. Besides them, the schools of Medina produced famous scholars like Sa'id ibn al-Musayyib, Ibn Shihab al-Zahri al-Quraishi and Malik ibn Anas. Ibn Shihab was held in high respect by Umayyad caliphs.

It is said that the scientific study of *Arabic language* and grammar began with a view to supplying linguistic needs to the new converts to Islam when they wanted to study the Quran. Asad-ud-Dowla who founded the Arabic grammar, flourished in Basra and died in 688 A. D. He was followed by Khalid bin Ahmad, another distinguished scholar of Basra. He was the first to compile an Arabic Dictionary named the *Kitab al-Ayan*. Khalid bin Ahmad was also credited with the discovery of Arabic prosody and its rules which hold good even today. His pupil Sibawayh, a Persian, composed the first systematic textbook on grammar and this became the basis of all native studies of the subject. The great Muslim mystic Hasan al-Basri was the chief ornament of the religious life of Basra. Malik ibn Anas also settled down at Basra. He earned his reputation as a traditionist. During the Umayyad period the schools of Basra produced some of the well-known personalities like Mohammad ibn Shireen and others. Intellectual ferment, thinking about religious practices and religious faith in a rational manner also started at Basra.

The contributions of the Kufans to Arab culture

was almost as brilliant as those of the Basarites. Among the celebrated traditionists who hailed from Kufa, the name of Abdullah ibn Masud stands out prominently. Ibn Masud is said to have been responsible for 848 Hadith. It is said that the school of Ibn Masud produced many well-known students of the Quran. Of these, Al-Qamah, Al-Aswad, Ubaydah al-Harith ibn Qayas were the prominent. These scholars were also distinguished Jurists. Amir ibn Sdurhabil al-Shabi and Abu Hanifa were other distinguished traditionists of this period.

Most of the great writers, poets as well as grammarians, thinkers as well as traditionists, came from these towns. It was here that the science of Hadith was founded. Rules for explanation of the Quranic verses, sifting of traditions of the Prophet, the elements of Muslim Law, the beginning of Muslim Sufism all had their beginning in either of these three centres of cultural activities.

Mosque as Centre of Learning

In pre-Islamic period, there was no school in Mecca and Medina. After the advent of Islam, schools used to be in the mosques. Khuda Bukhsh says, "For Muslims the mosque does not bear the same exclusive character as does a church for Christians. It is not merely a place of worship. The Muslim, indeed, honours the mosque, but he does not hesitate to use it for any laudable purpose." At first, the mosque had been associated, besides prayer, with the study of the Holy Quran and Hadith. The Prophet is represented as sitting in the mosque with his '*halqa*' (audience) of listeners who repeat with him the Quranic verses three times in order to memorise them and people come and ask him about this or that Hadith. There were nine mosques at Medina even at the time of the Prophet and they served the purpose of schools. The people who lived in and about Medina sent their children to these mosques. The Prophet, sometimes, personally supervised the schools in the mosques.

Hazrat Umar, the second caliph of Islam, appointed a number of learned men to lecture in mosques on Islamic teachings in the new cantonments of Kufa, Basra, Damascus, etc. He sent in the 17 A.H. teachers of the Quran to every region and people attended the lectures in the mosques every Friday. Lectures of this kind were called "Mua'iza". In this way, the mosques became not only a place for worship but also a centre of education. The number of such lectures increased and became the nucleus of a future mosque-madrassah.

The Umayyad caliphs had taken interest in some branches of science known to foreign nations. Their centres of imparting education were no other than the mosques. The Umayyad caliph Hazrat Umar II sent a learned 'Maula' to Egypt in order to teach Egyptians the 'Sunnah'. They taught their pupils Islamic sciences. The poet, al-Kumait, taught students in the mosque of Kufa about the beginning of the 8th century A.D. Students circled about their teachers in the mosque of Damascus.

During the Abbasids, mosques had become places for public lectures not only on theology and tradition but also on other branches of art and science. There were numerous mosque-schools in the city of Baghdad. According to Yaqubi, there were in Baghdad 30,000 mosques and each mosque was a potential school in the modern sense, but carried on all this educational work in the mosque. Al-Makkari, the chief historian of Arab Spain says, "The people of Andalusia (Spain) have no schools to help them in the quest of learning, because they study all branches in the mosques by the payment of fees." He further says that he himself taught students in the mosque of Cordova and that of Az-Zahara. From the beginning of Islam, mosques were used as schools in Baghdad, Damascus, Jerusalem and other places. The poet and traveller Nasir Khusro writes that the mosque at Cairo was daily visited by aboue 5,000 men, who heard lectures on various subjects, but the main subjects of study were the Quran, tradition and theology.

We can easily maintain that after the advent of Islam mosques became not only a place for worship but also an educational institution. Every Muslim could enter the mosque and attend a lecture. There were small primary and secondary schools attached to the more important mosques. Girls and boys of tender age were educated in the same school. It is also evident from the facts that the mosques also served the purpose of hostels. Pious people could spend days and nights there, when they came to the town. All branches of Islamic sciences found an asylum in the mosques. This was the meeting place of all learned men for study, worship and discussion. Thus the traveller found a shelter there, and the learned a lecture hall and the judge a court of justice.

Architecture

The Umayyad Caliphs were the great patrons of architecture and they engaged their attention towards its development. Architecture in Islam began with the construction of the mosque which remained, for long, the best specimen of Arabian architecture. The Umayyad rulers made Damascus their capital, where they built palaces and mosques. In order to make the mosque beautiful and attractive minarets were introduced. They were made of stones. Mosques were also built in Kufa and Basra by the Umayyad provincial Governor Ziyad. "He rebuilt the mosque of Kufa on which occasion he removed the gravel from the floor and replaced it by a solid pavement, to prevent the flinging gravel from hands after the performance of prostration at the time of Namaz" (W. Muir).

Architecture reached its high water mark during the reigns of Abdul Malik and his son Al-Walid I. Abdul-Malik built in 691 A.D. the great mosque at Jerusalem called the Dome of the Rocks (Qubbat ul-Sakhra), a mosque which stands to this day as a glory of early Muslim architecture. It was a large stone-built mosque, constructed in a style which shows traces of Byzantine influence.[1] It was the earliest Muslim mosque covered with a Dome. The columns were transferred from other buildings. The walls were built with semi-circular stones. The dome was made of timber, but covered outside with lead and painted inside with plaster. Near the Dome of the Rocks, the Caliph erected another mosque named the Aqsa Mosque (690 A.D.). Its arches are large and vividly painted. The size of the columns was made up by higher square ties over capitals which were under the range of other arches, under which wood ties had been built.

Walid I constructed a mosque at Damascus about the beginning of the 8th century A.D. Its chief sanctuary contains the aisle, (crossed by transepts) at the end of which is the Mehrab or prayer niche. The arches are of the horse-shoe pattern, and the interior is decorated with marbles and mosaics. The geographer Al-Masudi writes that it was decorated with gold and precious stones representing trees and cities and bearing beautiful inscriptions. Besides these mosques, the palaces of the caliph and the houses of the wealthy people show traces of ideas borrowed from Arabian and Syro-Byzantine architecture. Walid I enlarged and beautified the mosque of Mecca, rebuilt that of Medina, "erected in Syria a

1. A.M.A. Shustery : *Outlines of Islamic Culture*, p. 171.

number of schools and places of worship and endowed institutions for the lepers, the lame and the blind". (Tabari).

Among the earliest mosques known in Egypt is the one built in 643 A.D. by Amr bin As, the conqueror of Egypt. It had an open court 240 feet square. Its prayer hall is 106 feet deep, its columns and capitals were transferred from other buildings, carry arches of semicircular, horse-shoe and pointed form.

Umayyad dynasty ruled in Spain and has left historical monuments in the shape of architectural buildings of note. The Umayyad caliphs built the mosque of Cordova, the Almohade Giralda tower and a portion of the celebrated palace known as the Al-Cazar at Seville. The mosque of Cordova, built by the Umayyad caliph Abdur Rahman II in 756-788 A.D. comprises eleven aisles of 21 bays over it and a number of lateral aisles. Hisham, the next caliph, built the minaret, Hisham II added eleven more aisles. Professor Shustery says : "It was an imitation of the mosque at Kairawan in Tunis."

Among palaces, the Al-Cazar of Seville is so much altered and modified that its original plan has been lost to us. But that it was one of the glories of the palace there can be no doubt. The palace of Alhamra (in Granada,) which may be called the Taj Mahal of the Western Muslim monuments, is still intact. Its Hall of Justice, Hall of Ambassadors, Hall of the Two Sisters and its courts of the Myrtle and the lions are all charming and beautiful for the delicate workmanship they display.[1] Its walls are build of earth, supported with courses of bricks, and its wooden ceilings are masked by hanging stalactiles of painted gypsum. The walls are ornamented with glazed tiles in which gold has been used. The columns are of marble, the ceiling beams and doors are of wood. The principal entrance is

1. A.M.A. Shustery : *Outlines of Islamic Culture*, p. 178.

through the Gate of Justice, which is built of concrete. Close to Alhamra, there was another palace built in the centre of a beautiful garden, with fountains in which water flowed through streams descending from the surrounding mountains. The decoration was of a conventional character, consisting of Arabic inscription, foliage, geometric patterns and painted tiles. The palace of Az-Zahra built by Caliph Abdur Rahman III (8th Century A. D.) and continued and completed by his son was the marvel of the period. Az-Zahirah was another palace built at Cordova by Al-Monzar, the Regent in 978-81 A.D. Among other palaces, there were those known as the Palace of the Flowers, of Contentment, of Lovers, of Damascus and so on. The mosque and the monuments with their artistic excellence exercised a spell upon the imagination of the spectators.

Social Life

Damascus, the capital of the Umayyads, was one of the most beautiful cities of the world and the metropolis of the Islamic empire. "The position of the town," says Von Kremer, "is so exceedingly favourable that it must, doubtless, have become early in its history an important centre of the intercourse of nations and exchange of wares, as also a cradle of political and social life of those neighbourhoods." Palatial mansions built of white marbles, ornamented with inlaid stones of various colours, adorned the city. The water supply of the city is an imperishable memorial of the Umayyad rulers. The Umayyad caliphs lived in great pomp and grandeur and maintained a gorgeous court after the fashion of the Byzantine emperors. Most of the rulers of Damascus were sporting, pleasure loving and insatiable drinkers to whom the unavoidable cares of rulers must often have been very uncongenial and irksome. Despite the prohibition of Islam, it was not long before people indulged in wine and the court of Damascus summoned singers from Mecca and Medina—the centres of the art of music and song, with the result that under Yazid and Walid II, the evening parties degenerted into downright drinking bouts and carouses.

In the Umayyad society, the Arabs formed the autocracy and the neo-Muslims, though theoretically equal, ranked as second to the Arabs, but practically they did not enjoy full rights of Islamic citizenship. A Muslim was supposed to pay no tribute. There is no doubt, that throughout the Umayyad period, holders of land, whether believers or unbelievers were made to pay land-tax. The lowest class in the society was the non-Muslims, called the *zimmis*. Among the *zimmis*, the Christians and the Jews called Ahl-ul-Kitab enjoyed a better position than the idolators, fire-worshippers and others who had no divine book. The *zimmis* enjoyed a wide measure of autonomy and toleration. John, a Christian, rose to the position of minister in the caliphate of Abdul Malik. Revenue administration was practically done by the *zimmis*.

Umayyad society had great love for music and Mecca, Medina and Damascus were the centres of the art of music and song. "In this reign," remarks Ameer Ali, "the love of music grew almost into a craze, and enormous sums were spent on favour of its singers and musicians who were summoned to court from most distant parts" Thus dancing and singing became common. It resulted in the demoralisation of the society and led to the segregation of the females. Dancing and singing together with the introduction of wine were borrowed from the Persians. Von Kremer says, "The actual Harem system commenced only under Walid II, who, in imitation of the Byzantine custom, introduced eunuchs into his household. From that time, these unfortunate creatures played a conspicuous part in the oriental courts as confidential servants and guards of female honour."

The custom of the female seclusion, which was in vogue among the Persians from very early times, made its appearance among the Muslim community in the reign of Walid II. Still women enjoyed large dimensions of freedom and the chivalrous Arabs held fair sex in high esteem. Fathers were proud of assuming surnames after their accomplished and beautiful daughters; and brothers and lovers still rushed to battle acclaiming the names of their sisters and lady-loves. The highbred Arab maiden could still converse with men without embarrassment and in absolute unconsciousness of evil. To her the beautiful lines of Firdausi[1] were still applicable :

Lips full of smiles, countenance full of modesty,

Conduct virtuous, conversation lively.[2]

She entertained her guests without shyness and as she knew her own worth she was respected by all around her. Obscure poets made love even to princesses and they fearlessly sang of such love in their poems. Abu Dahbal composed some poem on Atika, the daughter of Muawiya and the would-be wife of Abdul Malik when the former saw her at Dhu Tunah, a place outside the town on the caravan route to Medina. Presently, love affair came about between the princess and the poet. He followed her to Damascus but in vain.

It is apparent that the position of women at the court of the Caliph, was entirely different at that time to the deep degradation which later on fell to the lot of the fair sex in Muslim countries.

Even in the state affairs, the final decision was often pronounced by women, and the wife of the Caliph was, at times, the real ruler. History furnishes the fact

1. The Homer of Persia.
2. "Do lab pur Khandah, do rukh pur ze sharm,
Ba-raftar neko, ba guftar garm,"

that Abdul Malik was completely under the influence of his fair and self-willed wife Atika. Umm-ul-Banin, the wife of Walid I, and sister of Umar II, was another remarkable woman of the time. Her influence over her husband was considerable, and was always exercised for the good of the people.

In the Umayyad society, women distinguished themselves as scholars and poetesses of wit and virtue. Sakina and Umm-ul-Banin were highly accomplished ladies of the time. The famous saint Rabia surnamed Umm-ul-Khair lived about this epoch. She is described as one of the most eminent among the holy persons of the time.

Men's dress had undergone much change from early times, but evidently the tight-fitting Kuba was now coming into use. The dress differed not only in quality and quantity according to the means of the wearer but varied in style and shape according to the profession. The costume of a *Fakih* (pleader) or a *Khatib* (clerk) differed widely from that of the soldier.

The Umayyad society made use of napkins and spoons. Chair and table also came into fashion.

At the bottom of the society stood the slaves. These persons were so much respected in times of the Prophet and under the early pious Caliphs that they were raised to the status of commanders. Similar treatment was not meted out in later days.

CHAPTER XII

CULTURAL HISTORY OF THE ABBASIDS

Social Life

The Caliph was the head of the society. He commanded the highest respect of the people. Below the Caliph stood the high officials of the court.

In the early part of the Abbasid society, the women enjoyed the same position and liberty as their Umayyad sisters. But towards the close of the tenth century, they lost their liberty and had to observe strict seclusion and absolute segregation of the sexes become general. In the early part, women exercised great influence in the affairs of the State. We read in history that Al-Khaizran, wife of Mehdi and mother of Rashid, Harun's sister Ulayah, Zubaidah, Rashid's wife and Amin's mother all these women achieved great distinction in that early period. They were fond of splendid dress, ornaments and jewelleries. Caliph Harun's sister Ulayah introduced the fashion of wearing a new ornament called the fillet.[1] She also set in fashion a dome-shaped cap for women. Empress Zubaidah was the first lady to ornament her shoes with precious stones. She would tolerate at her table no vessels not made of gold or silver and studded with gems.[2] The art of tinting the cheeks and lips was in fashion. The Arab maidens, in order to be considered beautiful, had to be tall, of slender figure, well-proportioned and with large and black eyes.

The women distinguished themselves in different walks of life. They took part in battle and even com-

1. P. K. Hitti : *The Arabs, A Short History*, p. 85.
2. Ibid., p. 85.

manded soldiers in the battle field. Many women excelled in literary and intellectual attainments. Empress Zubaidah was an accomplished lady and a gifted poetess. Ubaydah excelled in music. Fazl was a gifted poetess in the reign of Mutawakkil. Zainab was a distinguished lawyer. Taqqiyyah, daughter of Abul Faraj, was a talented poetess. The females in general were fairly educated and they could teach their own children.

In those days, a gentleman's dress consisted of wide trousers of Persian origin, shirt, vest and jacket with outer mantle. The theologians wore black turbans and mantles, the Jubbah. Aristocratic ladies used the dome-shaped cap and fillet as head-dress and ornaments. Anklets and bracelets were in great fashion among the women of the time. Boots and shoes were in use in the society.

Drinks were the common feature of the Abbasid society. Even Caliphs, Wazirs, Princes and Judges indulged themselves in revelry accompanied with drinks, convivial parties, and songs were not uncommon in the Abbasid society. The drinking room was made fragrant and the songstresses who participated in all these gatherings, were of loose character.[1] These songstresses were a menace to the morals of the youth of the age. People dined at tables placed by the side of the diwans or sofas. For each person there was a napkin.

Music was patronised by the Abbasid Caliphs. It was a noble profession in the society. Both men and women had great love for music. Princess Ulayah was an accomplished musician of the time. Princess and ladies of high families held music majlis in their houses. Dancing was also much honoured in the society. Caliph Amin introduced the wonderful saracenic ballet.

1. P. K. Hitti : *The Arabs, A Short History*, p. 97.

Under the Abbasids, hunting was the favourite outdoor pastime of all classes of people. Al-Amin was fond of hunting lions. Chess was the popular indoor game of the Abbasid society. Other notable outdoor games were polo (*chougan*), hockey (*sulajan*), throwing of spears (*jerid*), horse-racing, wrestling, and fencing on foot and on horseback. Cricket was not unknown, and rackets and tennis (*lub-ul-kurah*) were played by both sexes, and women also practised archery.

The nobles held social reunions and literary gatherings in their houses. Literary clubs, however, had sprung up since the time of Mamun, where scholars flocked and discussed philosophical subjects. The booksellers occupied an important position in the society in those days, and their shops were the resort of students and the learned generally. Authors, publishers and booksellers were held in high respect in the Abbasid society.

EDUCATION

The Abbasid rule proved itself the golden period of Muslim learning.[1] The Abbasid caliphs not only encouraged learning but also enjoined public discussion and founded schools where, besides Arabic literature, theology, philosophy, grammar, rhetoric, mathematics, physics astrology, astronomy and other branches of science were studied. Let us examine the system of education that was prevalent during the period of the Abbasid rulers.

Under the Abbasids, the child education started at home. At the age of six, boys were admitted into schools and according to Al-Ghazzali, "it was then that his formal education began." Elementary schools grew up quite naturally in the peninsula. The schools were held in mosques, in private houses and sometimes

1. A. M. A. Shustery : *Outlines of Islamic Culture*, p. 121.

in teacher's own house. Besides the mosques, there were Maktabs which served as elementary schools.

The education given in the early Abbasid period bore some resemblance to contemporary church education in Europe. In Europe, the scriptures were the final authority for everything and even philosophy and science had to be reconciled with Christian theology, so with the Muslims, the Quran and Islamic teachings were the bases for everything.[1] The curriculum of the elementary school consisted of reading, writing, grammar, traditions of the Prophet, elementary principles of arithmetic and some devotional poems. Hitti says that throughout the whole curriculum memory work was specially emphasized. Senior students studied Quranic criticism, the science of Apostolic tradition, jurisprudence, scholastic theology, lexicography rhetoric and literature. Advanced scholars engaged themselves in the study of Astronomy, Philosophy, Geometry, Music and Medicine.

Co-education was in vogue during the Abbasid period. Girls and boys of tender age were educated together in the same school. The girls were expected to read the Quran and acquire religious knowledge. Those who continued and became masters of theology and other subjects, took to teaching as a profession and we find some women theologians as great public teachers. A brilliant woman named Amrah, used her house as a school. The benefit of teaching was equally extended to poor; even slaves in some cases were admitted to schools. The system of appointing private tutors for children was in vogue among the wealthy persons of the society.

There were three types of teachers under the Abbasids. The first type of teachers simply taught the Quran to children in the elementary school and was

1. Ibid., p. 122.

called "Muallim." The social position of the Muallim was not considered very laudable. "Seek no advice from teachers" of elementary schools, acquired proverbial usage. The second type of teacher may be called a tutor, "Muaddib", representing a class which was engaged in teaching the sons of the higher strata as well as those of princes and caliphs. This class of teachers was superior to those of elementary schools. Thirdly, came the professors of higher learning. They were specialists in the teaching of logic, mathematics, rhetoric and jurisprudence. The higher grade teachers were held in high respect by the public.

The teachers received their payment from the pupils. The pay of the teacher was very low. Prof. Shushtery writes, "Teachers were supported by the income derived from endowments attached to mosques, shrines, hospitals and in some cases from the wealthy classes. Some of them received allowances from the Royal Treasury."

At the age of 15 the boy who had acquired elementary knowledge usually set out for the next great town to attend lectures there. Scholars were used to travel and take long journeys in search of knowledge. There was no regular curriculum or a fixed syllabus. The founders of the schools had the right of appointment and removal of professors. In the choice of subjects, the teachers enjoyed perfect freedom. The state interfered only in a case where religion was in danger.

Experienced professors knew the text by heart and could lecture without referring to any book. The number of students varied from a few to thousands. Ink and paper were kept ready to take notes from the lectures delivered by professors. "In the lecture hall at Nishapur, there were 500 ink-stands kept ready for the use of students" (Shushtery). The lecturer was not satisfied merely with delivering his lectures, he also wanted that the students should follow and understand him. For this purpose he put questions to the students and asked them to put questions to him. Khuda Bakhsh writes, "Many teachers while discussing the subject, left their seat and mixed with the students." Study in the high schools was thus not merely a hearing of lectures, but also a thorough drilling in the subjects. The lecturers were highly respected and followed by their pupils. The students after satisfying their teachers that they had learnt their subjects well, could ask and obtain certificates.

The education of the Abbasids was not only confined to that of children in primary schools. During the reign of Harun and his son, a large number of richly endowed schools were opened, a university was founded, libraries were organised, an observatory was set up. Mamun founded an academy named '*Bait-ul-Hikmat*', where the higher branches of learning were pursued. According to Prof. Hitti, "Besides serving as a translation bureau this institute functioned as an academy and public library and had an observatory connected with it." "*Bait-ul-Hikmat* may claim," says Totah "the honour of having been the first University of both the medieval and modern world, for it bore the torch aloft long before Boloqua, Paris, Prague, Oxford and Cambridge." The college Bait-ul-Hikmah boasted of a library with a librarian who was a noted mathematician and astronomer.

Something should be said here about some of the translators. Many of the translators were also original contributors. Hunayn bin Ishaq (809-873) was a Christian-Arab and a doctor. He translated the works of Galen, Plato, Aristotle and Ptolemy. He is credited with having written 31 books. His ability as a translator is affirmed by the report that he received about 500 dinars per month and that al-Mamun paid him in gold the weight of the books he translated. Other noted translators were Yahya bin al-Bitriq (815 A.D.), Sabit bin Qurrah (836-901), Qusta bin Luqa, etc.

The real academy in Islam which became the model for later schools of higher learning was the Nizamiyah established by Nizamul Mulk, the Persian Wazier of the Seljuq Sultan, Malik Shah. He organised a system of education and started regular Madrasah and founded several important colleges and universities and endowed them adequately with munificent grants from the Government. To these the Caliph Mustansir added a magnificent college with library and other arrangements under the name of 'Mustansariyyah'. There were 30 high schools in Alexandria and 17 centres of learning in Spain with 70 public libraries.

It can safely be concluded that the system of education under the Abbasids proved a turning point in the educational history of the modern world. In all the higher institutions of theology, the science of tradition lay at the basis of the curriculum and memory work was specially stressed upon. To build a Madrasah was a pious act for the Muslims. Madrasahs were endowed with land and property, the income of which went for the support of teachers and poor students. Ibn Zubair says that there were 30 schools in Baghdad and more than 500 students drawing daily rations from the funds of the mosque of that city. There were three kinds of institutions, which served the purpose of boys of different ages and calibre. The educational system during this period was not only confined to Quran and Hadith, but advanced students had to stduy philosophy, astronomy, astrology, medicine, music, history, geography, mathematics, botany, etc.

ARCHITECTURE

During the Abbasid period, the Islamic architecture began to develop in its own synthetic and novel designs. Baghdad became the capital of the Abbasid empire and it was noted for a large number of palaces, mosques and other buildings constructed by the Caliphs. It was the capital of Harun al-Rashid. Here Mansur founded a round shaped city enclosed by a double wall of four gates. There were one hundred thousand craftsmen and labourers employed for four years. The fort with the palaces was completed in 766 A.D., the Caliph thereafter shifted his residence to his new capital. The walls and the buildings were made of sun-dried bricks. The main features of the city were the palace of the Caliph, called the Golden Gate, crowned by a great dome of green colour, about 120 feet high, surmounted by a horseman, and visible from a long distance. Within this dome was the Audience Hall about 30 feet square, with a vaulted ceiling about 30 feet high, above which there was the Sacred Hall of the same dimension. A second palace called the Khuld,[1] was built after a few years, and became a favourite residence of Harun al-Rashid. The royal mosque was built of sun-burnt bricks, with a roof resting on wooden columns, which, in their turn, were supported by round capitals. Asad-ud-Dowlah of the Buwaihid dynasty built a fine hospital. It was a large building constructed on the banks of Tigris, containing many halls, separate wards, furnished with all the necessities of comfort. Caliph Mutadid (892-902) constructed a new palace called the Crown (al-Taj), which was completed by his son al-Mukhtafi (902-908). Its external shape was like a crown supported on fine arches resting on ten columns, each about five feet high.

In short, of the architectural monuments which once adorned the capital city of Baghdad, we can mention the names of the "Golden Gate" the "Palace of Eternity", and the "Rusafah Palace", built by Caliph

1. The imperial palace of Khuld had a golden gate and a hall surmounted by a green dome 80 cubits high, which was the crown of Baghdad.

al-Mansur; the palaces of Bermekides at Shamsiyah, the unique mansion of al-Muqtadir designated the Dar-us-Shajar (Hall of the Tree), on account of the gold and silver tree that stood in its pond.[1] But these architectural monuments were so completely destroyed by the invasion of Hulaku Khan in 1258 A.D., that no trace of them has been left to give us an inkling of their splendour. The Abbasid architecture was influenced by Persian architecture in contrast to the Umayyad structures which bear clear traces of Byzantine art.

MUSLIM INDEBTEDNESS TO THE GREEK AND INDIAN KNOWLEDGE OF SCIENCE

With the spread of Islamic sway, the Muslims became masters of many of those countries which served in the past as the centres of civilization and culture. In a word, Muslims were in possession of Persia, Greece, India, Chaldea, etc. It was the influence of Persio-Hellenic culture that helped the Muslims to play an important role in the intellectual firmament of the world. "The awakening," says Hitti, "was due in large measures to foreign influences, partly Indo-Persian and Syrian, but mainly Hellenic and was marked by translations into Arabic from Persian, Sanskrit, Syriac and Greek." The Muslims who had very little knowledge of science, philosophy or literature of their own became in course of time the heirs and carriers of ancient civilization. In only a few decades the Arab scholars were to assimilate what the Greeks had developed in centuries and in about three-quarters of a century after the establishment of Baghdad the Muslims were in possession of the chief philosophical works of Aristotle, of the neo-Platonic Commentators and most of the medical writings of Galen as well as of Indian scientific works.

Hellenism became the most vital of all foreign

1. P. K. Hitti: *History of the Arabs*, p. 417.

influences in Arab life. In the transmission of Hellenic ideas to Arab world the Syrian Christians played an important role. They translated the Greek works into Syriac and then into Arabic. At Al-Mansoor's court were some very notable scholars, and their efforts were not limited to translations.

Caliph Harun al-Rashid (796-809 A.D.) was a magnificent patron of science, art and literature and many more Greek works were translated by his order. He enlarged the 'Bait ul-Hikmah' founded by Jafar al-Mansoor for the translation of scientific works into Arabic. It was in Harun's time that Baghdad became "a city with no peer throughout the whole world." The apogee of Greek influence was reached under Mamun (813-833 A.D.). He was even a greater patron of letters and science than Harun al-Rashid. His court became the resort of philosophers, astronomers, physicians, scientists and other men of letters, of every caste and creed. He enlarged the translation bureau and raised it to a great academy for study and research. Mamun was greatly influenced by the Greek culture. It is said that he sent a mission to the Byzantine emperor, Leon the Armenian, to procure Greek manuscripts which he then had translated. The medicine of Galen, mathematics of Euclid and Ptolemy, and philosophy of Plato and Aristotle served as the starting point of the voyage of intellectual discovery by the Arabs.

Qusta bin Luqa (923 A.D.) was the translator of mathematical and philosophical works. He not only translated a number of mathematical and philosophical works but also wrote a number of books of his own. He was one of those who brought Greek Mss. from Asia Minor. He had a reputation for writing both Greek and Arabic in fine style. Abul Hasan invented a telescope from a tube. These 'tubes' were used afterwards in observations of Marougha and Cairo. An observatory at Shamsiyah on the plains of Tadmore for the study of astronomy and geometry. Astronomical observations made a great stride during this reign.

The most famous translator of Greek works was Hunayn bin Ishaq (809-873 A.D.). He was a Christian Arab and a doctor. He is admired for the high quality of his Arabic, Syriac and Greek. He is also known as the 'Shaikh of the translators'. He was one of those who were sent by to colleet Greek works for translation. His honesty as a translator is unquestionable. He was appointed by Mamun as the Superintendent of the Baitul-Hikmah. Hunayn was a man of tremendous energy. In addition to his translations, he is credited with having written 31 books.

India acted as an early source of inspiration. Muhammad ibn Ibrahim al-Fazari translated *Siddhanta* (Sindhind, a Sanskrit treatise on astronomy) into Arabic by the order of Jafar al-Mansoor. The famous mathematician Muhammad ibn Musa al-Khwarizmi (d. 850 A.D.) based his astronomical tables on al-Fazari's work. The decimal system is another important contribution of India to Arab mathematical science. Dulean, the Brahmin, translated the Indian books of mathematics and astronomy into Arabic and thereby opened the gate of knowledge on Indian Science, to the Arab minds.

In the art and literature Persian influence was felt in Arab culture. *Kalilah wa Dimnah* (originally the Panchatantra of India) translated from Sanskrit into Persian and a valuable work on polity was done into Arabic by Ibn a-Muqaffa (d. 757 A.D.), a Zoroastrian convert to Islam. From Arabic, *Kalilah wa Dimnah* was, in course of time, translated into practically all the languages of the civilized world and exerted a deep influence on the literature and imagination of a number of modern nations, as for instance La Fontaine's acknowledging it as a source of his famous Fables. The original work in its complete form is stated to be lost.

In short, the Muslims preserved the culture of ancient world through translation while Europe was shrouded in the darkness of the middle ages. "The researches of Aristotle, Galen and Ptolemy would have been lost the world, if the Muslims had not kept them preserved by translation."

The epoch of translation was followed by one of creative activity and this has been discussed in detail in Chapter XI.

CHAPTER XIII

CONTRIBUTIONS OF MUSLIMS TO SCIENTIFIC THOUGHT

History

The Arabs had a natural liking for history and took endless pains to collect historical data and test their accuracy by certain standards that worked all right when applied to their own sources. Most of the early works were practically statements of events in their chronological sequence but expressed in an elegant style and above all with fair and often impartial criticism. The work of writing history and biography began at a period when the Arabs were curious to know the history of the Prophet and this perhaps led them to the culture of history in those days. Nicholson writes, "The sacred book offered many difficulties both to the Arabs and specially to Persians and other Muslims of foreign extraction. For their right understanding of the Holy Quran, a knowledge of Arabic grammar and philosophy was essential and this involved the study of ancient pre-Islamic poems. The study of these poems entailed researches into genealogy and history, which in course of time became independent branches of learning." Abul Hasan Ali al-Masudi (956 A.D.) was the first to revolutionise the art of writing history. The modern method of dealing with different dynasties or countries or peoples with critical examination of the matter handled may be traced to the same writer.

Before the advent of Islam, there was no systematic way of writing history among any nation of the world. It was done under the Muslims who recorded the sayings of the Prophet, and the revelations revealed to him, just after his demise. In the front rank Muslim historians comes Muhammad ibn Ishaque (d. about 767), the author of *Sirat Rasul Allah* which has reached us only through a revision of Ibn Hisham (d. 834).[1] Then came the works dealing with the early wars and conquests of Islam by various writers, among whom the names of Musa ibn Uqabah (who wrote *Kitab-ul-Maghazi*) and al-Waqidi may be mentioned. Adbul Hakam's (d. 834) *Fath-al-Misr wa Akhbaruha* and Ahmed ibn Yahya al-Balazuri's *Futuh-ul-Buldan.* His *Ansab-ul-Ashraf* deals with the lineages and pedigrees of persons of distinction.

Amongst other writers of history may be mentioned Ibn Muqaffa who translated several books on Iranian history from Persian into Arabic, including *Kalilah wa Dimnah* which was for the first time translated by Burzuya, a contemporary of Khusroe. *Siyar-i-Muluk-al-Ajam* is one of the most important historical works. In respect of language and description this historical work occupied a unique position. Abu Hanifa Ahmad Dinawari wrote the *Kitab-ul-Akhbar-at-Tavil* (long histories). Other noted authors on history are Al-Yaqubi, (author of *Kitab ul-Buldan*), Abul Faraj, Abul Fida, Ibn Katib and Miskawayh (d. 1030 A.D.), author of universal history (*Tajarib al-Umam*) from the earliest times down to about 980 A.D.

Abu Jafar Muhammad ibn Jarir al-Tabari (838-923) is the most celebrated historian of the Muslim world. He was born in Tabaristan (Iran). His monumental work *Tarikh Rasul wal Muluk* is a work of detailed and accurate information. He travelled all over Asia and Egypt to gather material for his book from original sources, and according to Yaqut wrote 40 pages daily for 40 years.[2] His history beging with the

1 *Ibn Khallikan*, Vol. I, p. 520

2. *Yaqut*, Vol. VI, p. 424

creation of the world and comes down to 915 A.D. Al-Tabari arranged the events chronologically and tabulated them under the successive years of the Hijrah.[1] The original edition of al-Tabari's history is said to have been ten times as long as the surviving edition. Later historians have made free use of this authoritative work.

Abul Hasan Ali al-Masudi[2] is famous both as a historian and geographer and was one of the versatile writers of the 4th century. He was born at Baghdad. He travelled far and wide in practically every Islamic country in Asia from Baghdad and even went to Zanzibar, settling down finally in Egypt. He died at Fustat in 956 A.D. His work *Muruj al-Dhahab wa-ma 'Adin al-Jawahar* (Meadows of Gold and Mines of Precious stones) is a record of his travels, experiences and observations from the creation up to 947 A.D. It is not confined purely to chronological facts but gives interesting geographical information as well.[3] Prof. Hitti says, "Arabic historical composition reached at highest point in al-Tabari and al-Masudi and after Miskawayh started on a rapid decline."[4]

Ibn al-Athir was a historian of wide repute, who wrote *Kamil*, a history of the world up to 1231 A.D. Ibn Khallikan (born in Irbil in 1211 and died at Damascus in 1282) was the Qazi of Syria and author of a most delightful dictionary of national biography (*Wafayat al-A'yan wa-Anba' Abna al-Zaman*) dealing with the lives of 868 prominent Musalmans—a marvel of accuracy and eloquence.

The Muslim Spain had no scarcity of historians.

1. P. K. Hitti : *History of Arabs*, p. 390.
2. A descendant of Abdullah ibn Masud.
3. M.A. Rahman Khan : *Muslim Contribution to Science and Culture*, p. 31.
4. P. K. Hitti : *History of the Arabs*, p. 391.

Among them Ibn al-Qutiyah, Abu Marwan, Hayyan ibn Khalaf, Al-Farabi and Ibn Khaldun are famous. The last one flourished in the 14th century A. D. Abdul Rahman ibn Khaldun (1332-1406) was the most renowned of all historians of Western Islam. His history is preceded by a prolegomena. It is a masterpiece of historical criticism on the effect environment on national development, etc., and an introduction to the philosophy of history. He was born in Tunis in 1332 A.D. and was in the midst of all the revolutions of which Africa was the theatre in the 14th century A.D. He held responsible posts at Fas and later at Granada. The fame of Ibn Khaldun rests on his *Muqaddimah*, the first volume of his work *Kitab-ul-Ibar* which deals with the Muslim history of Arabia, Persia and North Africa.

Geography

The Muslims made much progress on the subject of geography. Their contributions to it were of immense value in the history of the world. While the Europeans believed in a flat earth, contemporary Muslim geographers had measured the circumference of the globe. The institution of the holy pilgrimage, the orientation of the mosques towards Mecca and the need for determining the direction of the Ka'bah at the time of prayer gave religious impetus to the Muslim study of geography.[1] The interest of the Muslims in geographical matters was largely born of the environment in which they lived. The Arabs had to have a knowledge of the fixed stars, the movements of the planets and other heavenly bodies and of the change of weather. These were undertaken for the purpose of travel over the vast expanses of the desert. The knowledge about the position of the stars led to the determination of latitude and longitude. Thus mathematical

1. P.K. Hitti : *History of the Arabs*, p. 383.

geography and cartography came in for early interest.

The scientific study of Geography in Islam began under Greek influence. Greek works were translated into Arabic by the Arabs and the result of the widespread activity in translation of Greek works, which at the beginning of the 9th century made the Muslims the spiritual heirs of Ptolemy. Caliph Mamun had gathered a large number of scholars on Geography. Ptolemy's works were translated into Arabic and independent researches were also made by Muslim scholars who paid great attention to his '*al-Magest*' and 'Geography'. The Muslims not only translated Greek works into Arabic but they also preserved, cultivated and, on a number of important points, developed them.

Muhammad bin Musa al-Khawarizmi was an outstanding geographer whose work laid the first foundations of Arabian geographical science. His *Kitab Surat al-Ard* (shape of the earth) which served as a basis for later works was written in the first half of the 9th century A.D. He made a measurement of the earth by the order of Mamun. The first map of the world was drawn up, in which the world was divided into seven *Iqlims* or climes.

The oldest known work on geography in Arabic is the one written by Ibn Khurdadhbih (850 A.D.), entitled '*al-Masalik wal-Mumalik*' (on routes and kingdoms). It gives a summary of the main trade routes of the Arab world and the description of distant lands such as China, Korea and Japan. Al-Istakhri, another Iranian, wrote a similar work named *Masalik-al-Mumalik*. In his work, maps play an important part. The work of Istakhri was revised and enlarged by Ibn Hawqal. Ibn Hawqal was a widely travelled man whose travels lasted not less than 30 years. He gathered a store of knowledge and experience through his travel.

Al-Maqdisi (856 A.D.), a native of Palestine in his book *Ahsan al-Taqasim fi Ma'arfat al-Aqalim* (the best of divisions for the knowledge of climes), gives a fair description of the places he visited during the 20 years he travelled in different regions included in Islamic territories. He divided the lands of Islam in 14 divisions or provinces. He prepared separate maps for each division and in these maps he used symbols and methods of representation of relief, etc.

Ibn Wadih al-Yaqubi, a Shiite, was a distinguished geographer and flourished in Armenia and Khorasan. He toured over India and Maghrib (N. W. Africa). He wrote a book entitled *Kitab-ul-Buldan* (Book of Countries) in which he gave details about numerous places and stated facts of physical geography, explaining the human geography of many areas. He was specially interested in the statistical and topographical aspects. He is better known as 'father of Mulim geography'. Al-Hamadani wrote two works named *al-Iklil* and *Jazirat al-Arab*, which contain valuable information on pre-Islamic and Islamic Arabia. It is often quoted by Masudi and Yaqubi.

Al-Biruni was the first Muslim geographer to give the geography of Siberia and North Europe. Much information was gathered through merchants taking the risk of travelling into distant countries. His keen sense of geographical observation is revealed through his famous work, *Kitab-ul-Hind*. Al-Qazwini was a renowned geographer of an Arab family (N. Iran). He wrote on Cosmography and Geograply. Another original geographer who flourished in the 14th century was al-Dimishqi. He is an important authority for Arab's knowledge of South India.

The Western Caliphate in Spain also produced many eminent geographers whose works and travels went a long way to contribute to the knowledge of geography. The best known geographer of the eleventh century was Al-Bakri of Cordova (1094 A. D.). His voluminous geography *al-Masalik wal-Mumalik* was written in the form of an itinerary. This book still survives but in part.

The most brilliant and the best geographer of the twelfth century and the entire medieval period was Al-Idrisi. He was a descendant of a royal Spanish Arab family and got his education in Spain. He travelled practically around the entire inhabited globe to compare the geography of the world.

He was the chief ornament of Roger II's court in Sicily after the fall of Arab rule in the island. He wrote a book at the court of Palermo entitled "Amusement for him who desires to travel round the world," also known as *Kitab-i-Rogari*.

His book on geography was supplemented by maps of different places and countries. He constructed for his Norman Patron a disc-shaped map of the world. Roger built for him a beautiful palace and granted a handsome monthly pension to him.

Other Arab geographers were travellers and their work is mostly based on travels and lesson research and originality. The best known among these travellers was Ibn Jubayr who undertook a journey from Granada to Mecca and back visiting Iraq, Egypt, Syria and Sicily. His *Rihla*, the account of his journey, is one of the most important works of its kind in Arabic literature.

Yaqut bin Abdullah (1197-1229), whose ancestors were Greek, compiled the celebrated geographical dictionary named *Majma ul-Buldan* in six volumes. Masudi, the author of *Meadows of Gold* was the Pliny of the Arabs. In this book, he has described earthquake and the first windmill which was also invented by a Muslim. Abu Abdullah Muhammad bin Battuta was the famous medieval traveller, who travelled throughout the Muslim countries. He is better known as a distinguished descriptive geographer.

Cartography

The Muslims opened a brilliant chapter in the history of cartography (the science of map-making). They had vast knowledge of geography and their original contributions to it along with the translation of Greek works have been highly recognised by the civilized world. In the field of cartography the Muslims represented the world on a map when the Western scholars could not think of it.

Ptolemy was undoubtedly the greatest and by far the best cartographer in the ancient world. But the fundamental error he made in making the maps was his mistake in under-estimating the size of the earth. In his estimation Europe and Asia extended over one-half the surface of the globe which in reality cover only about 1300 degrees. In the same manner he counted the length of the Mediterranean as 62 degrees, whereas in reality it is only 42 degrees. The Arab geographers and the marine chart-makers of the 13th century had corrected this inaccuracy.

Among the earliest map-makers of the Islamic world was al-Khawarizmi whose *Kitab Surat al-Ard* was written in explanation of the maps. He also made a map of the Nile. He participated in the scientific activity for the preparation of the map of the world, during the reign of Mamun.

Al-Balkhi was the next distinguished map-maker in Islam. His 'Atlas' contained a world map, a map of Arabia, the Indian Ocean, maps of Maghrib (Morocco, Algeria, etc.), Egypt, Syria and about a dozen other maps of the central and eastern Islamic world. His geographical works were written in explanation of his maps. K. Miller calls it 'The Islam Atlas'. Maps of Istakhari and Ibn Hawqal were based upon the work of Balkhi. He divided the lands of Islam into 14 divisions and showed each one in a map. In his maps routes were coloured red ; the golden sands, yellow ; the salt seas, green ; the well known rivers, blue ; and the principal mountains, drab ; so that everybody understood the description.

Al-Beruni made a round map of the world in his book *Kitab-ul-Tafhim*. In this map he illustrated the position of seas. He also devised a method for the projection of maps of the sky and the earth in his famous treatise, "Chronology of Ancient Nations".

Al-Idrisi was unquestionably the last map-maker the world ever produced. He is said to have made 70 maps of his 'climatic' divisions, a celestial sphere and globe of silver—on the globe he indicated his seven latitudinal "Climatic" Divisions. He also made a map of the world on a silver plate.[1] These maps of Idrisi indicate the western Islamic world better than eastern. The world maps of Qazwini and al-Wardi were made after the world map of 'Balkhi school.'

Medicine

Before the advent of Islam, the Arabs knew the medicinal value of plants and of certain stones found in Arabia. The pre-Islamic physician was Haris bin Kalda. He studied medicine and philosophy in the college of Junda-Shahpur in Iran. After the advent of Islam, the first and the greatest physician of the Islamic world, nay, the whole world, was Hazrat Muhammad (صلعم)). He understood the use and value of medical arts. He recommended the practice of medicine to his com-

1. Nafis Ahmed : *Muslim Contribution to Geography*, pp. 70-71.

panions and *Sahih Bukhari*, an authentic work on the traditions, contains two chapters on how to cure various diseases. Though the Umayyad rulers (661-720 A.D.) encouraged medical study, but real progress in Arabian medicine began with the coming of the Abbasids (750-1258 A.D.). The medical college at Junda-Shahpur had Greek, Iranian, Syrian and Indian elements. The work of translation from Greek into Syriac and Pahlavi had begun in the fifth century A.D. and in the 6th century, the works of Hippocrates and Galen[1] were translated into Syriac language. The college of Junda-Shahpur continued to be the scientific centre of the Islamic world. Hence the Abbasid caliph looked towards Junda-Shahpur for translation of medical works into Arabic. For the elevation of Medical works into Arabic. For the elevation of Medical education regular organised hospitals and schools under official control were instituted in Baghdad and other important centres of the Islamic empire. The development of Islamic medicine may be divided into four periods: The first period is the age of translation from 750 to 900 A.D. in Arabic and the following are among the best known translations:

(1) Masorjawaih, an Iranian Jew, translated Ahron's work into Arabic.

(2) During the caliphate of Mansur the task of Greek science was taken up in right earnest at Junda-Shahpur. He invited Jurjis bin Bakhti Yashu, the chief physician at Junda-Shahpur to his court. Successive members of his family became celebrated at physicians and continued to study the science of medicine from father to son, for about 250 years. It way they who established the first apothecary shop, founded the

1. Hippocrates, born at Cos, 400 B.C.: a contemporary of Socrates and Plato, was of wide spread renown as a physician Galen, a famous Greek physician, born in 131 A.D., went to Rome and became physician to the Emperor Marcus Aurelius, L. Versus, and Severus. Of his voluminous writings, 83 treatises are still extant.

earliest school of pharemacy and produced the first pharmacopoeia.

(3) Hunayn bin Ishaq (809-73) was an Arab of the tribe of Ibad but Christian by religion. He translated seven books of Hippocrates. Galen's medical and philosophical books have also been translated by him. It was he who gave Galen his supreme position in the middle ages in the Orient. Besides several independent works of his own, he translated the great synopsis of Oribasius and the Materia-Medica of Dioscoride's. Among the Arabs and the Persians the most famous of his works were the questions on Medicine and ten treatises on the Eye.

(4) Other famous translators were Isa bin Yahya, Ishaq bin Hunayn, Qusta bin Luqa, Yuhanna bin Masavaih and Thabit bin Qurra. The latter has written independent work, which has been published at Cairo. The work is divided into 31 sections, on Hygiene, diseases from head down to the breast, stomach and intestines, their causes, symptoms and cures.

The second period is the age of independent observation, criticism on Greek and other past authors. The Muslims had so long been the translators of Greek Science. But from 900 A.D. they began to rely upon their own sources and to develop from within. The science especially medicine now rapidly passed from the hands of Christians and Sabians[1] into the hands of the Muslims. The medical authors of this period were Persians in nationality but Arabs in language. The most famous physicians of this period were Ali ibn Rabban of Tabaristan, Al-Razi, Ali ibn Abbas and Ibn Sina.

(1) Ali al-Tabari's father was a scientist at Merv. Ali entered the service of Caliph Mutawakkil and wrote

1. Sabian—a worshipper of the host of heaven—sun, moon and stars.

his celebrated work named *Firaaus-ul-Hikmat* (The Paradise of Medicine). This work deals not only with medicine but also included other subjects such as Philosophy, Zoology, Psychology, Astronomy, etc. and its sources are from Greek, Iranian and Indian works.

(2) Abu Bakr Muhammad al-Razi (Europeans call him Rhazes) was the greatest physician of the medieval period. He was born at Rai near Tehran. He studied philosophy and at an advanced age specialised in medicine.[1] He wrote as many as 200 works on various subjects. One of the most celebrated works of al-Razi is *Al-Hawi* (the Comprehensive Book). For each disease he gives references to his Greek, Iranian, Arabic and Indian authors, and then his own opinion. This work was translated into Latin by the order of Charles I of Anjou (Naples) in 1279 A.D. under the title of Continens.[2] He has also written on alchemy a book named *Kitab-al-Asrar*. His treatise on smallpox, measles, stone in the bladder and kidney, his descriptions of the eye, the nose, the ear and the heart were well known in Europe. This treatise was considered an ornament to the medical literature of the Arabs. It served to establish Al-Razi's reputation as one of the keenest original thinkers and greatest clinicians not only of Islam but of the middle age.

(3) Ali ibn Abbas (European's Haly Abbas) wrote an encyclopedia named *Kitab-e-Maleki* (Liber Regius). This book deals with both the theoretical and practical sides of medicine. It begins with a criticism of previous Arabic and Greek medical treatises. This book was dedicated to the reigning Buwahid king Asad-ud-Dawlah.

(4) Abu Ali Hussain ibn Sina was most illustrious

1. A.M.A. Shustery : *Outlines of Islamic Culture*, p. 140.
2. P.K. Hitti : *History of the Arabs*, p. 366.

figure in medical science. He was known in Europe as Avicenna. He was born near Bokhara in 980 A.D. and died in Hamadan in 1037 A.D. His great work on medicine known as the *Canon of Medicine* was a medical Bible for several centuries. This work deals with general medicine, drugs, diseases, pathology and pharmacopoeia. It was translated by Gerard of Cremona (1114-87 A.D.) into Latin and it displaced the works of Galen, al-Razi and al-Majusi. His canon was supreme in Medical science for centuries in Europe. In the words of Dr. Osler[1] it has remained "a medical Bible for a longer period than any other work."

While the Eastern Islamic world was acquiring supremacy in medicine, the Muslims of Spain and North Africa produced a number of distinguished physicians, whose labours became models for European scholars during the period of European Renaissance. Among these were: Abul Qasim Zahravi (European's Abul Casis) wrote his work entitled *At-Tarif* (Medical Vade Mecum) at Cordova in 30 sections. Ibn Baja, Ibn-ul-Wafd, Ibn Rushd (known in Europe as Averroes) were famous physicians of Spain.

In Egypt, Syria and Mesopotamia there were much medical activity in the 11th century A.D. Ali ibn Rizwan of Cairo produced a fine medical topography of Egypt. Among the other physicians were Ibn Butlan of Baghdad, Abu Ali Hussain al-Haitham (Al-Hazem) of Basra, and Abu Mansur Mowaffiq of Herat. Optics was developed by al-Hazen, whose work on this subject survives in Latin. Western writers on optic based their works on this work. He also wrote on light, the rainbow, the halo. He is specially well-known for his discovery of atmospheric refraction.[2]

1. William Osler: *The Evoluton of Modern Medicine*, p. 98.
2. A. M. A. Shustery: *Outlines of Islamic Culture*, p. 143.

Third period (1250-1850 A.D.) is the age of decline of Arabic medicine and the rise of European science in Western Asia. All important works in science had been translated from Arabic into European languages. Their shortcomings and defects had been noted and rectified. Europe received from Eastern scholars its knowledge of drugs, the qualities of minerals, ideas about the science of optics and a better developed chemistry, but has managed to return all these with compound interest during the 19th and 20th centuries.

In the fourth or the present period, the East has to sit at the feet of Western scholars. The old Arabian method of treatment, known as '*Yunani*' appears to be incomplete. Its perfection is only possible by the absorption of newer Western methods. Though some of the Indo-Pakistani physicians are taking interest in the Yunani, there is very little hope of their success. The Muslims taught them with their original contributions to Europe. Thus Muslims became the teachers of Mediaeval Europe but today they are the pupils of Western scholars.

Astronomy

The Muslims made a great progress in astronomy. Their contributions in this field are the basis of future development.

Muslim contribution to astronomy is unforgetable and valuable. The greatest discoveries and studies were made by the Muslims under the Umayyads and Abbasids. They made wonderful discoveries about the movements of solar system and other astral bodies. They ascertained the size of the earth, the variation of the latitudes and the precession of the equinoxes. Abul Hassan discovered atmospheric reflection and al-Maimun determined the obliquity of the ecliptic. Ibn

Jannus, Nasir Tusi and al-Bani constructed astronomical tables of great value.

Under the second Abbasid caliph, al-Mansur, the centre of the Muslim culture was Baghdad (762 A.D.). The plans of the town Baghdad were drawn up by the astronomers Naubakht and Mashallah. Yaqub bin Tariq, an astronomer, presented at the court of Al-Mansur a Hindu astronomer named Nanka who introduced an Indian work on astronomy called the *Siddhanta.* This work was translated by Mohammad ibn Ibrahim al-Fazari and used as a model by later scholars.

Al-Fazari dedicated himseif not only to the theory and publishing of books on the armillary sphere, the calendar, the astrolabe but also to the making of apparatus. Ahmad of Nehawand (Iran, 835 A.D.) compiled tables which are known as Mushtamil.

The astronomical work flourished by leaps and bounds. during the reign of Al-Mamun. It is recorded that the Muslim intellectual activity reached its *zinith* in the 9th and 10th centuries. Al-Mamun etablished a Bait-ul Hikmah for the translation of foreign works. In addition to this, he erected at Baghdad near the Shamsiyah Gate an astronomical observatory under the directorship of Sanad Ibn Ali and Yahya ibn Mansur. Mamun's establishment of an astronomical observatory was followed by many an Abbbasid rulers. There is no denying the fact that "the system of erecting observatories was imitated from Muslims by Europeans, who improved it on a large scale."

Al-Khawarizmi's tables became the basis of the other works both in the East and the West. Habash al-Hasib's (770 to 870 A.D) apropos of the solar eclipse is supposed to be the first determination of time by an altitude. He also introduced the notion of *Zil* (shadow), equivalent to the European tangent. Ali ibn Isa al-Ustarlabi made astronomicalobservations at Damascus and Baghdad and wrote treatises on astrolabe. Al-Farghani (Al-Fraganus) was one of the greatest astronomers during the caliphate of Mamun. He was the author of Elements of Astronomy.

Under the Abbasids, there flourished a number of scholars who threw a vivid light on astronomy. Abu Ma'shar Jafar of Balkh wrote *Kitab-ul-Madkhal* (An Introduction to Astronomy). Four of his works were translated into Latin. He was well-known in Europe as astronomer and is often quoted by Western writers. Al-Nairizi (died in 922 A.D.) compiled astronomical tables and wrote a book on atmospheric phenomena.

Al-Battani (Latin : Albatenius) was one of the greatest astronomers that Islam produced. The Latin scholars of the Middle Ages and Renaissance admired him most. He was an original research worker. On comparing his own observations with those of Ptolemy, he discovered the motion of solar Apsides and wrote a comprehensive book on Astronomy which was regarded as the standard work till the 16th century. Ptolemy used chords for the calculation, of which he had only one main theorem, a very clumsy one. Al-Battani substituted the sines for the chords. He used tangent and co-tangent and he was familiar with two or three fundamental relations in trigonometry.

Among the numerous astronomers who lived at Baghdad at the close of the 10th century Ali ibn Amajur (generally known as Banu Amajur) and Abdul Hasan were the prominent. They were famous for their calculation of the lunar movements. Ibn Yunus, inhabitant of Cairo, was the greatest astronomer of his time. He may in fairness be regarded as the foremost Muslim astronomer of the world. He was provided with good opportunity of research in astronomy by the Fatimid sovereigns of Egypt. The 6th sovereign al-Hakim founded an observatory in Cairo, where Ibn

Yunus prepared his Hakimid tables. His observations are recorded in a book known as *al-Zijal Kabir al-Hakim*.

Thus the Arabs were born astronomers. Astronomy was a favourite recreation with the early Muslims so that even private persons with independent means installed observatories at their homes. There were astronomers in the Middle Ages who engaged themselves on ecclesiastical observations.

Mathematics

The Arabs were keen students of Mathematics. They made marked advance in this subject. The use of the cipher which was obtained by them from India, was passed on by them to Europe. Prof. Arnold says, "They were undisputably the founders of plane and spherical trigonometry which properly speaking did not exist among the Greeks." The Arabs gave the world the science of Algebra in its perfect form. Algebra is one of the proudest achievements of the Arabs and it was cultivated with so much absorbing interest that within two centuries of its invention it had reached gigantic proportions. Hajjaj bin Yusuf translated the first six books of Euclid into Arabic ; he also wrote a treatise on geometrical problems.

Their contribution to the development of mathematics is great. Algebra, Statistics, conic sections and other branches of applied mathematics are the discoveries of the Muslims. They for the first time applied Algebra to geometry. They discovered equations of the second degree and developed the theory of quadratic equations and the binomial theorem. The Arabs not only collected and translated the works of the Greek mathematicians but also illustrated them and made valuable commentaries of them.

There were a good number of mathematicians among the Muslims who contributed much to mathematics during the middle ages. Of the mathematicians Al-Khawarizmi (Muhammad bin Musa) was the principal figure in the early history of the Arabic Mathematics. His studies on Arithmetic and Algebra made a deep impression in Europe. His work on Algebra explains Algebraic multiplication and division. His work *Hisabal Jabr wal-Muqabla* was used until the 16th century as the principal mathematical text book in European Universities and served to introduce in Europe the science of Arithmetic and Algebra. Al-Kindi, the Arab philosopher, also wrote several treatises on Mathematics. Abu Abdullah Muhammad ibn Isa al-Mahani of Iran was a famous mathematician and wrote commentaries on Euclid and Archimedes. He is credited with the invention of Modern Algebra. He made observations of the solar and lunar eclipses and planetary conjunctions. Thabit bin Qurrah ibn Merwan al-Harrani (826 A C.) lived in Baghdad and died there in 901 A C. He was a Harrani medical-man and mathematician. He founded a translation bureau where among other books, Apollonius's conic sections, works of Archimedes, Euclid, Ptolemy, Galen and Eutocius were translated into Arabic. Abdullah of Farghana (885-933) and his son known as Ibn Amajur were mathematicians and astronomers. Abu Kamil Shuja of Egypt was the mathematician who completed the work of al-Khawarizmi on Algebra. Abu al-Wafa of Iran was one of the greatest Muslim mathematicians. He wrote commentaries on Khawarizmi, Diophantos and Euclid. His contribution to the science of trigonometry is invaluable. It was he who first pointed out the generality of the sine theorem in relation to spherical triangles. He made a special study of angles and prepared a table of tangents and made use of the secant and cosecant Abu Said Ahmed ibn Muhammad Abdul Jalil of Sijistan was alive between 951 and 1024 A.C., a master of mathematics and specially of the problem of intersection of a conic section and circles.

Abu Raihan Muhammad al-Beruni (973-1048) was also a mathematician. He wrote a book named *A Summary of Mathematics*. Al-Beruni gave the clearest explanation of Hindu numericals and collected a vast store of astronomical knowledge. He solved the most complicated mathematical problems of his time that came to be known as Al-Berunic problems. He also invented a simple method of stereoscopic projection. Among the Spanish Muslim mathematicians were Al-Kirmani and Abul Salmah, who lived at Granada and wrote a book on mental arithmetic, commercial arithmetic, geometry, mental calculus and the nature of numbers.

Ibn Yunus, inhabitant of Cairo, was the greatest astronomer of his time. He was also a mathematician and wrote on Arithmetic and contributed much in the field of trigonometry. Abu Bakr Muhammad bin Hussain was also a mathematician who wrote on Arithmetic and Algebra and solved quadratic equations and dio-phantine equations.

Umar al-Khayyam was born near or in Nishapur sometime between 1038 and 1048 A.C. He was an expert mathematician and astronomer, in addition to being a fine Persian poet. He divided cubic equations into thirteen classes. He wrote several treatises on arithmetic, algebra and astronomy.

Chemistry

Like other fields of science, the Muslims also made scientific contributions in chemistry. Chemistry is generally supposed to be an accidental product of alchemy. However, the Muslim Scientists did much to improve and advance it. The Muslims' contribution to the world's store of knowledge was the accumulation of scientific facts and the advancement of scientific theories. They developed the process of crystallization and precipitation, distillation and sublimation and were thereby able to obtain a number of substances (old and new) in a state of comparative purity, like mercury, ammonia, soda, lead and antimony. It was in Muslim Spain that chemistry was first established and had the Muslims not been defeated at Poitiers, it would have reached its zenith there. The Muslim contributions to chemistry has also been admitted by Humbolt who says, "Modern chemistry was admittedly the invention of the Muslims, whose achievements in this sphere were of unique interest."

The bulk of this knowledge came to be associated with the name of Abu Musa Jabir of Tarsus (the Geber of Christian writers) who flourished mostly in Kufa in 776 A.D. He is the true father of modern chemistry. His name is the greatest in the field of medieval chemical science.[1] His name is memorable in chemistry, since it marks an epoch in that science of equal importance to that of Priestly and Lavoisier. He clearly recognised and stated the importance of experimentation than any other early alchemist and made noteworthy advance in both theory and practice of chemistry. He wrote some five hundred treatises on chemistry and some of his books bear fanciful names, e.g., *Book of the Kingdom*, *Book of the Balances*, *Book of Eastern Mercury*. He put forward a sulphur-mercury theory on the six metals. He discovered for the first time the practical applications of chemistry like "refinement of metals, preparation of steel, dyeing of cloth and leather, varnishes to water-proof cloth and protect iron, and distillation of vinegar to concentrate acetic acid". He improved on the methods for evaporation, filtration, sublimation, melting, distillation and crystallization.[2] From his studies, he was able to predict

1. P.K. Hitti : *The History of the Arabs*, p. 380.
2. Ibid. p. 381.

the vast part which gas would be found to play in the make-up and composition of elements and more complex substances. He was followed by others, whose originality and industry, profoundness of knowledge, and keenness of observation, evoked the astonishment of the students.

Besides Jabir, other important chemist of that period was al-Razi (Rhazes), who has left behind him valuable studies on chemistry. His great Book of the Art of Alchemy is worth reading. Razi classifies all chemical substances as belonging to vegetable group or animal, and mineral groups, a conception which comes from him into modern thought. The class of minerals he divides into spirits, bodies, stones, vitriols, boraxes, and salts. He distinguished volatile 'bodies' and non-volatile 'spirits', placing among the latter sulphur, mercury arsenic, and salmiac. Razi became celebrated all over Europe and was considered the foremost authority and master of chemical science by all men of learning.

Ibn Sina, a famous doctor, helped systematize medical chemistry.

Thus, when the Arabs were making epoch-making discoveries in their world, the Europeans were placing a premium upon every conceivable kind of social and political evil. Syed Ameer Ali is correct in his statement when he says, "Chemistry, as a science, is unquestionably the invention of the Muslims."[1]

Calligraphy

Calligraphy is the art of fine writing. According to *Encyclopaeaia Britannica*, it may be defined "as free hand in which the freedom is so nicely reconciled with order that the understanding eye is pleased to contemplate it. Hence, we immediately recognise the beauty resulting from right proportion of the components to

1. S. Ameer Ali : *The Spirit of Islam*, p. 384.

the whole of a letter and between the parts to the whole of a word".

The art of calligraphy in Islam occupies a unique place in the history of the world. It must be remembered that compilation and composition of arts commenced in Islam from the very outset. In fact, it existed in Arabia even in pre-Islamic days. Populous cities like Basra and Hijaz provide us with many examples. The Hamarians composed many books about themselves which were engraved on stones. Balazuri describes in detail how three men Mora Mur bin Murra, Aslam bin Sidra and Amir bin Jadra assembled in Baqqa and invented the script and how the people of Anbar, Hira, Mecca and Wadi ul-Qura learnt it from these men. After the advent of Islam there were seventeen men in Quraish who knew the art of writing. The Prophet himself, though considered to be unacquainted with either reading or writing, used to encourage his followers in the art of learning particularly in writing.[1] Thus the Muslims cherished the idea of writing and beautifying their script from the very beginning.

The scripts adopted by the Quraish originally were of two kinds: a stiffer one with more angular letters and a round, cursive one. The first type of writing is known as Kufic, from the town of Kufa in Mesopotamia which was the religious and intellectual centre of the Arab world. The second type is known as Naskh (round script). Both the types were known in the 7th century. "In the letters of the Prophet written to the Kings and heads of States preaching Islam, the Kufic script was used." But in the beginning there were no *Fatah*, *Zama*, *Kasrah* or dots on the words. In 670 A.D. Abul Aswad Doiby invented dots or *Nuqāt* but these dots were used only to serve the purpose of *Erab* (اعراب). When Islam spread in Egypt the letters similar in shape created great

1. A.M.A. Shustery : *Outlines of Islamic Culture*, p. 207.

difficulty in the study of the Quran. Also many differences arose in the perusal of letters and daily writings. To remove the handicap, Abdul Malik ordered Hajjaj, the Governor of Iraq, to improve the script. Nasr bin Hakim according to the Hajjaj's orders invented points (dots) to differentiate the letters. He declared that dotted letters should bear black points (dots) and for *Erab*, points of purple colour should be used. Khalil bin Ahmad Oruzi (d. 786) invented special shapes of *Erab*. Due to their simplicity they became very popular in Governmental offices, business affairs, schools and educational institutions. In the meantime many changes and improvements occurred in Kufic script. For about 500 years the Kufic characters existed side by side with the round script and were used almost exclusively for copies of the Holy Quran, inscriptions on stones and coins and for a short time also in official documents especially of legal character. In the eleventh century the use of Kufic script was replaced by Naskh. The cause of its downfall was that in the words of B. Mortiz, "standing unrelated to the needs of practical life it was artificially cultivated", and was often found difficult by the scribes, thus leading to its complete extinction. Among the better known calligraphists of the Umayyad period were the following:

Qutba, the son of Ubaidulla; Khalid, the son of Hajjaj; Salim, the scribe of Caliph Hisham; Hassan Basri; Abdul Hamid, a Secretary of Aarwan, the last Umayyad ruler.

Abu Ali Muhammad, known as Ibn Muqla of Baiza in south Iran (8 5-940 A.D.) is considered the most celebrated calligraphist of Muqtadar-Billah, an Abbasid Caliph. The Naskh script was one of those six scripts and according to Shustery seven or eight scripts which Ibn Muqla invented. Miss Khalida Bukhari writes, "He was unrivalled in the art of calligraphy." The scripts he invented and improved were Raihan, Sulus,

Naskh, Tauqi, Khat-e-Muhaqqaq, etc. Every type depends on two things: *Satah* and *Daur*. The stroke of pen, if straight, is called *Satah*, if round is called *Daur*. The Naskh script was devoted to the writing of the Quran only, but Muhaqqaq, Raihan and Kufi for writing headlines and Tauqi and Riqqa for kingly orders and correspondence.

Urdu Rasm-i-khat by Muhammad Sajjad Mirza developed and flourished with popularity towards the end of the Fatamid rule. During the Ayyubid period its use was in fact confined to stone monuments. The peculiar round and well proportioned forms in which it appears, *e.g.*, on Saladin's inscription (Mihrab of Jami al-Akra of 1187-1188, a scriber of 1168-69) give it a character entirely its own, so that we are justified in speaking of a separate Ayyubid style of writing. Later on, Mamluk ruler also paid sincere and devotional attention to it and spent lavishly for the sake of getting copies of the Quran written in this script. The following were among the most celebrated calligraphists of the Abbasid period:

Ishaq, the son of Hamnad; Fazl, the Iranian Wazir of Al-Mamun; Ibn Muqla and his brother Hassan: Ibn Bawwab; Abu Abdullah Muhammad, the son of Ismail known as Bukhari; Abul Fazl of Khurasan who improved the type known as 'Riqa': Ahmad, the son of Hassan of Seistan, the Wazir of Sultan Mahmud of Ghazni; Abul Hasan Rawandi; Asad-ud-Dowla, a king of the Buwaihid dynast; Yaqut the last great calligraphist of the Abbasid period. It is said that when Baghdad was captured by the Mongols and its inhabitants massacred, Yaqut took refuge in a mosque and was glad with the thought that he could write the most beautiful "Kaf" (the letter ک).

In North Africa the Maghrib script was very common. It was originally called Kairawan after the name of the town where a University had been established.

A new force of writing arose in Spain after the centre of the Maghrib script had been shifted from Kairwan to that country. It was called Andalusian or Cordovan and is distinguished from the still somewhat stiff and angular script of Kairawan by the remarkably round forms of its letters. Timbuktoo became the intellectual centre of Africa in 1213. Its script is called the script of Timbuktoo or Sunani. Its letters are large and thick.

The practice of Arabic script and beautiful handwriting existed throughout the Islamic world. Numerous types of writing reflect the depth of devotion which attached to calligraphy. The causes of miraculous nobility and respectability of this art in Islamic culture may be traced in the writings of Mr. Arnold who writes in his work *Painting in Islam*: "The art of writing is an honourable and soul-nourishing accomplishment; as a manual attainment, it is always elegant and enjoys general approval." Imagine its honour and importance when God Himself says in the Holy Quran (68 : 1) : Nun (inkstand) : By the pen and by the (record) which men write. After Allah, Hazrat Muhammad (صلعم) always encouraged the Muslims saying "Go in quest of knowledge even into China" (Ibn Majah). 'The word 'China' implies "that one can here seek other types of learning besides religious knowledge and even from non-Muslims." A wise man has said, "Fine utterances in elegant handwriting are a pleasure to the eye and a joy to the heart and fragrant to the soul."

Thus calligraphy became an important art in Islam and worthy of serious study. The calligraphists enjoyed a higher reputation and honour than painters in the society.

Music

Music is the expression of the aspirations, emotions and passions of man through the medium of sound. It is a highly symbolic art. Its very abstract nature makes it best suited to express one's hidden feelings and urges. It also serves as an outlet to our religious emotions. This function of music is perhaps the oldest.

Music may be divided into two categories: Vocal music and Instrumental music. As far as Vocal music is concerned, we have no hesitation in saying that subject to the general moral qualifications, it is in itself quite permissible. For singing is nothing but a very delicately balanced combination of sweet sound, lilt, harmony and melody, and all these elements are not only permissible and tolerable, but desirable and praiseworthy.

Instrumental music :—The instruments which are delicate and complex in their sounds and shapes usually have the power of evoking in men and women sexual passions and they are looked upon by Islam with strong disapproval. It is of these that the Prophet said "Allah has commanded me to destroy the lute and guitar".

The However music continued to progress during the rule of the pleasure-loving Umayyads and reached its highest excellence during the golden days of Caliph Harun and Mamun. During these periods music was developed as an art free from any restriction. The Umayyad rulers: Yazid I, Abdul Malik, Walid I, Yazid II, Hisham and Walid II were fond of music and other enjoyments of life. Their subjects copied them in this respect and the demand for singers and players of musical instruments, particularly for young and beautiful women became great. These singers sometimes enjoyed great influence over their masters. History bears eloquent testimony to this fact that the music was highly patronised by the Umayyad Caliphs. Large sums of money were spent on singers and musicians, who were summoned to the court from the most distant parts. By the time of Yazid I, the taste for music had grown on a large scale, and the holy cities of Mecca and Medina had become centres of music and song where flocked the Persian and Byzantine singing girls in increasing numbers and from where musicians were recruited for the court of Damascus. It would not be out of place to mention here that Caliph Yazid II was so passionately attracted to Salma and Hubbaba, two singing beauties, that the could not leave them and attend to the affairs of his vast empire. And when one of them died, the Caliph could not survive her death and died in his grief.

There were many reputed musicians and singers who flourished under the Umayyads. The earliest Muslim professional musician was Tuwais (632-710 A.D.). He was the inhabitant of Medina and was considered the father of song in Islam. It is said that he was the first to introuduce rhythm into Arabic music. He is supposed to have been first to sing in Arabic language to the accompaniment of an instrument called the tambourine. Tuwais had a number of students, chief of whom was Ibn Suraij (634-726 A.D.). Ibn Suraij who belonged to Mecca, was "regarded as one of the four great singers of Islam" (Aghani).

Sa'id ibn Misjah (d. 714 A.D.) of Mecca is generally regarded as the first person to adapt Persian music to Arabic.[1] He was perhaps the greatest musician of the Umayyad period and was responsible for a new theory of Arabian music.[2] He is said to have travelled

1. S. Khuda Bakhsh : *History of Islamic Civilization*, pp. 14-15.
2. *Legacy of Islam*, pp. 356-357 ; P.K. Hitti : *History of the Arabs*, p. 275.

in Syria and Persia and to have been the first to put the Byzantine and Persian song into Arabic. He was the court musician of Abdul Malik.

Muslim bin Muhriz (d. 715 A.D.) was a prominent musician of Persian origin. He received his first lessons in the art of music from Sa'id ibn Misjah. He used to live at Medina and Mecca alternately. He travelled in Persia and Syria and learnt the tunes of Persian and Byzantine music. After this he combined the best of all the diverse elements and out of this amalgam he derived the airs which he put into Arabic verses. He was called the Sannaju'l-Arab (the cymbalist of the Arabs). He was the first to sing Arabic verses in pairs, an example which was imitated by later musicians. He was of opinion that single lines of verse could not produce a complete melody.[1]

Ma'bad (d. 734 A D.), a Medinite, held a special favour of the courts of Walid, Yazid II and Walid II. Among the songstresses, the name of Jamilah (d 720 A.D.) draws our attention first. In short, during the Umayyad period, Mecca and Medina became the centre of song and the best singers used to flock at the Damascus court.

The Muslim music reached its highest excellence during the Abbasid Caliphate. Mehdi seems to hav been the first among the Caliphs of the Abbasid dynasty, to show special interest in music. He patronised th musician Siyat[2] of Mecca (739-785 A.D.) "whose song warmed the chilled more than a hat bath".[3] The musica art in Islam reached its perfection in the reign of Harun al-Rashid. His court musician, Ibrahim of Mosul, wa the master of classical music. Harun's municifen patronage of music attracted skilful men of the pro

1. S Khuda Bakhsh : *History of Islamic Civilization*, p. 14, f. note.
2. *Aghani*, Vol. V, p. 7.
3. Hitti : *History of the Arabs*, p. 424, *Kitabul-Aghani*, Vol. VI, p. 8.

fession from far and near to his court who formed a brilliant galaxy of musical stars.[1]

Ishaq bin Ibrahim of Mosul (767-850 A.D.), a versatile genius like his father, carried on the tradition of classical music in the courts of Mamun and Mutawakkil. As an all-round musician he was "the greatest that Islam had produced".[2] Princess Ulayyah was one of the most accomplished musicians of her time. She had an exquisite taste for music. Ibrahim bin al-Mehdi acquired the greatest fame as musician-singer. Al-Wasiq (842-847 A.D.) was the first Caliph musician who performed on the lute and composed a hundred melodies.[3] After him came al-Muntasir (861-862 A.D.) and al-Mu'tazz (866-8 9 A.D.) who showed some poetical and musical talent. In the words of Masudi, "the only real Caliph musician was al-Mu'tamid (870-892 A.D.), in whose presence the geographer ibn Khurdadh bih delivered his oration on music.'.

During the Abbasid period, many books on music —*Kitab al-Masail* (Problemata) *Kitab fi'l-Nafs* (De-Anima), *Kitae al-Nagham* (book of melody), *Kitab al-Musiqi al-Kabir* (opus major on music)—were translated from Greek into Arabic. Al-Kindi was the first Muslim philosopher to write a book on the composition and tone of music. Al-Farabi was the greatest writer on the theory of music. He wrote a book entitled *Kitab al-Musiqi at-Kabir* which is considered as a very important contribution to the study of music.

After the fall of Baghdad (1258 A.D.) the master writers on music ceased to exist. Farmer writes : "Their place was taken by a host of legists who argued for or against the permissibility of music."

1. Hitti : *History of the Arabs*, p. 425.

2. H.G. Farmer : *Arabian Music*, p. 125. Hitti : *History of the Arabs*, p. 426.

3. Hitti : *History of the Arabs*, p. 426.

CHAPTER XIV

MUSLIM PHILOSOPHERS

AL-KINDI

Among the earliest Muslims philosophers and the only great representative of the Arab race in philosophy was Abu Yusuf Yaqub ibn Ishaque of the Kinda tribe. He was born in Kufa in 813 A.D. His father was the governor of Kufa under al-Mehdi, al-Hadi and Harun. He was first educated in Kufa and then in the university of Baghdad. Besides Arabic, he knew Greek and Pahlavi also. After completing his studies, he was selected by Caliph Mamun for the work of translating Aristotle and other Greek writers into Arabic. Thus, he got the patronage of Caliph Mamun, Mustasim and Wasiq. In 847 A.D. he was dismissed by Caliph Mutawwakil (847-861) and his library was confiscated. Since then he lived a retired life and died in 873 A.D.

Al-Kindi was the greatest scholar of his time. In the words of Prof. Hitti, "Al-Kindi was more than a philosopher. He was astrologer, alchemist, optician and music theorist." He wrote as many as 263 works, large and small, on different subjects. His principal works are: Commentaries on Analytica, Posteriora, Sophistica Elenchi, the Categories, the Apocryphal Apology of Aristotle, Almagestia of Ptolemy and the Elements of Euclid. He also made an abridgement of Aristotle's Poetica and Herneutica and Isagoge of Porphyry, besides writing essays 'On the Intellect' and 'On the Five Essences'.

His Philosophy

Al-Kindi began his career as a Mutazilite and was first interested in theological questions. But later on, he devoted himself to the study of Greek philosophy. He translated many Greek philosophical works in Arabic and thus paved the way for new fields of speculation. The main trend of his thought was to reconcile Islam with Greek philosophy and with intention in view, he thoroughly studied Greek philosophy, translated the great works into Arabic, wrote commentaries on it and tried to explain it in the light of the teachings of the Quran. Al-Kindi based his philosophical discussion on the Quran, Aristotelian philosophy, Neo-Platonism and Neo-Pythagoreanism. According to him none can be a philosopher unless he knows Mathematics. He applied Mathematics to the science of medicine. Though he regarded reason as a sufficient source of knowledge, yet he believed in the truth of Revelation and he tried to reconcile reason with revelation.

Aristotelianism

Al-Kindi's philosophy was greatly influenced by Aristotle's works. In the long list of his works, Aristotle takes a prominent place. He studied Aristotle in original, translated him into Arabic, commented on him and tried to reconcile his thought with the teachings of Islam. He popurialsed Aristotle in the Muslim world. The theology of Aristotle greatly influenced his philosopical discussions and his treatise 'On the Intellect' was the result of this influence. The Aristotelian physics with the commentary of Alexander of Aphrodisians had also great influence upon Al-Kindi. He did not believe in the science of alchemy. According to him Nature can alone produce things and man has no power to do so. In his opinion, the man who gives himself up to alchemical experiments, is an imposter, who deceives either himself or others. This view of Al-Kindi was refuted by Al-Razi.

Importance of Al-Kindi

Undoubtedly Al-Kindi was the first great philosopher of the Muslim world. He was well-versed in the field of philosophy. It was Al-Kindi and not Descartes who first held that mathematical knowledge was essential for philosophical enquiry. He preserved Greek philosophy and acquainted the Muslim world with it. He tried to interpret Greek philosophy in the light of the teachings of the Quran and made an attempt to reconcile it with tne religion of Islam. Al-Kindi is regarded as the real founder of Falsafa or Philosophical School in Islam. His influence upon the later Muslim philosophers was very great. Roger Bacon and Cardanus held him in high esteem. Thus for him great contributions towards the development of Muslim thought Al-Kindi is regarded as the father of Muslim Falsafa (Philosophy).

AL-FARABI

Abu Nasr Muhammad al-Farabi (870-950 A.D.) according to Ibn Khaldun, was "a celebrated philosopher, the greatest indeed that Muslims ever had". He was born at Wasij, a village near Farab in Transoxiana in 870 A.D. His father was a general. Zabiullah Safa has explored many sources relating to Farabi's life and works. He has arrived at the conclusion that he was a Persian by origin and not a Turk as is stated often enough. He had his education at Farab and at a tender age he left Farab and reached Baghdad, the then greatest centre of learning and culture. At Baghdad he studied the Arabic language and afterwards took logic under Abul Bashar Matta, son of Yunus. To study philosophy, he went to Harran, and became a pupil under Yuhanna, son of Yunus and soon he acquired mastery over Greek logic and philosophy.

He was so fond of philosophy that he read Aristotle's "De Anima" two hundred times and the physics 40 times. After travelling in Syria and Egypt, he settled down at Damascus where he was in such poor circumstances that for sometime he served as a watchman and had to read by the light of the garden lantern. Saif-ud-Dowla, the prince of Damascus, was very much pleased with the brilliant calibre of al-Farabi and offered him high post and handsome pension. But the philosopher accepted from the prince a poor pension of 4 dirhams per day. Content with this limited income, he passed the remaining days of his long life in seclusion, studying and writing a series of books. He died in Damascus in 950 A.D. at the age of about eighty.

Al-Farabi was a versatile genius. He is regarded by D.B, MacDonald as the very base of the pyramid of Muslim philosophy. According to Ibn Khallikan, no Muslim thinker ever reached in philosophical knowledge the same position as al-Farabi His system was a creative synthesis of Platonism, Aristoteleanism and Sufism. He was not only a philosopher, but was a fair physician and mathematician and an excellent musician. Prof. Hitti recognises him as the greatest of all Arabic music theorists. Prof. Shustery says that his style is not clear and this is one reason why he is not well-known as a musician. He wrote more than hundred books on different subjects, half of which were commentaries and criticisms on past thinkers and the rest were original works. Of his works and commentaries the following were famous ;

(1) Introduction to Logic.
(2) Abridgement of Logic.
(3) Isagoge of Prophyry's.
(4) Commentaries on De Anima of Aristotle.
(5) Almajest of Ptolemy and Elements of Euclid.
(6) On the Intelligence and Intelligibility.
(7) Kitab al-Musiqi al-Kabir.
(8) Ash-Shir.

(9) The Gems of Wisdom.

(10) Fususul Hikm, etc.

He could speak in all the principal languages of the world—70 in number—as the saying goes.

His Philosophy

Al-Farabi was first a devotee and a pious man and next a philosopher. Al-Farabi's philosophy is dependent in certain parts on Neo-Platonism. He has reconciled the views of Plato and Aristotle with the teachings of Islam. He quoted freely from the Quran and tried to prove that the current philosophical views fully agreed with its teachings. According to him philosophy is the science of all being. It is the only all-embracing science, which gives us the true knowledge of Allah and His creation. The aim of philosophy is to know Allah, the Creator, through rational and logical arguments. The study of philosophy should be preceded by the knowledge of Logic and Mathematics. Al-Farabi considers that the greatness of the devotee of Philosophy lies in his righteousness.

His Logic

Al-Farabi is considered a great logician among Muslim thinkers. He studied Greek Logic, modified it, and on its basis he developed the Muslim science of logic which was later on followed by the great thinkers like Ibn Sina, Ibn Rushd and even by many Western philosophers of the pre-Renaissance period.

According to al-Farabi Logic is a subject leading to the knowledge of the unknown from the known. It distinguishes the real from the unreal and the good from the evil. Therefore, the object of studying logic is to perfect and purify the soul and to obtain true happiness and satisfaction.

He divided Logic into two parts. The first deals with the doctrine of Ideas and Definitions and the second with Judgment, Inference and Proofs. The function of Logic is to begin with known and well-established ideas, and from them to deduce something which was formerly unknown. It thus passes from the known to the unknown. It begins with concepts which it synthesises into judgment and inference. But in the higher stage, logic turns into a science of ultimate realities, which are universally valid. Here it tries to ascertain the 'norms' of the principles of universal truth. Thus logic ends in Philosophy.

Al-Farabi divided everything into two grades, the Possible Being and the Necessary Being dependent for its existence on a cause. The existence of every Possible Being presupposes a cause from which it has come into being. This cause is the result of another preceding cause and so on, until we reach the final cause, itself independent of any other cause. The final cause is the uncaused cause or the first cause. It is the Necessary Being, self-caused, self-existent, unchangeable and most perfect. The Necessary Being is One and only One, for if there be more than one such being, the simplicity of One will be limited by the others. A being which is most perfect must be one and only one. This theory of al-Farabi corroborates the doctrine of the Quran.

The Necessary Being is the First Cause of Allah, the Creator of the universe. He cannot be proved to exist, because He Himself is the Proof of His existence. His existence is the same as His Essence. He is beyond any definition and none can compare or identify Him with anything. He is the Greatest, Noblest, Highest and Most Powerful Being.

Conception of Soul

According to al-Farabi, man is composed of two substances, *viz.*, soul and body. The soul is the essence and body is the support. The soul is imperishable and unchangeable, but it causes change in matter. It does not require sensible organs, but uses them in order to make the functions of the body complete. Thus it causes completencess of the body. While soul gives completeness to the body; mind or spirit gives completeness to the soul. Therefore, spirit or mind is the real in man.

He believes that human soul consists of four faculties. These faculties form an ascending series. The lower facutly becomes material for the higher one.

(1) The first foculty is called the latent intelligence or *Aql-i-Haiwani* by which man can understand the essence of material things.

(2) The second faculty is intelligence in action or *Aql-bil-fi'l*, which rouses the first faculty into action.

(3) The third faculty is the acquired intelligence or *Aql-Mustafad* which is acquired by man under the inspiration of the agent intellect.

(4) The fourth faculty is the agent intelligence or *Aql-i-fi'l* which is an external power and enters into body by emanation from Allah. It is the constructive faculty in human beings, without which man is degraded to the rank of animal. It is the real man. After the death of man, the agent intelligence will go back to its source and be re-absorbed in the omnipotent source from which it has come. This proves the immortality of the soul. With death, body perishes but the soul returns to the source from which it has come.

As a Sufi, al-Farabi believed that beyond the material objects and their knowledge and intellectual experience, there is a particular faculty called 'Love' through which everything in the universe, including man, reaches to its highest perfection.

In its politics, al-Farabi follows Plato in many points ; he believrd that a wise prince with divine knowledge must rule the nation. "His conception of the model state," says MacDonald, "is a strange compound of the republic of Plato and Shiite dream of an infallible Imam."

It is difficult to overestimate the importance of al-Farabi He was the master in all branches of philosophy known in his time. In the judgment of Ibn Khallikan, "No Muslim ever reached in the philosophical sciences the same rank as al-Farabi ; and it was by the study of his writings and by the imitation of his style that Ibn Sina attained proficiency and rendered his own work so useful."

"All the later philosophers including Ibn Sina and Ibn Rushd acknowledged their indebtedness to him. His order and enumeration of the principles of being and his doctrine of the double aspect of intellect and perfect beauty become the basis for his Muslim successors for buiding up their Philosophy".

IBN SINA

Husain bin Abdullah bin Hassan bin Ali bin Sina, better known to the West as Avicenna (Latin version of Ibn Sina derived from Hebrew Aven Sina) was born at Afshana near Balkh in 980 A.D. His father belonged to Balkh, capital of one of the four quarters of Khurasan. In the 9th century A.C. it was the biggest city of the Province according to Yaqubi. The celebrated Buddhist temple (Nau Bahar) was situated just outside the city limits The Barmecides, who professed the Buddhist faith, were originally placed in charge of the temple. Ibn Sina migrated to Bukhara during the reign of Nuh bin Mansur (Samani) and joined the service of the state.[1] He

1. Saman Khuda (ساماںخدا), a noble man of Balkh, originally a Zoroastrian, joined the service of اسد بن عبدالله القسری the Governor of Khurasan and was appointed ruler of his native city in 116 A.H.

was subsequently appointed Collector of Khurmeshun which was the district headquarters of a rural area in the vicinity of Bukhara. Ibn Sina studied Quran and Humanities (literature) from his father. During his youth he was converted to Ismailia creed. His father invited him to become a convert, but he would not listen to him. So his efforts proved absolutely fruitless. Sometimes his father would talk of Philosophy and Geometry, occasionally giving a discourse on Mathematics as known to India and the Indians. By this time he had also studied Muslim Theology and Jurisprudence from Ismail Zahid. Then, there came to Bukhara great Philosopher, Abu Abdullah Nateli. Ibn Sina became his disciple and studied with him the works of Aristotle and Ptolemy and elements of Logic, five or six figures of Geometry of Euclid, and soon he surpassed his teacher in these subjects. He also studied Isagoge under the direction of Nateli and instituted a probe into the definition of 'genus'[1] with the result that his teacher was forced to admit his ignorance of the question that he had raised. Next he studied medicine and read all the books that had so far been written on this subject. He took the practice of medicine as his profession and gained clinical experience. At the age of 17, he became so famous as a physician that he was summoned to the court to cure the chronic disease of the Samanid Sultan, Nuh bin Mansur (reigned 976-997). Ibn Sina succeeded in restoring the health of the Sultan and obtained from the grateful Sultan the privilege of access to the Royal Library in order to enhance his knowledge of the science of medicine. Endowed with extraordinary powers of absorbing and retaining knowledge, Ibn Sina devoured the contents of the Royal Library and at the early age of 21 was in a position to embark on his career of writing. This included the systematizing of the knowledge of his time.

1. Genus was defined as "an object comprehending various species."

After the death of his father, he fell on hard times. He was forced to accept an office in the service of the Sultan of Bukhara. The great thinker had to live in constant danger. His last resort was Isfahan where he lived under the patronge of Buwaihid Prince Ala-ud-Dowla. He died in Hamadan in 1037 A.D.

Ibn Sina was a man of extraordinary genius. He has composed about 125 books on Philosophy, Medicine, Geometry, Astronomy, Theology, Philology and Art.

Among his books the following are very famous:

1. *Hikmat-i-Mashriqqiya* or Oriental Philosophy.
2. *Qanun fi al-Tibb*, a comprehensive work on medicine. It was the greatest authority on medicine in Medieval Europe and is still the chief authority of medicine.
3. *Kitab al-Shafa* or (Book of Healing).
4. *Al-Najat* or Salvation, a book on philosophy.
5. *Danish Nama* (in Iranian) on philosophy.
6. On Logic dedicated to Abul Hasan Sahli.
7. *An Arabic Lexicon* in 5 volumes.
8. *Sadidiyya* (also on medicine) in five volumes.

He wrote besides a large number of smaller treatises on various subjects coming under the heads of Science and Natural History. Of all his works, *Kitab al-Shafa* and *Qanun fi al-Tibb* are masterpiece works.

His Philosophy

Ibn Sina was one of the greatest thinkers of the Islamic world. He was the last of great Aristotelean philosophers in the East. With him the studies of Aristoteleanism reached its zenith. In the domain of Aristotelean philosophy he was the disciple of Farabi. With the help of Farabi's works he grasped the meaning and purport of the writings of Aristotle. Ibn Sina collected his materials from various systems and utilised them in developing his own system of philosophy. To build up his own system, he synthesised the materials collected from different sources. He produced a synthesis of Aristotelean and Neo-Platonic philosophy. He had not written commentaries on the writings and doctrines of others, but also developed his own system of philosophy, and thus he gave a new form to the old doctrines. In his writings he blended Oriental with Greek philosophy. In his opinion philosophy is quite independent of and separate from religion. Its function is not reconcile faith with reason; its function is to explain the ultimate problems of life with the help of reason. This tendency was the common attitude of all the thinkers after Farabi. Ibn Sina emphasised this tendency in his writings. According to him, complete and perfect knowledge can be attained by the study of philosophy and therefore, it is the duty of every man to study philosophy.

His Logic

Ibn Sina considered his Logic an introduction to all other subjects of science and philosophy. Logic discusses the nature of intellectual existence. It is the science of the regulative principles of thought .To Ibn Sina, Logic is a system used more in a negative way than positive. His treatment of Logic is an improvement on Farabi's and Razi's system. Ibn Sina combined both. According to him the end of Logic is to give a man a standard rule, by observing which he is preserved from error in reasoning. Logic directly helps us to avoid error and indirectly guides us to attain truth. According to him, knowledge can be attained only through the logical development of the rational faculty, and thetefore he laid special stress on the study of Logic.

His Conception of Being

According to Ibn Sina, Allah is the Necessary Being. He is beyond space, time and motion. There are two kinds of beings: possible and necessary. A possible being is that whose existence is not inherent in it, but received from some other being. A necessary being, on the other hand, is that which is independent of everything. A possible being has a cause or causes but the necessary being has no cause whatsoever. Everything whether of this world or of heaven is possible being, which pre-supposes the existence of a necessary being, which is the source of all existence and from which the stream of existence flows. The existence of possible being is momentary but the existence of necessary being is eternal. This necessary being is Allah. In upholding this conception Ibn Sina followed Farabi and he was followed by Spinoza. The necessary being is one and only one. The essence of the necessary being is identical with His existence.

His Importance

Ibn Sina was one of the greatest thinkers of the Islamic world. As a philosopher, he was great. In the words of Ameer Ali, "He was unquestionably the master spirit of his age, and in spite of the opposition raised against him by fanaticism and self-interest, he left his impress in undying characters on the thought of succeeding ages. His voluminous works testify to the extraordinary activity of his mind. He systematised Aristotelean philosophy and filled the 'void between God and Man' in Aristotle's fragmentary psychology by the doctrine of the intelligence of the spheres conceived after a scientific method."

Ibn Sina was one of the greatest commentators on Aristotle and tried to reconcile the Aristotelean philosophy with Islam. Most of the later philosophers both in the East and the West were greatly influenced by his philosophical thought. His theory that there exists an intimate connection between the human soul and the primary absolute cause, was followed by Jalaluddin Rumi. Even the great German Philosopher Kant was influenced by the philosophical speculations of Ibn Sina.

IBN RUSHD

Ibn Rushd or Averroes (Abul Walid Muhammad Ahmad, 1126-1198) was born at Cordova in 1126 A.D., and belonged to a distinguished family which had produced several theologians and Qazis. Ibn Rushd was a Jurisconsult. In 1169-70, he himself was Qazi of Seville and two years later of Cordova. In 1182 he was called to Marrakesh by Abu Yaqub Yusuf to replace Ibn Tufail as court physician. Yusuf's son and successor Yakub al-Mansur banished Ibn Rushd in 1194 on a suspicion of heresy due to his studies in philosophy, but later recalled him to his office in Marrakesh, where he died in 1198. Ibn Rushd was without question one of the greatest scholars and philosophers the Arab world has produced and "one of the profoundest commentators," says Munk, "of Aristotle's works." Among his works are the following :

1. *Mabadi-ul-Falsafa*, or the Beginning of Philosophy, in 12 parts. Besides this, there are over 25 other works on different subjects in philosophy.
2. *Destruction of Destruction*, Philosophy.
3. *On the Agreement of Religion and Philosophy.*
4. *Kulliyat fil-Tibb*, a work on medicine.
5. *Kashf ul-Adellah*, scholastics.

He is known as a commentator "among European scholastics." His philosophy is a commentary on Aristotle. He aimed at reconciling Aristotle's teachings with the doctrine of Islam. With his writings, Spinoza appears to have been well acquainted.

His Philosophy

Ibn Rushd agrees with Aristotle's belief in the eternity of the world. According to him, "Pure matter and form are created." Allah transfers to matter a pure potentiality which brings it into existence by motion. All the intelligences emanated at one time are not equal in perfection or simplicity. Matter contains in itself the capacity of taking form. Both matter and form are eternal and necessary and permanent. It does not resolve, but the apparent motion is connected with the stars fixed in it. The heaven of the planets has two motions : one particular to each planet and the other its daily movement. Sun and the stars contribute to life on earth by their warmth. In these theories, Ibn Rushd differs from Ibn Sina, who believed in the universe but also as the matter of the forms. He differs from Suhrawardi, who taught that sun and the stars affect the earth by their warmth but by their light.

Each heavenly body possesses its intelligence or soul which it forms. Their intelligence is never tired. Like mankind, they do not see, hear or touch but possess the knowledge of their own self and of the external world.

Divine Knowleage

The Supreme Being loves Himself and has knowledge of His own existence. In His essence, He knows all things and perceives them in Himself. His knowledge embraces the whole universe.

Predestination

On the question of predestination he held that

man was neither the absolute master of his actions nor bound by fixed immutable decrees. But the truth lies in the middle. Our actions depend partly on our own free will and partly on causes outside us. We are free to wish and to act in a particular manner, but our will is always restrained and determined by exterior causes. These causes spring from general laws of nature. Allah alone knows their sequence.

Political Theory

Ibn Rushd's political theories were directed against human tyranny in every shape. He regarded the Arab republic under the Rashidin Caliphs as the model government in which was realised the dream of Plato.

His Importance

No Muslim thinker influenced the West more than Ibn Rushd. The main ideas for which he was vehemently opposed by the scholastics of the East and those of the West and most enthusiastically welcomed by the radicals in thought from the 12th to the 14th century and which opened the door to the European Renaissance, were : (1) Allegorical interpretation of the scriptures, (2) The theory of two truths, which in the words of Macdonald, "ran like wild-fire through the schools of Europe", (3) Pan-Psychism which implied immorality of the Universal soul of humanity, and morality of the individual soul, (4) Eternity and potentiality of matter, and (5) Emancipation of women.

Ibn Rushd's theory of two truths, combined with the doctrine that matter is eternal and potent to produce all from within itself, was a God-send for the scientifically-minded people in the West who were as a rule condemned and persecuted by the orthodox church and the state. They found in the above theses which passed as

Averroism their best support. For this reason De Wulf calls Ibn Rushd the Doctor of Anti-scholastics.

Averroism became rapidly the ruling mode of thought in the West. Scholars of Medieval Europe were agitated by Ibn Rushd's Aristotle as by no other author. From the end of the 16th century Averroism remained the dominant school of thought, and that in spite of the orthodox reaction it created first among the Muslims in Spain, then among the Talmudists, and finally among the Christian clergy. "His writings . . . after being purged of objectionable matter by ecclesiastical authorities, became prescribed studies in the University of Paris and other institutions of higher learning.

CHAPTER XV

POSITION OF WOMEN IN ISLAM

Arabia of the pre-Islamic age has been generally looked down upon as a country where men neither respected women nor allowed them any social status. They were treated as chattels and with contempt. Women could not have any share of the property of their husbands or their fathers. She was marketable and transferable to others on the sweet will of the head of the family. In a word, no religion before Islam did anything for the betterment of women.

It was Islam, which recognised the position of women to be the same as that of men. Good works bring the same reward, whether the doer is a male or a female : "I will not waste the work of a worker among you, whether male or female, the one of you being from the other." Hazrat Muhammad (صلعم) emancipate the women from the bondage of males and raised their status and dignity in the society. Denied of any right to property and individuality, the women all over the world were degraded to the position of slaves to their fathers, brothers and husbands, and were subject to injustice, contempt and oppression. The Prophet of Islam first felt for this half of the human race. In his social justice he gave women equality with men and conferred on them the property rights and many other rights which had been exclusively enjoyed by the males. As a result women came to occupy a position of dignity and respectability in the society. The Prophet of Islam also stopped the inhuman custom of burying their daughters alive under severe penalties. Thus the killing of daughters was stopped for ever.

Women's Position as Wives

In the 6th century A.D. the Arabs held their wives in very high esteem and believed it to be one of the blessings of God to have given them wives to live with and to have established mutual love. The Holy Prophet gave women the same position as he gave to prayer and perfume. Allah says in the Quran, "If ye hate women, it may happen that ye hate a thing wherein God placed much good."

Unlike the Christian teaching that "women should submit themselves unto their husbands as unto the Lord", the Arab women were taught : "Be to him like a slave, so that he may be a slave to you."

Women had equal status with men in everything. They were free to carry on any work they liked, to make any contract they desired, to dispose of their properties as they wished, nor are their individualities merged in that of their husbands. But they are at the same time recognised as undertaking new responsibilities of life, which carry with them new rights. Hadith describes their position with home as that of a *raiyahs* or rulers : "Every one of you is a ruler and every one shall be questioned about his subjects ; the Amir (the King) is a ruler, and the man is a ruler over the people of his house, and the woman is a ruler over the house of her husband and his children, so everyone of you is a ruler and everyone shall be questioned about his subject." (Bukhari).

Her pledge commanded respect from her husband even when she gave protection to his enemy. Within the family she was highly respected and was the "mistress of the tent."

The Prophet laid equally great stress upon good treatment of a wife : "The most excellent of you," he is reported to have said, "is he who is best in his treatment of his wife." The husband is allowed to exercise his authority against the wife and this is an occasion when the wife's conduct is openly immoral.

Women as Mothers

A brave, generous or eminent Arab was always praised with reference to his mother and every eminent man acclaimed himself as the son of a worthy mother giving credit to his mother what he was worth. The Arabs were proud of their noble maternal descent. We find Zubair proudly retorting, "And I am son of Safia" when Manzar bin Zabban arrogantly proclaimed, "I am son of Fahtam."

The Prophet of Islam said, "Paradise is at the feet of the mother."

Women in the Field of Education

Cultivation of a taste of poetry was freely allowed to women. Arabia produced many women known for the beauty of their poetry and excellence of their oratory. The following are among the more important of them :

Fatima, the daughter of the Prophet, was celebrated for her pious life. She was a most obedient daughter, a devoted and faithful wife and a very kind mother. She composed verses on several occasions.

Fatima Ani, a well-known poetess and calligraphist.

Laila, daughter of Abdullah, a noted poetess, who flourished at the beginning of the Umayyad rule.

Laila, daughter of Turaif, poetess and warrior. She fought against the army of Caliph Harun-al-Rashid.

Princess Khadifa, daughter of Caliph Mamun.

Sakina, daughter of Imam Husain, the martyr of Kerbala.

Zainab, daughter of Tathriya, a prominent poetess in the Umayyad period.

Asma, daughter of Yazid Ansari, was a well known poetess.

Khansa was celebrated as the greatest poetess of Arabia. Her birthplace was Najd. She came to Medina and embraced Islam at the hands of the Prophet.

Khayzuran, a well-known poetess in the Abbasid period.

Ulayyah, sister of Harun-al-Rashid, was a celebrated poetess.

Zubaidah, the wife of Harun-al-Rashid, and Buran, the wife of Mamun, were talented women and celebrated poetesses.

Oratory and eloquence were the chief characteristics of the Arabs and the Arab women did not lag behind in this respect. The following are among the more important of them : Ayesha, the wife of the Prophet : Fatima, the daughter of the Prophet ; Darimiyya, a poetess, and a propagandist in the cause of Ali against Muawiya ; Zarqa, daughter of Ali, was a good orator and took part in the battle of Siffin against Muawiya.

Polygamy

Polygamy is a legacy from times immemorial and this practice seems to have been accepted as a matter of course. In the beginning it was perhaps a custom in Arabia to keep as many wives as one could afford, since women were entirely dependent upon men for their living and protection. The number of Arab women far exceeded the men in every tribe because of the killing of males in inter-tribal feuds. Such a condition of society of those days made this practice imperative.

The Prophet of Islam only restricted polygamy but did not prohibit it. The very large number of women left destitute and helpless had to be provided for and the institution of polygamy was the only honourable solution of this difficult problem. In this respect, Allah ordains in the Holy Quran :

"If ye fear, ye cannot act justly between two, three and four wives, marry only one."

It is evident from the above verse that polygamy is allowed in Islam only as an exception. As complete equity and other conditions attached to it is not possible for everybody to fulfil them in the present-day set-up, the Quranic injunction amounted in reality to a prohibition.

Divorce

The custom of separation in the pre-Islamic Arabia was that the husband used to say to his wife : "Thou art to me as my mother," and the result of this pronouncement was a total estrangement of the wife, but the woman was not free to remarry. This had almost no restrictions in divorcing and it seems could get wives wherever they went and could leave them whenever they pleased, though it was not looked upon with favour.

"Husband as well as wife had the right to divorce."

The Arabs had recourse to this practice when it was found convenient. Divorce was resorted to only when the wife did some grievous harm to him or when she was quarrelsome or when she did not agree on fundamentals and it was impossible either for the husband or the wife to pull on. In the event of divorce the wife was given a share of inheritance for herself and the children and she was at liberty to remarry. The modern tendency to interpret everything in a rigid form and give divorce a statutory recognition was not the spirit in which divorce was then allowed. Unless certain words were intentionally spoken to this effect thrice whether at the same time or at intervals, he could reconsider the matter and could change his mind and the marriage would still be valid. But when final pronouncement had been made they could not resume marital relations until the woman had once married some one else. This rigidity was kept perhaps to avoid divorce. Like men, women have the right to divorce their husbands on the ground of persecution, want of maintenance and such other causes.

Marriage in Islam

Marriage in Islam is a sacred contract which every Muslim must enter into, unless there are special reasons to the contrary. The Arabic word for marriage is *Nikah* which means conjunction and understood in the sense of contract. Regarding marriage, the Holy Quran says, "And those among you who are single and those who are fit among your male slaves and your female slaves ; if they are needy, Allah will make them free from want out of His grace ; And Allah is Ample giving, knowing. And let those who do not find a match keep chaste until Allah makes them free from want out of His grace." In another verse, marriage relationship is given the same importance as blood relationship. "And He it is who has created man from water, then He has made for him blood relationship and marriage relationship." Hadith also lays stress upon living in a married state. The Prophet is reported to have said, "O assembly of young people, whoever of you has the means to support a wife, he should get married, for this is the best means of keeping the looks cast down and guarding the chastity ; and he who has not the means, let him keep fast, for this will act as castration." According to another Hadith, "The man who marries perfects half his religion."

The institution of marriage is responsible for the development of those feelings of love and service which are the pride of society today. The mutual love of husband and wife—a love based not on momentary passion but life-long connection and the subsequent paternal love for offspring leads to a very high development of the feeling of love of man for man. The natural inclination of the male to the female and of the female to the male finds expression through marriage and is developed first into a love for the children, then a love for one's kith and kin and ultimately into a disinterested love for the whole of humanity.

There were four kinds of marriages prevalent among the early Muslim Arabs, *i.e.*,

(1) Marriage with a close relation. It was considered that the children of such a marriage would be of pure blood. Those born of such marriages among the Quraish, were proud of their descent, especially if they were of a well-known tribe, such as Bani Hashim, from which the Prophet was descended.

(2) Marriage with a stranger, because it was thought that those born of such connection would prove strong and healthy. Women from war-like tribes and from families celebrated for their generosity were taken as wives.

(3) Women taken captives (in war) were either kept as prisoners or married off, such as Safiyya, who was captured in the battle of Khaibar and was taken as wife by the Prophet.

(4) Slave girls, noted for their beauty were sold in the open market by slave dealers and purchased at

high prices and after emancipating them they were married by their masters.

Marriage between cousins, both on the paternal and maternal sides is permitted in Islam. The Holy Quran forbids certain marriage relations : "Forbidden to you are your mothers and your daughters and your sisters and your paternal aunts and your maternal aunts and brother's daughters and sister's daughters and your mothers that have suckled you and your foster-sisters and mothers of your wives, and your step-daughters who are in your guardianship, both of your wives to whom you have gone in—but if you have not gone in to them, there is no blame on you—and the wives of your sons who are of your own loins, and that you should not have two sisters together, except what has already passed" (4 : 23).

Marriage among non-Muslims is forbidden. The Quran had made an exception for the women of tributaries (Ahl al-Kitab), whom Muslims were permitted to marry.

Preliminaries of Marriage

The very fact that marriage is looked upon as a contract in Islam, shows that before marriage both parties must satisfy themselves that each will have a desirable partner for life in the other.

The Holy Quran says, "Marry such women as seem good to you" (4 : 3). The Holy Prophet is reported to have said, "When one of you makes a proposal of marriage to a woman, then if he can, he should look at what attracts him to marry her" In another Hadith, it is reported that when Mughaira ibn Shubah made a proposal of marriage to a woman, the Holy Prophet asked him if he had seen her and on his replying in the negative, he enjoined him to see, because "it was likely to bring about greater love and concord between them."

The Jurists are almost all ageed upon the *istahbab* (approval) of looking at the women whom one intends to marry. The consent of the parties is the first condition essential for the validity of the marriage. In this respect, however, much will depend upon the customs prevailing among a people and satisfaction may be obtained either personally or through female relatives, as is generally the way in the East.

Every marriage starts with *mangani* or betrothal after negotiations for the marriage. The bridegroom's parents after ascertaining the personal beauty, learning, character, health, age and descent of the proposed girl, go in person or appoint a relative to meet the bride's parents and settle the terms and, if satisfactory, come to a settlement. *Sherbet* or dates are given to the party by the bride's father and a ring or other presents are given to the bride-elect by the bridegroom's parents.

No particular age has been specified for marriage in the Islamic law in fact, with the difference of climatic conditions, there would be a difference as to the marriageable age in the different countries. It is evident from the facts that the age of marriage is the age of majority, when a person is capable of excercising his choice in matters of sexual liking or disliking.

The marriage contract is entered into by mutual consent expressed by the two parties : the husband and the wife, in the presence of witnesses and that is only essential. This mutual consent is techichally called *Ijab* (affirmation or declaration), and *Qubul* (acceptance or consent) in Fiqah. The Qazi, after receiving the consent of the bride or her agent and after acceptance of the terms of marriage by the bridegroom recites *khutba* and ends with blessing for both, in which the others present also join. Sweets and dry dates are distributed among the assembled guests. This ceremony is a very ancient one, dating from the times of the Prophet.

The second most important thing in marriage is the *mahr* or dowry. The dowry paid by the husband is assigned by the Quran to the wife, and no longer to her father, but various arrangements put it after all at his disposal. It is usual for a half only, or possibly two-thirds, to be paid at the time of contract, the balance may not be exacted till after the consummation of marriage, and is still payable after a marriage has been broken. If the husband breaks the marriage before its consummation, he must leave half the dowry in the possession of the wife.[1] No limits have been placed on the amount of *mahr*. The Holy Prophet paid varying amounts to his wives. The *mahr* of his daughter Fatima was four hundred dirhams. The lowest amount mentioned in Hadith is a ring of iron, and a man who could not procure even that, was told to teach the Holy Quran to his wife (Bukhari).

Generally, however, *mahr* is treated simply as a check upon the husband's power of divorce, and very high and extravagant sums are sometimes specified as *mahr*. This practice is against the spirit of Islamic institution. The *mahr* is an amount which should be handed over to the wife at marriage or as early afterwards as possible ; and if this rule was kept in view, extravagant *mahr* would disappear of itself.

After *nikah* is over, the bride is conducted to the husband's house and this is followed by the marriage feast called *walimah*. This feast is a step in the publicity of the marriage, and hence the Prophet laid stress on it. On the occasion of his own marriage with Safiyyah, when returning from Khaibar, he gave a feast in which every one was required to bring his food with him (Bukhari). He also invited his friends to a *walimah* feast on the occasion of his marriage with Zainab, which is said to have been the most sumptuous of all his *walimah* feast and yet he slaughtered only one goat

1. D.M. Gaudefroy : *Muslim Institutions*, p. 129.

(Muslim). This shows the great importance given to the marriage feast.

The most important duties of a married woman are:

Looking after the household, including the kitchen and preparation of food for her husband, though Islamic law does not allow the husband to force her to prepare meals for his guests. She is not asked to earn her livelihood or find means for maintaining her children. An ideal wife is described as one who is content, submissive, clean and devoted to her husband.

A man, who has more than one wife, has to provide for each. The convenience of each wife has to be provided for according to his wealth and status. In his sexual relation, he is expected to be strictly just and treat all wives alike. If he cannot do this, he must be content to choose only one wife.

Mutah or Temporary Marriage

Among the ancient Arabs there existed the custom of entering into conditional as well as temporary contracts of marriage. It went under the name of *mutah*, meaning profiting by or enjoying a thing. These loose notions of morality exercised a disastrous influence on the condition of the society within the peninsula.

After the advent of Islam, *mutah* marriages were tacitly allowed. But the Holy Prophet prohibited *mutah* at the time of Khaibar expedition. There is some confusion in Hadith about the *mutah*. Bukhari has the following as the heading of the chapter on *mutah*: "The Prohibition by the Holy Prophet of *mutah* finally." Under this heading he cites first a Hadith which says that "Ali (the reporter) said to Ibn Abbas that the Holy Prophet prohibited *mutah* and the eating of the flesh of domestic assees at the time of Khaibar expedition. It is then related that Ibn Abbas being asked if the permission to practise *mutah* related to the time of distress and when the number of women was very small, replied in the affirmative. The third Hadith is that of Salmah ibn Akwa who says that they were in an expedition when a messenger of the Holy Prophet came and said that they were permitted to contract temporary marriages, at the end of which Bukhari adds, and 'Ali has made it clear, reporting from the Prophet "that this was abrogated." Abu Daud has two Hadith from Sabrah, the first stating that the Holy Prophet prohibited *mutah* in the year of the Farewell Pilgrimage (10 A.H.) and the second simply that he prohibited *mutah*. There is no mention of *mutah* having ever been allowed. Muslim has several contradictory Hadith. But even in these it is admitted that though *mutah* was permitted on certain occasions it was finally prohibited.

The Shia School of Law recognises *mutah* marriage. A Shia of the male sex may contract a *mutah* marriage with a woman professing Islam, Christian or Jewish religion or even with a woman who is fire worshipper, but not with a woman following any other religion. But a Shia woman may not contract a *mutah* marriage with a non-Muslim.

It is essential to the validity of a *mutah* marriage that (1) the period of cohabitation should be fixed and this may be a day, a month a year or a term of years, and that (2) some dower should be specified. When the term and dower have been fixed, the contract is valid. But if the dower is specified and the term is not fixed, the contract, though void as *mutah*, may operate as a 'permanent marriage'.

The following are the incidents of a *mutah* marriage:

(1) A *mutah* marriage does not create mutual

rights of inheritance between a man and a woman, but children conceived while it exists are legitimate and capable of inheriting from both parents.

(2) When the cohabitation of a man and a woman commences, in a *mutah* marriage, but there is no evidence as to the term for which the marriage was contracted and the cohabitation continues, the proper inference would, in default of evidence to the contrary, be that the *mutah* continued during the whole period of cohabitation, and that the children conceived during that period were legitimate and capable of inheriting from their father.

(3) A *mutah* marriage is dissolved *ipso facto* by the expiry of the term. No right of divorce is recognised in the case of a *mutah* marriage, but the husband may at his will put an end to the contract of marriage by "making a gift of the term" (*Hiba-i-Muddat*) to the wife, even before the expiration of the fixed term.

(4) A woman married in the *mutah* form is not entitled to maintenance under the Shia law.

Thus all the Muslim sects agree in holding temporary marriage to be unlawful, with the exception of Akhbari Shias, but even according to them it is not a very honourable transaction. To quote Ameer Ali, "It is declared to be abominable, though not actually prohibited, to marry in the *mutah* form a virgin girl who has no father . . . . the reason being that as such a marriage is to her prejudice, and she has had no paternal advice or guidance in the matter, she should not be subjected to the degradation of a temporary union.

Concubinage in Islam

Concubinage is regular sexual connection with a female who does not hold the legal status of a wife ;

in other words, keeping a woman in the position of a wife without marrying her. There is a general impression that Islam gives an unlimited licence to have as many concubines as one likes, so long as the concubine is a slave or a prisoner of war and not a free woman. Concubinage, the union of people standing to each other in the relation of master and slave, without the sanction of matrimony, existed among the Arabs and it may have been practised by some Muslims until the revelation came to the Prophet. The Prophet in the beginning did not denounce the custom, but with the coming of revelation, concubinage was put to an end. The Quran says, "And you are permitted to marry virtuous women who are believers, and virtuous women of those who have been given the scriptures before you, when you have provided them their portions, living chastely with them without fornication, and not taking concubines." Thus a plain injunction had been received that all male and female slaves must be married. If any master of a female slave kept her as concubine after that, it was against the Quranic injunction.

It must be borne in mind that neither the Holy Quran, nor the Hadith, anywhere speaks of the right of the master to have sexual intercourse with a slave. In other words, ownership is nowhere recognised as legalising sexual relationship. The only thing that legalizes sexual intercourse is a contract between the two parties to undertake the responsibilities of each other, and thus marriage, whether with a free person or a slave, is the only means of legalizing sexual connection.

Now the question is that the Prophet had taken two women as wives out of the prisoners of war, *viz.*, Suffiyah from among the Jews and Juwairiyah from among the Bani Mustalaq. Were they not concubines? The answer would be in negative. They were lawfully married wives, taken as wives in an honourable manner as any of the others. If there was any difference, it was that their freedom was considered as their *mahr* (dowry). The Prophet's example, however, shows that when a prisoner of war was elevated to the dignity of wifehood, she was also set free.

The Holy Quran and the Hadith are thus all agreed that slave girls must be married ; there is no exception to that rule whether her husband is a slave or a free man or the master himself. It is only in Fiqah that we find the rule laid down that a master may have sexual relations with his slave girls simply because of the right of ownership which he has in her. But even Fiqah maintains that cohabitation with a slave girl is only allowed if all those conditions are fulfilled which must be fulfilled if she were to be taken in marriage as a wife. Again, just as a man cannot have two sisters as wives at one and the same time, a master, according to Fiqah, cannot cohabit with two slave girls who are sisters. This shows that even the Eiqah, though allowing cohabitation on the ground of ownership, recognises such cohabitation as the equivalent of marriage.

APPENDIX—A

MUSLIM FESTIVALS

There are, in Islam, two great festivals having a religious sanction. Both these festivals go under the name of *Id* which means a recurring happiness. The first of these is called *Idul-Fitr*, the word *fitr* meaning to begin, from which is also derived *fitrah* meaning nature. The other is *Idul-Azha*, meaning a sacrifice. It is thus clear that both these festivals are observed by Muslims all over the world.

1. *Idul-Fitr* : It is celebrated on the first of Shawwal, the tenth Arabic month, after Ramazan, the month of fasting. It is religious in character, and dates from the time of the Prophet. The preparation for *Id* is similar to the preparation for the Friday service. One must take a bath, put on one's best clothes, use scent and do everything possible to appear neat and tidy. One must attend the festival prayer, *i.e.*, two *rakats* at the Idgah (or the mosque), and embrace the Muslims present in the place. No Azan is called out for the Id prayer nor any *iqamah* for the arranging of the lines (Bukhari). The time of Id prayers is any time after sun rise and before noon. The Id sermon is delivered after Divine service is over.

While celebrating the great Id festivals, a Muslim not only remembers Allah, but he is also enjoined to remember his poorer brethren. The custom of giving things in charity is associated with both Ids. On the occasion of *Idul-Fitr*, every Muslim is required to give *Sadaqah Fitr*, which amounts to two and a half seers of wheat, barley, rice or any staple food of the country per head of the family. The payment is to be made before the service is held, and it is obligatory.

2. *Idul-Azha* : It means the feast of sacrifice. This feast is observed on the tenth of the last Arabic month named Zulhijja. It is a pre-Islamic feast celebrated by the pilgrims who visited Mecca and allowed by the Prophet. The pilgrims assembled in the valley of Mina, close to Mecca, and offered animals, by way of sacrifice, according to their means. On the day of Idul-Azha, Muslims take a bath, change their dress and go to the Idgah or place of prayer. The Imam then leads them in prayer of two *rakats*. Then the Khatib addresses the audience, praising the significance of the day, and when it is finished, people embrace each other and return home. On returntng, all those who can afford to do so sacrifice animal.

In the case of a goat or a sheep, one animal suffices for one household. In case of a cow or a camel, seven men may be partners. The animal sacrificed must be free from apparent physical defects and fully grown. The goat or sheep should be a year old, the cow two years and the camel five years. As regards the meat of the slaughtered animals, the Holy Quran says : "Eat of them and feed the poor man who is contented and the beggar." The skin of the animal must, however, be disposed of in charity.

Besides these two there are other festivals observed by the Muslims. Among these are :

Milad, which is the birthday of the Holy Prophet Hazrat Muhammad (صلعم), is annually celebrated on the twelfth of Rabi-ul-Awwal. In Pakistan and India, the date is not fixed. It may fall on any day in the month of Rabi-ul-Awwal or the following month.

The *Shab-i-Barat* (the night of record) falls on the 14th day of Shaban. It is supposed that on that date the shares of living and fortune for the coming year are fixed and registered in Heaven. The young children celebrate it by using fireworks. According to Muslim tradition, on the night of Shab-i-Barat, the tree of Sidratul Muntaha is shaken. Each leaf contains the name of a person and according to the fall of the leaf, the death of a person named is settled. On the 14th, a variety of food is prepared in memory of deceased relations with recitation of Fateha and is distributed among the poor or served to the members of the family.

Akhri Chahar Shamba or the last Wednesday is observed in the month of Safar, the second Arabic month. On that day, people take bath and put on *Tawiz* to protect themselves against impending bad luck. It is thought that the Prophet, on that day, recovered from a serious illness and took a bath.

Muharram: In commemoration of Hazrat Hussain's martyrdom, the Shia Muslims observe every year the first ten days of Muharram as the days of lamentation. Orthodox and religious-minded Muslims spend the first ten days of Muharram in reading the account of the martyrdom of the heroes of Kerbala and in offering prayers for their spiritual benefit. The various elements of the present day Muharram 'Passion-play', namely, the Taziyas or miniature models of the mausoleums of the martyrs of Kerbala, the relics of the heroes and thh wailings and demonstrations take place.

Trade and Commerce

Arabia is a mountainous desert. The soil being barren, there was little of agriculture in the country. The people could not fully depend on her for their livelihood. They were to seek fortune elsewhere. The economic factor compelled them to carry on trade with the neighbouring countries. To solve this problem, they risked the voyage as far as Coromanddal, Ceylon, and further East in the Indian Ocean. In the West, they explored the East African Coast and had established several colonies in that continent. Their chief seaport and centre of trade was Arabia Felix (Southern Arabia called by Ptolemy as Arabia Felix), the modern Aden. Job, a Jewish writer, has said that the Arabs imported balm, spicery, myrrh, and other articles from western India and exported them to Egypt and Palestine. The ancient Arabs were traders in the coast of the Red Sea, the Iranian Gulf and the Indian Ocean. Gherra was the chief port for Indian trade in East Arabia. The merchants of Arabia imported gold, gems, silver, sandal, spices and ebony into Palestine.

On the advent of Islam, the Prophet and most of his early converts were merchants. They exported goods from Hijaz into Syria and imported them from Syria into Hijaz. Mecca was the city of bankers and money-lenders.[1] Even the Arab women used to carry on business side by side with men. Khadija, the wife of the Prophet, was a wealthy merchant lady. Hinda, mother of Muawiyah, the first Umayyad Caliph, had business transactions with the Kalbi tribe in Syria. Abu Jahl's mother was a trader in perfumery. Besides, there were many ladies in Arabia who adopted business as their profession. Large sums of money were invested in business. The Arab merchants imported Indian and Chinese products through Yemen, Syrian and Egyptian goods through the border towns of Syria; and Iranian articles from Mesopotamia, such as silk, cotton, and linen goods, arms, cereals, oil, etc. Many articles of imports during this period were skin, leather, currant, ingots of gold and silver, perfumes, spices, aromatics, guns, drugs, etc.

The rice of the Israelites under David and his son Soloman and the surrender of the Queen Saba (Yemen)

1. A. M. A. Shustery : *Outlines of Islamic Culture*, p. 147.

marked the beginning of the decline of the Yemenite ascendency. The Yemenites lost their influence and supremacy in the sea. But the rise of Islam brought fresh courage and vigour to them and the Arabs again became the foremost trading nation in the East. This time, their supremacy lasted several centuries, till the war of Crusades and the Renaissance of arts and sciences in Europe.

From the 10th century A.D. to the rise of the European maritime activity, the Muslims were the masters of the Mediterranean and the Red Sea, the Indian Ocean, the China Sea and the Pacific Ocean. Their trade and journey on land extended over a great area comprising the whole of the Northern and a part of the Central, Southern, and Eastern Asia, as far as the interior of China. They founded colonies from the Atlantic to the Pacific Ocean. Important places such as Malaga (65 miles north-east of Gibralter ; now a Spanish seaport), Cartagena (on a bay of the Mediterranean), Alexandria, Basra, Baghdad, Barcelona (the second largest city in Spain) and Cadiz (Spanish port on the Atlantic) became flourishing ports. The Spanish Muslims had one thousand ships. They founded factories on the Danube and it was through Muslim merchants that the silk industry spread to Constantinople and Spain. Prof. Shustery writes, "This grand work of civilization was not limited to Arabs who were the earliest members of the Muslim brotherhood. It was the combined effort of Arabs, Iranians, Turks, Indians, Chinese, Africans and Spanish Muslims."

Basra was the chief port on the Iranian Gulf, from which vessels left *via* Muscat to the coast of western India, Ceylon and the islands of the Indian and Pacific Oceans in the East. Iranian trade centres were famous for fine carpets, silk, precious stones, textile manufactures, wool, cotton, household furnitures, dried fruits, etc. These articles were carried to Russia and through the European and Jewish merchants to England, Norway and Sweden. Through Khurasan and thence to Khiva traders entered into the mouth of the Volga as far as Kazan and the Don (river of Russia). Russian goods such as fur, wax, honey, etc., were exchanged for silk, cotton, and linen. Merv had become the centre of trade during the rule of the Seljuqs. It was noted for its textile fabrics and silk. Herat manufactured carpets, sword-blades and other war-like weapons. Balkh and Badakhshan were noted for precious stones.

Trade and commerce made a remarkable progress during the period of the Abbasid caliphs. Eastward, the Arab merchants ventured as far as China for silk and westward they reached Morocco, Spain, Germany, Russia, Sweden and Poland. The discovery of a large number of coins in those countries confirms the stories of the '*Arabian Nights*' that the Arabs of that age were enterprising traders and carried on a world-wide commerce. It is for the purpose of giving more impetus to commerce that Caliph Harun al-Rashid conceived the idea of digging a canal through the Isthmus of Suez, one thousand years before Ferdinand de Lesseps. The flourishing ports and cities of Baghdad, Basra, Siraf, Alexandria, Cairo and others indicated the commercial prosperity of the Abbasid empire.

Arab Spain made all-round progress in industry and trade. It was the Arabs who firts introduced in Europe manufacturing industries of hide, paper, sugar and gun-powder. The manufactured goods of the Arabs were held in great honour in all parts of Europe. Cordova, the capital of Spain, was famous for its leather trade, silver-smiths and filigree works. Its industry could support two hundred thousand families. The Muslims of Spain were noted as weavers and dyers of silk and wool. They were also masters in metal work. Qairwan was the centre of trade for the west, east and central Africa. There were other places in Africa which became the emporium of trade. Fez in Morocco was famous for manufacturing red caps and fabricating silk, and the gold thread. Africa exported gold-dust, ivory, ostrich feathers, etc., to different parts of the country. Fustat and Alexandria were the important ports through which the merchandise of the East passed to the West. Sicily enjoyed a prosperous trade. It had also flourishing industries. Eastern goods were imported to it and it passed them on to the European countries. It obtained wheat, vines, olives and fruits from Europe and exported them to the surrounding seaports of Africa. Europe and Asia. Thus in the words of Prof. Shustery, "The tapestries of Cordova, woollen stuffs of Murcia (Spain), silks of Granada, gold work of Toledo, sword-blades of Damascus and Ispahan were noted in the then known world."

APPENDIX—B

REFERENCES FOR FURTHER READING

Ali, Mohammad : *The Quran.*
The Religion of Islam.
A Manual of Hadith.

Ali, Allama Abdullah Yusuf : *The Meaning of the Illustrious Quran.*

Ali, Ameer : *The Ethics of Islam.*
The Spirit of Islam.

Ahmad, Nafis : *Muslim Contribution to Geography.*

Ahmad, Nur : *Glories of Islam.*

Akbar, A .U. : *The Orations of Muhammad.*

Amin, Muhammad : *Muhammad and the Teachings of the Quran.*

Arberry, A.J. : *Revelation and Reason in Islam.*
Sufism.

Ahmad, K. Jamil : *Heritage of Islam.*

Arnold and Guillaume : *The Legacy of Islam.*

Arnold, Thomas : *The Preaching of Islam.*

Ataullah, Shaikh : *Revival of Zakat.*

Baille, Neil B. E. : *Mohammadan Law.*

Baloch, Aziz : *The Sufi.*

Bhargava, K.D. : *A Survey of Islamic Culture and Institutions.*

Bilgrami, S.A. : *Tamaddun-i-Arab.*

Boer, De : *History of Philosophy in Islam.*

Bukhari : *Traditions.*

Demombynes, M.G. : *Muslim Institutions.*

De Lacy O'Leary : *Arabic Thought and its Place in History.*

Donaldson : *The Shiites Religion.*

Enan, M.A. : *Ibn Khaldun : His Life and Works.*

Friendlander : *The Heterodoxies of the Shiites.*

Fyzee, A.A.A. : *Outlines of Mohammadan Law.*

Galwash : *The Religion of Islam.*

Gedon : *Studies in the Religions of the East.*

Hakim, K.A. ; *Islamic Ideology.*

Hamilton, Charles : *The Hedaya* (A Commentary on the Musalman Law.)

Hammond : *The Philosophy of Arabi.*

Hashim ; *The Creed of Islam.*

Hell, Joseph ; *The Arab Civilization.*

Hitti, P.K. : *History of the Arabs.*

Ibn Ishaq : *Sirat Rasul Allah.*

Iqbal, Dr. M. : *Reconstruction of Religious Thought in Islam.*

Issawi, Charles : *Arab Philosophy of History.*

Ivanow ; *Imam Ismail.*
The Alleged Founder of Ismailism.

Kamaluddin, Kh. : *Sayings of the Holy Prophet.*

Karim, F. : *Al-Hadis.*

Kazvini, Mirza Mohammad : *Lawaih* (A Treaties on Sufism).

Khwaja : *Sufism in Islam.*

Khuda Bakhsh, S. : *Islamic Civilization,* (2 vols.)
Marriage and Family Life Among the Arabs.

Kirk, G.E. : *A Short History of the Middle East.*

Kuraishy, F.A. : *Islam : The Religion of Humanity.*

Lammens : *Islam : Beliefs and Institutions.*

Latif, S.A., : *Islamic Cultural Studies.*

Levy : *Sociology of Islam.*

Lewis : *The Origin of Ismailism.*

Macdonald : *Development of Muslim Theology and Jurisprudence.*

Mahmud, S.F. : *The Story of Islam.*

Matheson, D.M. : *An Introduction to Sufi Doctrine.*

Miller : *Treatises on the Principles of Shiites.*

Moors : *History of Religions.*

Maududi, S. Abul Ala : *Towards Understanding Islam.*

Nadvi, S.M., : *A Geographical History of the Quran.*
Muslim Thought and its Source.

Pickthal, M.M. : *Islamic Culture* **(Cultural Side of Islam)**
Rahman, S. : *An Introduction to Islamic Philosophy.*
Robson, Dr. James : *Mishkat al-Masabih.* **(English Translation).**
Sarwar, Hafiz Ghulam : *Philosophy of the Quran.*
Schacht : *The Origin of Muhammadan Jurisprudence.*
Sell : *Twelvers.*
Shahrastani : *Muslim Schism and Sects* **(Trans. by Seelye).**
Sharif, M.M. : *Muslim Thought : its Origin and Achievements.*
Sharif, M.R. : *Islamic Social Framework.*
Shustery, A.M.A. : *Outlines of Islamic Culture.*
Sharif, M.M. : *Studies in Muslim Philosophy.*
Siddiqi, M.M. : *Women in Islam.*
Development of Islamic State and Society.
Subhan, John A. : *Sufism : its Saints and Shrines.*
Suhrawardy, Abdullah al-Mamun : *The Sayings of the Prophet.*
Tritton ; *Muslim Theology.*
Umaruddin : *Ethical Philosophy of Ghazzali.*
Wensinck : *Muslim Creed.*
Watt, W. Montgomery : *Faith and Practice of Al-Ghazzali.*
Wickens, G.M. : *Avicenna : Scientist and Philosopher.*
Windellfaud : *History of Philosophy.*
Wulf : *History of Scholastic Philosophy.*
Yusuf, S.M. : *Some Aspects of Islamic Culture.*
Zaydan : *History of Islamic Civilization.*
Ziauddin : *Muslim Calligraphy.*

KITAB BHAVAN
Exporters & Importers
1784, Kalan Mahal, Daryaganj
New Delhi- 110002. (India)
Phones: 3274686, 263383
Telex No. 31-63106 ALI IN

First Published in India 1981
3rd Edition 1990

ISBN 81-7151-037- x (Set)
ISBN 81-7151-039-6 (Vol. I I)

Published by:
Nusrat Ali Nasri for Kitab Bhavan
1784, Kalan Mahal, Daryaganj
New Delhi- 110002

Printed in India :
at Lahoti Fine Art Press
1711,Sui Walan
New Delhi-110002

THE ADMINISTRATION OF JUSTICE IN ISLAM

AN INTRODUCTION TO THE MUSLIM CONCEPTION OF THE STATE

BY

AL-HAJ MAHOMED ULLAH *Ibn* S. JUNG, M.A., LL.D.

OF CHRIST'S COLLEGE, CAMBRIDGE ; TRINITY COLLEGE, DUBLIN ; BARRISTER-AT-LAW, LINCOLN'S INN, ADVOCATE, HIGH COURT, ALLAHABAD ; READER IN LAW AT THE UNIVERSITY OF ALLAHABAD

With an Introductory Discourse

By

MR. JUSTICE HAMOODUR RAHMAN,

Formerly Chief Justice of Pakistan

KITAB BHAVAN

New Delhi-110002